Nihonshu: Japanese Sake

Gautier Roussille

This book has been produced with the objective of spreading the knowledge of sake to the greatest number. If you wish to use the information contained in this book, please notify the author and quote him.

Follow us on facebook: www.facebook.com/nihonshusakejaponais/
Direct order from the author available at: www.nihonshu.bigcartel.com/

Cover picture: rice steaming in Sohomare kura by Gautier Roussille

Acknowledgements

This book could not have been created without the help of many people, first of all the team at Sohomare *kura* where I spent a season as a worker. I especially thank Mr. Jun Kono and his wife Junko, owners of the *kura* and Mr. Toru Akita, *toji*.

I also thank all those who, during my discovery of sake, have helped me to lift corners of the veil: Mr. Kuroda, Mr. Kimijima, Mr. Hamada, Mr. & Mrs. Kumada, Mr. Masumi, Mr. Utsunomiya, Mr. Huet, Mrs. Hiraide, Mrs. Yoshitake, Mr. Gauntner, Mr. Auld, all my fellow IWC judges and the IWC team as well as the Japanese organizations involved in sake promotion and education: MAFF, JA, NRIB, JSS, NTA, BSJ, Sake Samurai, etc.

I warmly thank all the participants in the crowdfunding campaign who contributed greatly to the printing of this book, especially Antony Moss, Estévan Reuse, Tzvetan Mihaylov, The Sake Ninja a.k.a Chris Johnson, Noel Pusch and Dagmar Maas for their generosity and support!

Thank you, finally, to all the patient editors, and most importantly my wife, without whom writing this book would not have been possible.

This book has been translated from its original language, French, by its author, but this could not have been possible without the help of proofreaders; Katie Worobeck, Ben Thomas and Johnny Drain. To them I say a very special thank-you!

Foreword

The purpose of this book is to instruct as many people as possible, be they amateurs or wine and spirit professionals, in Japanese sake's methods of production. It covers all subjects, from rice cultivation to tasting, in a clear, accessible yet rigorous language.

Attempting to organize and treat such a complex subject in a given order, when all its parts are intertwined, is a major intellectual challenge; just as it is impossible to treat fermentation before evoking raw materials, it is difficult to speak of raw materials without mentioning fermentation. Hence, you will find in this book numerous references and short repetitions, intended for the neophytes reading this book, as well as a consistent glossary that systematically refers to the page dealing in detail with each subject.

You will also find inserts that introduce technical, historical or cultural contexts, which are intended to embellish the reading of a book that, due to its subject, sometimes ventures into arid technical grounds. Some of these inserts that deal with some crosscutting themes may call upon subjects not yet dealt with within the book. Also, do not hesitate to return to these inserts during your reading if you feel the need.

On the other hand, you will find that the words "often", "generally", etc. are regularly included in this book. This is due to the mischievous (and fascinating) habit of sake producers to do things "in their own way". Thus, in all subjects concerning sake, it will be possible to find rare exceptions, which justify this caution. Nevertheless, the methods and practices described here are broadly representative of the daily life of sake producers.

Despite the efforts of all those who collaborated on this project to present a comprehensive, accurate and typo-free book, *errare humanum est* and I hope that you will forgive us for our possible shortcomings.

Wishing you as much pleasure in reading this book as I had in writing it,

Enjoy reading,

Gautier Roussille

Table of Contents

Chapter I: Raw Materials

Chapter II: Sake Fermentation

Chapter III: Fining Raw Sake

Chapter IV: Sake Tasting

Disambiguation: what is sake?

For the Japanese, "sake" is a generic term covering all alcoholic beverages. In this book we deal with Japanese sake, which the Japanese call "*nihonshu*" or, administratively, "*seishu*" (respectively Japanese alcohol or clear alcohol). Sake, as we conceive of it here, is therefore a traditional Japanese alcoholic beverage, usually translucent, colorless and containing 15-17% alcohol, resulting from the fermentation of rice. It should not be confused with baijiu or meikueilu, which are 40% ABV distilled alcohols served in shooter glasses with suggestive drawings in many Asian restaurants.

Sake or *baijiu*?

Japanese characters or "*kanji*" derive from Chinese characters. The term "sake" in particular is the Japanese pronunciation of the Chinese character "*jiu*".

A large number of Japanese restaurants, run by people of Chinese descent, serve the most famous of Chinese spirits: *baijiu* (literally "white alcohol"), a distilled alcohol produced from cereals.

For the sake of "authenticity", *baijiu* is read in Japanese as "*shiroki*" or "*shirozake*" (see the insert "Sake, *zake, shu*, etc." on the following page). The term *shirozake* being unknown, it is simplified as "sake".

This is how a good part of the European population and most Westerners came to confuse these two drinks with distinct origins and modes of production.

Let us note that, amusingly, "*shiroki*" (literal transcription of *baijiu*) is a historical but very real category of Japanese sake (see "Antiquity: the Court's sake", p.17).

Japanese characters may have, for the same meaning, several possible readings according to the context. Thus, the character "酒" meaning "alcohol" may be read "*shu*", "sake", "*ki*", etc.

The first reading is derived from the Chinese "jiu" which, over time, gave "*shu*" in Japanese. This type of reading is called "*on-yomi*" or "reading according to sound" (implying the Chinese sound of the character).

The second reading is derived from the Japanese language pre-existing the introduction of Chinese characters. This type of reading is called "*kun-yomi*" or "reading according to the meaning". For ease of pronunciation, this reading can be distorted into "*saka*" if placed as a prefix or into "*zake*" if placed as a suffix.

The third reading is old, and now used almost exclusively for the names of people or places. This type of reading is called "*nanori*" or "presentation reading". It will be found here only in the terms "*shiroki*" and "*kuroki*".

The choice of one reading or another can sometimes seem rather random (*ginjoshu*, *junmaishu* versus *namazake*, *nigorizake*, for example), however it is possible to draw some general trends:

- "*shu*" is used in compound words and refers to alcoholic beverages in general: *umeshu* (liqueur made of *ume*, a Japanese plum or apricot, fruit of *Prunus mume*), *koshu* (aged alcohol), etc.

- "sake" is more often used in groups of words, to evoke precisely Japanese sake (a logical use knowing its historical link to proper Japanese culture): *sakagura* (sake warehouse), *sakamai* (sake rice), *hanamizake* (sake drunk during the *hanami*), etc.

Reading Japanese terms

This book contains many Japanese technical terms whose pronunciation may be foreign to readers who have never encountered them before. The script chosen for this book is the most commonly used by the Japanese themselves, i.e. a simplified romaji, without distinction for long vowels. Fortunately for us, Japanese and English pronunciations are very close and only a few adjustments are necessary to obtain a correct pronunciation:

« u » is pronounced « ou » as in « you »
« g » is pronounced « g » as in « game »
« j » is pronounced « dj » as in « gentle »
« r » is pronounced in-between « r » and « l »
« ai » is pronounced as two separate vowels « a » + « i »
« e » is pronounced «eh » as in « sketch »

Hence, « *junmai* » is pronounced « dj-ou-n-ma-i », « *daiginjo* » is pronounced « da-i-g-in-dj-o » and « *shiboritate* » is pronounced « shi-bo-ri-ta-teh ».

Questions on the choice of certain spellings have arisen several times during the creation of this book. Depending on author, spelling or the use of hyphens may vary in the transcriptions of certain characters or groups of characters. Here, the author has chosen to use relatively common spellings, while limiting the presence of hyphens to cases where they emphasize the meaning of the groups of characters they separate.

The terms borrowed from Japanese have been considered invariable and are shown in italics, with the exception of proper names (rice varieties, names of places or books, etc.) and old borrowings accepted by English dictionaries (sake, shogun, Shinto, etc.).

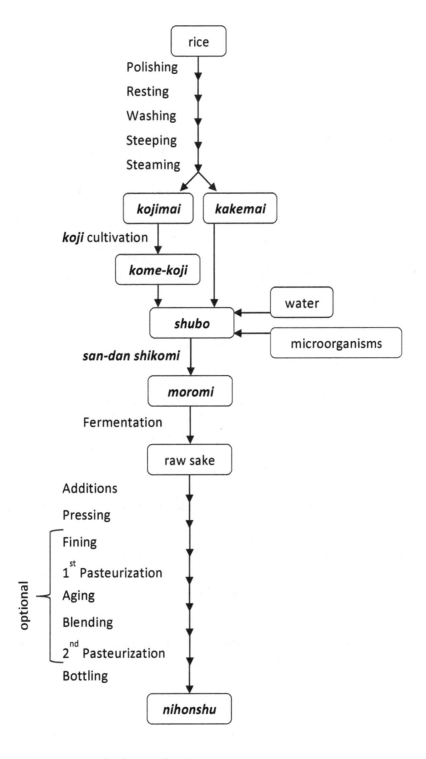

Figure 1. Summary of sake production.

In brief: production of sake and the main terms to remember

The first step to obtain sake is rice polishing. This requires removing a variable quantity of the grain's outer layers (generally between 15% and 65% in mass). Sake produced from rice of which more than 40% of the mass was removed during the polishing can be called "*ginjo*". The best sakes are usually in this category.

After a rest period, the rice is steeped in water for several minutes and then steamed. After cooling, a part of the rice, called "*kojimai*", is inoculated with a mold, the "*koji*". The growth of the *koji* lasts about three days during which the rice is regularly mixed to ensure a homogeneous development of the *koji* fungus. The rice on which the *koji* has developed is called "*kome-koji*" (*kome* = rice): it allows the transformation of rice starch into sugar, a necessary step for fermentation.

A mixture of *kome-koji*, steamed rice ("*kakemai*") and water is then prepared. This mixture, called "*shubo*" or "*moto*", is then inoculated with yeasts through various techniques. The yeasts develop for 1 to 2 weeks before their population reaches its peak. A new mixture of *kome-koji*, cooked rice and water is then added to the *shubo* 3 times over 4 days. This step is called "*san-dan shikomi*" (*san-dan* = three steps, *shikomi* = addition) and the resulting mixture is called "*moromi*".

A period of low temperature fermentation follows, ranging from 2 weeks to 1 month, at temperatures between 6 °C and 20 °C (43 °F / 68 °F). The process is completed by pressing the sake. The resultant raw sake is generally filtered and then pasteurized before commercialization.

Water, usually blended with distilled alcohol, can be added to the sake at the end of fermentation or after pressing in order to increase the volume produced and/or lower its alcoholic strength. A sake produced without addition of alcohol is called "*junmai*".

All these operations take place within the "*sakagura*" (literally the "sake cellar", and by extension the company producing sake) or simply "*kura*", under the direction of a "*toji*", the cellar master.

Sake, *nihonshu* or *seishu*

For centuries, the only alcohol available in Japan apart from the few foreign spirits sent as presents to the emperor or to high dignitaries was the locally produced sake. Although there were several kinds and production methods evolved over time (see "A short history of sake", p.16), it can be considered that all these sakes belonged to a single family, those of alcoholic beverages based on fermented grain.

Thus, there was no clear distinction in the minds of the Japanese between sake and alcohol, which were both designated by a single term: "sake". It was only with the development of international trade and the increased availability of foreign alcohols that the need to specifically designate Japanese sake took shape. "Sake" became a generic term for all alcoholic drinks, while "Japanese sake" became "*nihonshu*": *nihon* meaning Japan and *shu* being an alternative reading of "sake" (see the insert "Sake, *zake*, *shu*, etc.", p.11).

The term sake, however, remains strongly connected by this historical context to *nihonshu*. Hence, if you are talking about sake in Japan, your interlocutors will tend to assume that you are talking about *nihonshu*, but if the context or topic of conversation is not clearly established you should be more specific. So if you order sake in an *izakaya* (see insert "*Izakaya*, sake houses", p.188), it is better to talk about "*nihonshu*", but if you order a second round, an empty carafe in hand, you can say sake (or "*o-sake*" out of politeness) without risk of confusion.

The term *seishu* derives from the need to define a category of marketable and taxable products distinct from the self-consumed peasant sake (*doburoku*, see "The Middle Ages: the elite's sake", p.19). To this day, this term is still limited to official documents, particularly to taxation.

Since December 2015, the term "*nihonshu*" is recognized as a Geographical Indication in Japan (see "Sake and terroir", p.215). We can safely assume that this decision, which is primarily aimed at valuing the sake produced in Japan (paradoxically, since Japanese communication campaigns continue to use the unprotected term "sake"), will have no impact on the common use of this word, just as the term "Champagne" continues to be improperly used throughout the world.

A short history of sake

1. Origins: ritual sake

It is in the form of terracotta jars dated from 4000 to 3000 BC. that we find the oldest traces of production and consumption of alcohol in Japan. As in many other parts of the world, these jars were filled with wild fruits that fermented naturally. These primitive "wines" predate the invention of sake by several thousand years: the first mention of sake appear in a history book of the 3rd century to specify that the Japanese were fond of an alcoholic beverage they consumed especially during funerals.

If the appearance of fermented fruit-based drinks always precedes those of cereal-based beverages, it is because the latter require a more complex production process. Indeed, while abandoned fruits ferment naturally, this is not the case for cereals, as yeasts cannot ferment the starch of the grain by themselves; a primary stage of transformation from starch into sugar is necessary. In the case of beer and whiskey, for example, the means for this transformation are provided by a seed germination process called "malting". A different approach was developed in Japan.

In many cultures (Claude Levis Strauss makes the account for Latin America in his book "Tristes Tropiques"), this step is carried out thanks to salivary enzymes. The grain (ideally cooked) is chewed so that the salivary enzymes penetrate it and break down the starch into sugars. The dough thus formed is spat in a container that can then be fed with a larger quantity of grain. As with fruit, the fermentation is then ensured by yeasts naturally present in the air.

In Japan, *kuchi-kami-sake* ("chewed sake") was produced during Shinto ceremonies and consumed quickly. Depending on the period, the place and the specific ceremony, the work of mastication was carried out either by young virgins, by the *miko* (diviners and guardians of the sanctuary), or by the whole village. This tradition persisted sporadically until the end of the Second World War when the American occupation ended it under sanitary pretexts.

Kuchi-kami-sake is sweet and sparkling because of its on-going fermentation. The partially dissolved grains accumulate at the bottom of the container and (brought up by the bubbles) on its surface, making the consumption of the mixture difficult. This paste-like sake was therefore "eaten" with chopsticks rather than "drunk". However, traces of vessels equipped with straws, dating from the 5th century have been found. These vessels, allow for the liquid part of the *kuchi-kami-sake* to be drunk through the solid residues according to the Mesopotamian technique (4000 BC.).

In a second phase (3rd-4th century), methods based on the germination of grains (or malting, a technique imported from Korea) made a brief appearance but did not persist. They were quickly supplanted by the use of fungi, which gave rise to the *koji* method, as we know it today (see "Discovery and use of *koji*", p.95).

Most experts date the introduction of rice cultivation in Japan from Korea to the 5th century BC. Other theories trace its arrival to the 10th century BC. However, whatever the precise date of the first crops, it is clear that proto-sakes based on other grains and fruits pre-existed.

The main sources of starch available locally were fruits (nuts, chestnuts, acorns), rhizomes or tubercles (dog's-tooth-violet, yam, lily) and grains (millets). These were the basis of Japanese food but also the ingredients of "sake". Moreover, these starch sources stayed in use, blended with rice, long after the introduction of the latter.

It is therefore impossible to precisely date the "invention" of sake *stricto sensu*. Rather, we must consider the constant evolution of the ingredients, methods and techniques still in progress today.

2. Antiquity: the Court's sake

From the Yayoi era (400 BC to 250 AD), Japanese society began to structure itself and a ruling caste appeared. The consumption of sake, hitherto reserved for rituals, developed within this elite. In 689 the "*Sake no tsukasa*", or Department of Sake Production, was created within the Imperial Palace.

This office was run by the "*Sake no kami*", a high-ranking official, demonstrating the high place that sake now occupied within the Court and Japanese culture in general. The creation of this office was accompanied by a prohibition imposed on commoners. But, like any prohibition, it was subverted: the nobles had the authorization to produce sake so they unofficially marketed it, and those who could afford to, produced their own.

The management of the production of sake by the government triggered a technological boom and a diversification of the methods of production. The "Engishiki", a collection of regulations published between 905 and 927, described 13 varieties of sake produced for the different uses of the Court, of which *goshu, reishu* and *sanshuso* represented the best qualities, *tonshu, jyuso* and *kosake* were reserved for low-rank officials, *zakkyushu* was distributed to civil servants as part of their salary, *shiroki* and *kuroki* (white and black sake, respectively) were used during Shinto ceremonies, and, finally, *aesake* was used for cooking.

The description of these different sakes and their classification tells us about the tastes in vogue at the time as well as the persistence of a wide range of production methods.

Sanshuro still contains millet and malted cereals. *Reishu* is what we would today call an *amazake*, a non-alcoholic or low-alcohol sake. *Goshu* uses a unique recipe to increase its alcoholic strength: rice and *kome-koji* are added to the freshly squeezed sake to restart the fermentation, the pressing and refermentation operation being performed four times. *Shiroki* and *kuroki* are obtained through the same production method (a 10-day fermentation) but wood ashes are added to the *kuroki* to reduce its acidity (ash is an alkaline product).

Other sakes mentioned vary only in their polishing rate or the amount of *koji* used, with the direct consequence of variable production cost, and thus prestige. It should be noted that only the most prestigious sake was filtered.

From the 9th century onwards, the central government gradually lost power to clans and religious movements, which had become prosperous thanks to the gradual abandonment of the Taika centralizing reform (645). The shrines thus obtained the right to produce sake, initially only for ceremonies but, little by little, the production became commercially focused.

With the development of currency during the 12th century (until then barter and rice were the main means of trade), the sake trade became a major source of revenue for the shrines. Under the direction of the monks, many technical advances appeared in the world of sake.

A large part of these innovations were to arise out of the Shoryaku-ji monastery, located to the southeast of Nara: among them were *san-dan shikomi* (the three-step addition of rice, water and *koji*), *morohaku* (exclusive use of polished rice as opposed to *katahaku* where only the *kakemai* is polished), pasteurization at low temperature 300 years before Pasteur, and *fukurozuri* (pressing in cotton bags).

These innovations contributed to the production of sakes more suitable for conservation and, therefore, safe for transport. Until then, many batches of sake turned sour during summer due to the development of spoilage bacteria. A higher alcohol level (thanks to the *san-dan shikomi*), the destruction of the inoculum by pasteurization, and charcoal filtration and fining (the first written references to this technique dates from the mid-14th century) made it possible to circumvent these bacterial contaminations.

3. The Middle Ages: the elite's sake

The rise of the clans culminated during the 12th century with the Ginpei war, which ended with the nomination of Minamoto no Yorimoto as shogun (military dictator) in 1192. He became the *de facto* ruler of Japan, relegating the emperor to a religious and ceremonial role.

The shoguns held power until 1868. These almost seven centuries of feudal power saw the caste of the samurai who, together with their people, became an educated middle class, actively consuming sake.

The shogun's decision to banish home-produced commercial sake in the mid-13th century (1252) gives an indication of its popularity; each home was allowed to keep only one jar of sake. In Kamakura (capital of Japan at the time) 37,274 jars were counted for a total estimated population of 200,000 inhabitants (7 million throughout Japan). We can therefore consider that virtually every household with the financial means to do so, stored at least one sake jar.

Prohibitions on the production and commercialization of sake, although never respected, came and went until the 20th century, based on the need to control the rice supply, which was vital to the shogun's power. Farmers would then produce sake as soon as surpluses of rice were available.

This peasant sake, rustic and unfiltered, was then called "*doburoku*" (literally: cloudy sake) as opposed to the filtered *seishu*, on which the government levied taxes. The Japanese law keeps the memory of this distinction to this day (see "A special case: *nigorizake* pressing ", p.191).

From the 15th century onwards, technological advances foreign to the sake universe allowed for the industrialization of production processes and the professionalization of the sector. For example, Japanese coopers started to produce 1800-liter tanks, compared to the largest 180- or 360-liter terracotta jars that were used until then (see units of measurement for sake, "*koku*").

Since the Court was the first market for sake, Kyoto was at the forefront of these developments: as early as 1425, 342 *kura* were installed in the city. However, the establishment of a strict corporation system stopped this development in the 16th century.

The increasing professionalization of producers and the improvement of the conservation properties of the sake they made led to another revolution: seasonal production. It became possible to produce sake only in winter, when the agricultural workforce was available and low temperatures allowed for long fermentations without contamination, resulting in better quality sake. From year-round production ("*shiki-jozo*", literally production of the four seasons) came five distinct sakes:

shakeshu, aishu, kanmaezake, kanzake and *haruzake*; now, only one type of sake was produced, exclusively in winter ("*kanzukuri*" or production in the cold season).

Toji guilds

Agricultural workers specializing in sake production moved in winter to sake-making regions. Soon, they created a system of guilds by region and the most experienced or gifted workers took the title of *toji* (cellar master). Within these guilds, they exchanged ideas on the best production methods and created distinctive styles. Each guild gathered members and jealously guarded its methods and secrets of production. The most famous guilds sent their members to the four corners of the country at the request of *kura* wishing to improve the quality of their sake. They also became unavoidable recruitment agencies for the *kuramoto* (owners of *kura*) to hire not only a *toji* but also *kurabito* (brewery workers).

Today, only a few guilds remain in activity. They have preserved the names of their region of origin although those were renamed in the 19th century. The main three are Nanbu (Iwate prefecture), Echigo (Niigata prefecture) and Tanba (Hyogo prefecture), followed by Izumo (Shimane prefecture), Noto (Ishikawa prefecture), Tajima (Hyogo prefecture) and Hiroshima. Some of these guilds, including Nanbu, offer training courses and *toji* diplomas. Differences in style, although historically real, no longer make much sense insofar as the different methods of production have been unveiled. However, some *toji* continue to keep these traditions alive through the style of the *kura* where they operate.

The transfer of the capital city to Edo (now Tokyo) in 1603 shifted the center of consumption and production of sake. Initially, small quantities of Kyoto sake were transported by land. However, faced with increased demand and potential profits, merchants started to specialize in ensuring an increased supply of sake by sea.

Specialized boats, light and fast "*taru kaizen*" (that took 20 days to go from Osaka to Edo), were built to avoid sake from spoiling during transport. Their importance became such that they would compete with the regular "Hishigaki" line for Osaka-Edo shipping. Towards the end of the 18th century, these boats could carry up to 3000 barrels per trip.

Not unlike the development of the Bordeaux vineyard (for export to England) to the detriment of the South-West French vineyards, these flows favored a shift of production towards new areas, better suited for exportation because of their geographical location: initially Ikeda and Itami (located on the river), then Nada and Nishinomiya in the 18th century (by the sea).

Simultaneously, under the shogun's drive, the new capital also developed its own means of sake production: in 1666, there were 36 *kura* in Edo. This number may seem very low compared to those for Kyoto, but the Edo *kura*, unable to compete in prestige and quality with those in the Kyoto region, focused instead on large-volume production of entry-level sake to satisfy the thirst of the capital's middle classes.

At the same time, the *sankin-kotai* system (the alternate residence of provincial governors in their fiefdoms and in Edo every other year) promoted sake culture throughout the country, with daimyos favoring local production in order to replicate the pomp and habits of the court in their fiefs.

As for the rest of Japan, sake producers benefitted from more than two centuries of prosperity, in spite of the strict control enforced by the Tokugawa shogunate, which culminated with the distribution of licenses and a rice allocation system introduced in 1657. By 1698 Japan had more than 27,000 *kura*.

4. Modern times: the people's sake

At the turn of the 20th century, the liberation of production rights followed by a sharp increase in taxes on sake (which then represented 30% of the state's revenues) led to the creation, then disappearance, of a large number of *kura*. At the end of the 19th century, Japan had 30,000 sake producers, but by 1912 only 11,000 remained, and by the beginning of the Second World War, only 8,000 were left.

At the beginning of the 20th century, the use of glass bottles became more common. Until then, sake was transported and marketed in *taru* (casks made of *sugi*, Japanese cedar, with a capacity of 18 to 72 liters (see "*Taru* making", p.204) and consumers would fill their *tokkuri* (ceramic pitcher) at their local dealer.

The adoption of the glass bottle as the main container for transport and sales paved the way for the entry of sake into domestic households in a more durable form and democratized its consumption to excess.

This change had important consequences on sake distribution but also, cedar being a very aromatic wood, on sake's taste (try a modern sake produced in such barrels, or *taruzake*, for a glimpse into this radical change of style). The use of glass bottles gradually eliminated this typical taste and encouraged the production of fresh, dry and aromatic sake. This evolution was further favored by the progressive replacement of storage and fermentation tanks, from the historically used *sugi* to enameled steel, and more recently to stainless steel.

Sugi or Japanese Cedar (*Cryptomeria japonica*) occupies a special place in the Shinto religion and as a construction and woodworking timber in Japan. Particularly appreciated for its solidity, its resistance to putrefaction and its high and straight trunk, it was overexploited until the great fire of Meireki that devastated Tokyo in 1657.

Wood demand resulting from the destruction of 70% of Tokyo prompted the shogunate to draw up a precise map of the wood resources and to limit the use of *sugi*: its usage was banned for peasants and limited for the samurai, to which a number of *sugi* logs of standardized size was allocated for building construction.

In 1663, a new regulation prohibited the manufacture of small containers and household tools in *sugi*. In some regions such as Akita, these laws were coupled with even more restrictive local regulations. However, the production of *sugi* tanks, necessary for the production of sake but also of *shoyu* and *miso*, remained authorized.

Sugi is used for the construction of *koji-muro* (the room where the *koji* is grown), storage and fermentation tanks as well as *taru*. Since the appearance of glass bottles, enameled and stainless steel tanks, the taste of *sugi* has disappeared from sake (except for a few *taruzake*: sakes aged in *taru* or *sugi* barrels, see "*Taru*", p.203) and is considered an aromatic deviation.

Although *koji-muro* are still built in *sugi*, it is widely held that many years are needed before the *sugi* flavor from a newly built *koji-muro* stops tainting the *koji*, and only then will the sake produced be of good quality. The *sugi* also remains the symbol of sake stalls and *kura* via the *sugidama* tradition (*sugi* branch ball, see "Aging", p.198).

In 1904, the creation of the National Research Institute on Brewing (NRIB) marked the beginning of a new era that radically changed the style of sake thanks to a wide transfer of technical knowledge.

The promotion of certain production methods (use of enameled steel tanks, selection of yeasts, new *moto* methods) and the organization of national competitions (from 1911 onwards, following the prior existence of local competitions) also brought about, to some extent, a standardization of products.

Additionally in 1904, motivated by the shortfall in taxes, the government decided once again to prohibit (for good this time, the ban being still in force today) home-production of sake.

The Second World War severely hurt the sake sector and the quality of its products. Nearly half of the *kura* were requisitioned for the war effort and turned into weapons factories. The restrictions on rice forced producers to substitute an increasing share of sugar and distilled alcohol. This was especially true of sake produced overseas, mainly in Taiwan, Korea and Manchuria, then parts of the Japanese Empire, or its sphere of influence following the Sino-Japanese and Russo-Japanese wars and their aftermaths.

Sake production outside Japan, 1900-1945

Between the Sino-Japanese war and the Second World War, a growing number of Japanese citizens and military present in those regions triggered a high demand for sake. If at first the demand was met by importation and the developement of local *kuras* by Japanese entrepreneurs and pre-existing Japanese *kura*, the skyrocketing demand coupled with the cost and risks of shipping (then, sake would easily deteriorate, hence it needed a stabilizing adjunction of salicilyc acid), increases of import duty, lack of proper local sake rice and a shortage of Japanese rice, made it much simpler to combine glycerol, starch syrup, glucose, succinic acid, lactic acid, *mirin*, sake *kasu*, rice powder, and a number of other flavoring agents to readily available locally distilled spirits.

This gave birth namely to « Reproduced Japanese sake » in Taiwan or « New Japanese sake » in Manchuria (the latter being specifically produced for the Japanese military in up to 13 plants, giving us an idea of its popularity).

Rice came to represent only a very small proportion of the ingredients, sometimes only in the form of rice powder, or disappearing from the recipes entirely. The resulting beverage, "war sake", required additional corrections with acids, flavors, etc. and holds more to a diluted and flavored alcohol than to the sake we know.

Unfortunately, old habits die hard. After the war, despite the return of abundance and the economic boom that fully benefitted the sake industry, such techniques remained widely in use (see *"Sanbaizoshu"*, p.177). Sake sales exploded until the 1970s when beer and wine began to take its place. Peak sake production, of 1,766 billion liters (for 109 million inhabitants), was reached in 1973.

Since 1944, sake has not been taxed at production but rather at the final point of sale to the consumer. This incited small *kura*, in a bid to avoid taxation, to produce bulk sake and resell it to big, nationally recognized, brands. This delegated form of production, coupled with the old wartime habits and a strong market demand did nothing to improve quality.

The number of *kura* was already falling sharply (down 10% in the 1960s) due to rationalization and the increasing scale of sake companies; but in the late 1970s and 1980s, when sake demand slowed down, large *kura* stopped buying bulk sake and many local *kura* were forced to close (down 32% between 1970 and 1990).

In the early 1990s the economic bubble burst and the economic crisis hit, marking the beginning of a long desert crossing for sake with a continuous fall in production and *kura* numbers during the 1990s and 2000s (down 4% and 2% each year on average, respectively).

Kura and *meigara*

A *kura* can produce sake under one or more brands or "*meigara*", whose name does not necessarily refer to the *kura*. Thus Saura Co. Ltd. markets its sake under the *meigara* "Urakasumi" and Akita Seishu Co. Ltd. markets the *meigara* Dewatsuru, Yamatoshizuku, and Kariho. Between the 1950s and 1970s, this practice was justified, in particular by the large flows of sake between *kura*, allowing to distinguish proprietary and trade sake. This approach could be accompanied by an additional identification of proprietary sake; In Nada, for example, sake *junmai* produced and bottled in the same *kura* could be named "*ki-ippon*": (today the term can be used throughout Japan but has lost its appeal).

Today, the multiple *meigara* are rather used by large *kura* to segment their offerings: for example a "proximity" *meigara* with a rustic and local image, and a high-end *meigara* for "export" to Tokyo and other regions. Moreover, some *kura*, having bought bankrupt competitors, chose to keep their *meigara*, out of respect or for brand synergy.

5. Contemporary times: a resurgence?

In 2010, the volume of sake produced in Japan reached 447 million liters (4 times less than in 1973) for just under 1300 *kura*. Since the 1990s, the industry has largely restructured itself. The 10 largest *kura*, which still account for half the production, have turned to more industrial production methods (such as continuous cooking, liquid rice, *koji* machines, etc.) while the smaller *kura* tend to retain qualitative and traditional methods that they can advertise in their local distribution networks.

Since the beginning of the 2010s, the production volume and number of *kura* seem to have more or less stabilized, mainly thanks to export sales (which doubled between 2002 and 2012, then grew by 60% between 2012 and 2015) triggered by the fashionability of Japanese culture and cooking.

Furthermore, in the domestic market, trends for slow food, local consumption and organic produce are giving new direction to sake production. If the 1980s and 1990s were the years of major brands, *ginjo*, Yamadanishiki and ultra-aromatic yeasts, the 2010s and 2020s could well be those of *jizake* ("local" sake, see "Sake and terroir", p.215), *junmai*, local varieties of rice and high polishing ratios.

Chapter I
Raw Materials

Chapter I: Raw Materials

First and foremost, sake is made of rice, water and *koji*. Here, we will describe in detail all there is to know about these ingredients, their use in the production of sake and their impact on its quality.

a. Rice

While the first sakes were made with various sources of starch, they were progressively replaced with rice as it emerged as a central component of Japanese culture and diet.

i.   Table rice and sake rice

Any type of rice can be used to produce sake, but not all rice can produce quality sake. We distinguish rice especially designed for the production of sake (= *shuzo-koteki-mai*) from table rice or eating rice (*uruchi-mai* or *ippan-mai*). The latter, cultivated on a large scale, are widely available and inexpensive (15 to 20% cheaper, depending on the variety): their use represents between more than 50% of total sake production (for more details see annex 1). Furthermore, while *shuzo-koteki-mai* are produced only in Japan, table rice can be bought on the international market, from countries with lower production costs. It should be noted, however, that such practices are prohibited in the context of the "*nihonshu*" geographical indication (see p.213)

The prevalence of table rice could have increased as a consequence of the recent revocation by the Japanese government of sake rice production subsidies (this decision led to a sharp rise in prices, while table rice remained heavily subsidized in a country dangerously dependent on its mainland neighbors such as China for its food supply). However, due to the rising demand for high quality sake, demand for *shuzo-koteki-mai* remained more or less constant.

It should be noted, that just as the use of a sake rice is not a guarantee of good sake, it is quite possible to produce excellent sake using table rice.

About 270 varieties of Japonica rice are grown in Japan. Among these, a hundred varieties are considered *shuzo-koteki-mai*. This number is constantly evolving as regional research institutes or independent producers breed new, improved, varieties.

To be considered *shuzo-koteki-mai*, a variety must have characteristics that allow the production of a quality *kome-koji* and sake. Some varieties that do not produce a satisfactory *kome-koji* may be used as *kakemai* (rice added to the ferment directly after cooking, as opposed to *kojimai* used for *kome-koji* production) in combination with another variety (such as Yamadanishiki). Here are the main characteristics that distinguish quality rice:

1. Grain size

The weight of 1000 grains (*senryuju* or "1000-grain weight") is used as an indicator for the grain size. A rice whose 1000-grain weight is less than 22 g is considered to be of small size, of average size if it's between 22 and 26 g, and large if it's over 26 g. Large grains are preferred in sake production for deep polishing and the production of *tsuki-haze koji* (a kind of *kome-koji* obtained when the *koji* grows deep in the grain, see p.107).

The 1000-grain weight of a lot of rice can be determined using small counting boards preformed with a thousand holes, thus avoiding counting each grain individually. It is also possible to weigh around 30 g of rice and count the grains to calculate the 1000-grain weight through a simple rule of three.

Within a lot or a set of lots, we can observe a dispersion of grain weights. Ideally, this dispersion (standard deviation) should be kept to a minimum so that the average weight of the batch is representative. Here is an example of the dispersion of grain weights within a sample

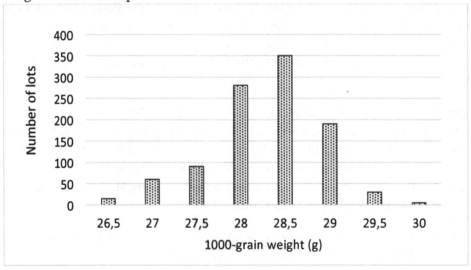

Chart 1. Example of grain weight distribution.
Sample: 1020 batches of 1000 Yamadanishiki grains harvested in 2014 in the Hyogo area, average weight = 28.1 g, min = 26.1 g, max = 29.9 g, standard deviation = 0.6, source: Hyogo Sake Rice Association.

Rice

2. Grain thickness

This measurement, which is complementary to the grain size, is an important qualitative indicator for polishing: a wide grain limits the losses attributable to differential polishing (a grain gets more polished on its long axis than on its short one, see Figure 7).

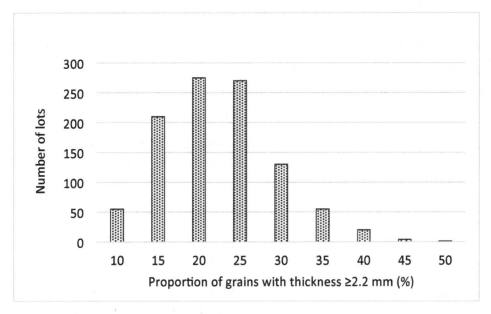

Chart 2. Example of grain thickness.
Sample: 1020 batches of 1000 Yamadanishiki grains harvested in 2014 in the Hyogo area, average percentage = 20.1%, min = 5.3%, max = 46.3%, standard deviation = 7.07, source: Hyogo Sake Rice Association.

3. *Shinpaku*

The *shinpaku* is a core of amyloplasts (starch storage cells) whose arrangement and richness in amylose give the grain particular characteristics. It can be observed with the naked eye in the form of a white heart in the center of the translucent (raw) polished rice grain.

This apparent coloring is due to the aerated structure of the *shinpaku* that disturbs the path of light through the grain. The structure and specific composition of the *shinpaku* create a gelatinous core at the baking stage, which allows the development of the *koji* at the center of the grain, a characteristic particularly sought after for the production of high-end sake (see *Tsuki-haze*, p.107).

Starch, amylose and amylopectin

Starch consists of two types of molecules: amylose and amylopectin, both exclusively made up of chains of D-glucose (a simple sugar). However, their sizes and structures differ:

-**Amylose** is composed of 600 to 1,000 units of glucose, organized in a straight, or scarcely and short-branched structure.

-**Amylopectin** is composed of 1,000 to 100,000 glucose units, organized into a highly branched structure with long branches.

The proportion of these molecules can vary according to the type of starch.

Moreover, with its linear and short structure, amylose is more rapidly digested by *koji* enzymes than amylopectin. Rice grains with a *shinpaku* will dissolve faster and more completely, avoiding loss of material.

Only certain varieties of rice have a *shinpaku*. Among these, one can judge its quality according to several parameters:

a. Occurrence

Even within rice varieties with *shinpaku*, not all grains have a *shinpaku*. It is necessary to consider an occurrence that differs according to varieties and, within a given variety, according to different rice lots.

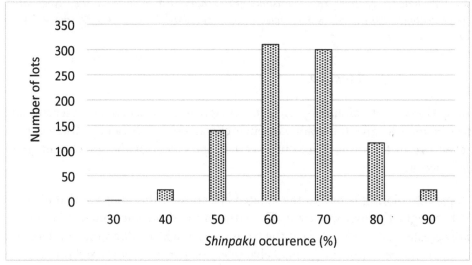

Chart 3. Example of *shinpaku* occurrence.
Sample: 1020 batches of 1000 Yamadanishiki grains harvested in 2014 in the Hyogo area, average occurrence = 59.8%, min = 26.4%, max = 89.8%, standard deviation = 10.48, source: Hyogo Sake Rice Association.

As the *shinpaku* favors the production of a high quality *koji*, a strong occurrence is desirable. For each variety there is a reference value, ranging from 0% for table rice to over 90% for some modern varieties.

However, as we can see in Chart 3, above, *shinpaku* occurrence can vary greatly depending on the rice lot. These variations are mainly explained by cultivation conditions. Lots with a high *shinpaku* occurrence (>70%) are favored, especially for the production of high-end sake.

b. Size

The *shinpaku* must be large enough to have an impact on the grain characteristics but not too large, so as not to alter its resistance to polishing. The ideal size of a *shinpaku* is considered to be about half the thickness of the grain.

c. Position and shape

There are 4 forms of *shinpaku*: "bellied" (eccentric toward the ventral position), "ellipsoid" (central and large), "linear" (central and elongated in the long axis of the grain), and "dot" (central and small).

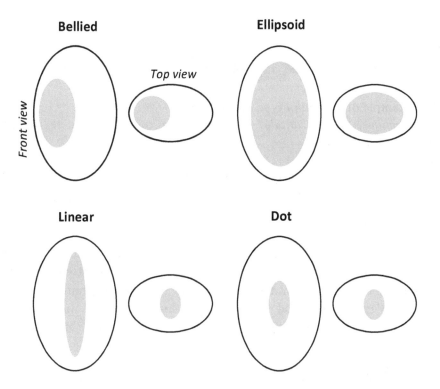

Figure 2. The four *shinpaku* shapes.

Ideally, the *shinpaku* should be central in order to be preserved after polishing, and large (except for deep polishing, as they can weaken the grain, see "Resistance to polishing", below). The ellipsoid or linear forms are therefore generally preferred, but a single batch of rice may present all the different forms.

The characteristics of a rice lot's *shinpaku* depend mainly on the variety and conditions of cultivation (weather, soil, cultivation methods, etc.).

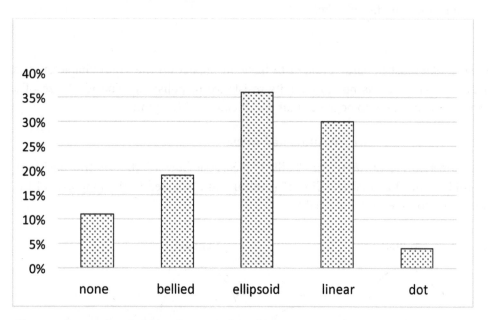

Chart 4. Example of *shinpaku* type distribution.
Lot of Hattannishiki 35 rice, cultivated in Hiroshima prefecture, 11% none, 19% bellied, 36% ellipsoid, 30% linear, 4% dot.

d. Resistance to polishing

This criterion has grown in importance over the last few years due to the *ginjo* sake trend, which favors deeply polished rice.

Some grains are broken by the friction of the grinding wheel. This may be due to pre-existing fragilities (cracks) or to the structure of the grain itself (such as low tissue density, or eccentric or large *shinpaku*). The broken grains expose their internal layers to polishing and represent a net loss of material. In the literature, polishing values are recommended for each variety, beyond which the risk of breakage is too high.

The great resistance of Yamadanishiki to extreme polishing is one of the features that has made it the most cultivated sake variety. There are, for example, sake made with Yamadanishiki polished at 12% or 21% (this is the remaining fraction, see "*Seimaibuai*", p.72, for more details). Other varieties make it possible to go even lower (see the "Extreme polishing rates" insert)

e. Steaming process tolerance

Before use, the rice is soaked and steamed: in order to ensure the quality and homogeneity of the rice after cooking, the raw rice must be allowed to absorb water (see "Cleaning, washing and steeping (*senmai* and *shinseki*)", p.84).

Moreover, in order to allow the development of the *koji*, sake rice must keep its integrity after cooking. The ideal consistency is elastic, firm and very slightly sticky.

f. Lipid and protein contents

Rice contains lipids and proteins, especially in its outer layers. When present in large quantities, these elements can have a negative impact on the aromatics of sake (see "Purpose of polishing", p.79).

Sake rice ideally contains a protein level of 5-6%, compared to 7-8% for standard rice (and 0.3-0.7% lipids).

g. Solubility

Not all rice dissolves as easily during fermentation. The dissolution is mainly carried out under the action of *koji* enzymes, which degrade starch.

As explained above, starch consists of two types of molecules, amylose and amylopectin. The amylose-rich grains dissolve more quickly because the structure of amylose is more accessible to enzymes. A high amylose content also guarantees a better grain integrity after cooking (glutinous rice contains 1% amylose versus 12-19% for short grain rice). Moreover, the presence of a *shinpaku* promotes solubilization thanks to its loose structure.

Matsuo-sama, Shinto, and sake production

Most *sakagura* have a *kami-dana* (Shinto shrine) dedicated to Matsuo-sama, the main *kami* of sake production. The workers greet him every day after washing their hands, and make regular food offerings (mainly rice and sake).

Shinto ceremonies can be organized to celebrate the beginning or end of the production season, the new year, or the success of the *kura's* sakes in a contest. The ancestral ties between sake and Shinto are thus perpetuated even within the most modern *kura*.

ii.   Sake rice cultivation in Japan

1. Historical and political context

Irrigated rice cultivation covers about 1.6 million hectares of the 4.2 million hectares of arable land in Japan. The area under rice cultivation has been halved since the post-war period, while yields have doubled due to modern agronomic methods.

The Japanese agricultural sector, and particularly rice cultivation, is highly controlled and subsidized by the state, in order to maintain a socio-economic fabric of part-time small farmers. Most of these farmers are members of the Japanese Agricultural Cooperative (JA) to which sake producers must address their request for rice.

However, this system showed its limits in the 1980s. At the time, new laws promoted high yields in the production of agricultural commodities. Cooperatives then set rice purchase prices without yield criteria, resulting in a sharp decline in quality and the abandonment of the less productive varieties. Sake rices, which yield 30-60% less than table rices, had been particularly affected, and some ancient varieties, such as Omachi, went close to disappearing.

The crisis of sake sales pushed producers to question themselves in the 1990s. While some looked for more and more industrial solutions to reduce costs, others, inspired in particular by the culture of wine that had developed in the country, reinvested in rice production. They established partnerships with cooperatives, or with independent growers, in the form of contracts setting not only a price but also a quality and expected yield. Today, a small number of *kuramoto* are also getting involved in rice cultivation and organic rice production is growing.

> ### JA and rice cultivation (1/2)
>
> In the aftermath of the Second World War (1946), the Japanese authorities, backed by General Douglas MacArthur, the Supreme Allied Commander, adopted a far-reaching agrarian reform. Among other measures, it limited land ownership to 3 *cho* (a little less than 3 hectares), removed the payment in kind of rents (which had always been paid in rice) and limited them to 25% of the harvest. In just three years, more than half of the country's arable land was taken over by the government and redistributed to peasants.
>
> At the same time, the agency responsible for collecting, storing and redistributing food in wartime (Nogyokai) became the JA (Japanese Agricultural Cooperative). Its legal functions and powers remained, however, virtually unchanged due to the food shortage.

Its action was in any case made necessary by the fragmentation of production induced by the agrarian reform. This history explains the JA's omnipresence in all aspects of Japanese agricultural life: from the supply of seeds and plant protection products, to the commercialization of crops, to banks ("Norinchukin bank" and "JA bank") and advice to producers.

The reform of 1946 radically changed the method of supplying rice to *kura*. *Kuramoto*, largely rich landowners, who had hitherto used their surplus rice for production, were now obliged to buy rice from the JA at a price determined by the state. It was not until 1995, when the "Stabilization of supply, demand and primary food stabilization act" was introduced to deregulate the market, that it became possible to buy rice directly from its producer. Furthermore, new legislation passed in 2004 and 2008 authorized *kura* to, once again, produce their own rice. However, few *kuramoto* have bought land. Indeed, the price of land in Japan is very high while the rental of it is almost free. This is explained by a system of subsidies conditional on the exploitation of these lands. The landlords thus lease their land for long periods of time, at rock-bottom prices provided they are cultivated, and satisfy themselves with Government subsidies. Moreover, the *kuramoto* do not necessarily have rice production knowledge. Thus, they prefer to establish long-term contracts with farmers, specifying quality criteria and possibly cultivation methods. About half of the *kura* have chosen this mode of operation, the others continuing to buy their rice via the JA. Many *kura*, however, use both systems because some rice is available only via the JA (like the Yamadanishiki in the Yokawa region, see "Hyogo-prefecture Yamadanishiki", p.69) or to ensure a certain volume.

In order to buy rice from the JA, the *kura* must specify in their order the quantity, quality and region of origin of the desired rice. Orders are usually grouped by local sake producer associations before being sent to the JA. Demand for rice is relatively constant and there is much discussion between producers and the JA to ensure that plantations match the need. However, shortages can occur, especially in the case of a small harvest, as in 2013.

2. Irrigated rice farming

Rice is grown during summer, usually alternating with a dry winter crop harvested in the spring, such as wheat. In cold northern areas where the vegetative period is too short for this rotation, rice can be grown two years out of three (rice growing two consecutive years, then wheat and soybean in the third year, for example). In the extreme south, on the island of Okinawa, two harvests per year can be obtained. However, cultivating rice continuously on the same plot may deplete the soil. This practice is therefore strongly discouraged.

Here, we will describe the main stages of irrigated rice cultivation, for a field in central Japan, alternating with a winter crop. The dates indicated in brackets are for illustrative purposes only and may vary from one to two months depending on the variety and latitude.

In spring (April) seeds are steeped for 4 to 12 days to activate germination. When seeded, the seeds are sown at high density in a nursery. After 30 to 50 days, the plants reach 20 to 40 cm in height and are ready to be transplanted (May). At the same time, the winter crop is harvested. Vegetative parts are usually ground on the spot and compost or fertilizer added to feed the soil. The plot is then plowed and irrigated in preparation for planting, which will be done in a fine mud. When the plot and the seedlings are ready, they are delicately plucked, cleaned, bundled and planted in rows. Manual planting can be done with a wooden jig that helps building straight rows and constant spacing between plants on the row and between rows. Several types of templates exist but the best known is a wooden frame equipped with four plugs allowing it to be fixed to the ground. When the plants have been positioned, the template is turned over on the axis formed by two of the plugs (imagine a ladder that would be turned over on one side). One side of the frame thus remains on the last row planted while the second side forms the new row, perfectly parallel to the previous one.

Manual transplantation is very labor intensive and mechanical solutions have been developed. The first automated transplanters were created in Japan in the 1960s and are now used by all farmers. They take the form of small hand-held or self-propelled tractors, equipped with a loading platform on which trays of young plants are placed. A system of claws sequentially separates off plants and then pushes them into the mud in the same movement.

This type of transplanter requires an adaptation of cultivation methods. The plants are now grown in standard 28x58 cm trays. These trays are filled in 3 layers: earth, seeds and then with a thin layer of clay. Approximately 120 g of seed are used per tray or some 4000 to 5000 seeds per tray, equivalent to 3 to 4 seeds per square centimeter. The trays are then placed in a germination chamber for 3 days and then in a culture chamber for 4 days. In the first chamber, the seeds are kept under ideal conditions for germination: a temperature of 27-30 °C (80-86 °F) and high humidity. In addition, the trays are stacked on top of each other, creating a pressure on the seeds favorable to germination. In the second chamber, conditions promote growth and photosynthesis: the trays are separated in order to give the young plants access to sunlight.

At the end of these 7 days, the plants reach a few centimeters and the entangled roots create a carpet of plants that can be handled without a tray. The plants must then keep on growing until they reach 20 centimeters, the ideal size for mechanized transplanting. As we have seen above, traditional varieties reach this stage after 1 to 2 months. However, thanks to varietal improvements, twenty days are now enough to reach this stage. This duration is shortened (15 days from germination) for automated transplanting, which requires smaller plants (8-25 cm depending on the conditions).

Cultivators with small areas and dual activity cannot always provide the necessary care for nursery plants. However, they can choose to buy their seedlings directly from an agricultural cooperative that also manages the distribution of harvested rice to final customers as well as sells seeds, seedlings, fertilizers and pesticides.

Regardless of the planting system, a gap of 30 cm between rows of plants is typically used. The distance of the row can vary between 12 and 21 cm, but is generally around 15 cm. In the case of manual planting, only one plant is positioned per site, sometimes two if they are small or feeble. In the case of mechanical planting, the claw drives and plants 3-5 seedlings per site.

Once the plot has been planted, it is flooded (see the "Rice cultivation inputs" insert on the next page). A water layer of 10 cm is generally maintained during the first week, then the plot is drained and kept with between 3 and 5 cm of water until one month before "heading" (that features the appearance of the ears).

A new wet phase (with 10 to 15 cm of water) that lasts 3 weeks begins after heading (August). The flowering and grain filling periods are critical for the quality of the rice. The air temperature directly affects the quality of the starch and therefore the digestibility of the rice. A warm season (with temperatures above 25 °C / 77 °F) will favor the production of long chains of amylopectin difficult to hydrolyze, while a cool season (with temperatures below 25 °C / 77 °F) will favor short chains and thus a better digestibility of rice.

Harvesting takes place in September with combine harvesters. The grain must be harvested at the right maturity: too early harvesting will yield green grains, a late harvest will give dry, brittle grains. Mild weather during flowering favors grain homogeneity and therefore facilitates the choice of a harvest date. However, a crop is never perfect and a crop with 85% mature grains is considered to be of high quality (see "Rice quality assessment systems", p.66).

After harvesting, the grain is dried in order to reduce it from 20-25% moisture at harvest to 15% moisture, a content more suitable for storage. Then, it is husked (the elimination of the husk, see "Rice grain structure", p.72), bagged and shipped, ready to be used by the *kura.*

> ## Rice cultivation inputs
>
> Throughout the vegetative period, rice requires care to deal with the various ills that can afflict the crop:
>
> Despite the water layer that limits the development of other crops, rice remains susceptible to weed competition and therefore requires regular manual or chemical weeding control (every 10 to 15 days during the growing season). Similarly, fungicides and insecticides are used to prevent attacks of bacteria, fungi and insects. Various fertilizers can also be added to increase yields and avoid soil depletion.
>
> Rice is also subject to lodging, i.e. the fall of the plant under the weight of its grains, favored by the wind or certain diseases. It is necessary to control the nutrition (especially nitrogen) of the plant through planting density and an adapted fertilization program in order to produce short and solid stems. The tallest varieties are the most susceptible to lodging.
>
> Although conventional rice farming still prevails, many alternative methods to chemical pesticides and fertilizers exist. The most famous is the Aigamo method, which introduce ducks in the fields to eat weeds, insects and feed the rice plants by their droppings. Fishes and algae can complement this method. The higher cost of alternative methods can be more than offset with adequate communication of the features of the final product.

3. Rice varietal improvement

Today, farmers choose cultivated varieties based on two main factors:

1/ the variety's **agronomic qualities** and **adaptation to a given terroir**.

2/ **market demand** and **selling price**, both depending on the variety's processing qualities and, sometimes, latest trends in the sake market.

Significant research efforts have been made by the Japanese government to obtain varieties that meet both criteria. These new varieties have been developed through public research, funded by the Ministry of Agriculture, Forestry and Fisheries (MAFF) or its regional offices, and private research.

They are obtained by crossing old varieties, with the aim of improving their agronomic qualities, their adaptation to the climate and their ability to produce sake. The main criteria for improvement are as follows:

-Early or late varieties
-Germination rate
-Resistance to cold, lodging and diseases
-Yields
-Processing qualities

These new varieties are obtained mainly by crossbreeding preexisting varieties but also through mutagenesis or genetic engineering.

Rice is a self-pollinating plant (see next page's insert). Cultivated varieties of rice are therefore pure lines, strongly influencing available methods of improvement.

The bulk method is a classical method of varietal improvement for self-pollinated species. Its principle is described in Figure 3, below.

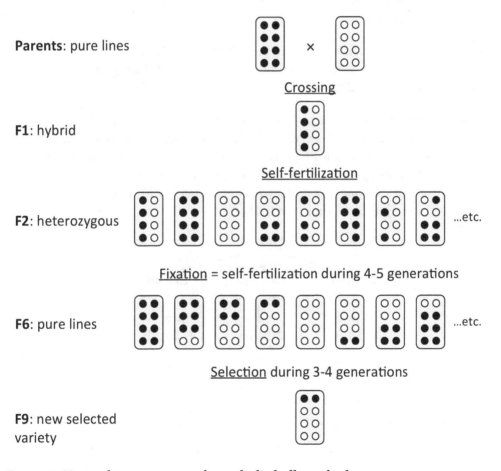

Figure 3. Varietal improvement through the bulk method.

Rice genetics, autogamy and pure lineage

For plants as for animals, pairs of chromosomes carry the genotype formed by the genes of an individual. Two versions of a given gene, called alleles, are thus present in an individual, each carried by a chromosome of the pair. For a given gene, a genotype is represented by two letters corresponding to the alleles: "AB" for an individual carrying the A and B alleles, for example, the blood groups in humans.

An individual randomly receives for each gene an allele from his father and an allele from his mother. This principle explains the differences between descendants of the same parents: a pair of parents "AB × AB" can give "AA", "AB" or "BB" descendants.

Rice is a self-pollinating plant. That is, in more than 90% of cases, a given plant is self-fertilizing. This phenomenon is due in particular to the late opening of the rice flowers: the stamen (male organ of the flower) pollinates the pistil (female organ of the flower) before the pollen from other individuals can do so.

Consequently, rice tends to form pure lines, that is to say individuals possessing twice the same allele (homozygosity) for all their genes (in the above example AA or BB):

A self-reproducing AB (heterozygous) individual gives a mixed AA, BB and AB offspring while an AA or BB individual only gives respectively AA or BB descendants. Thus, the proportion of AB in the population decreases rapidly until it disappears (in fact, a small part remains in the case of rice because of the rare natural crosses between plants which represent less than 10% of the reproduction in the field).

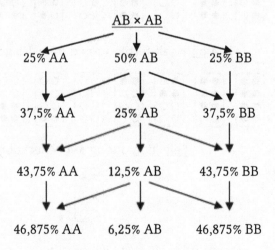

This method consists first of all in crossing two pre-existing and complementary varieties of pure lineage. At the end of this crossing, a hybrid (F1) is obtained which, by self-fertilization, gives a wide variety of heterozygous (F2) lines. These lines are cultivated for 4 to 5 years and give new pure lines (F6) by self-fertilization (see the insert "Rice genetics, autogamy and pure lineage"). This phenomenon is called "fixation". The evaluation of the agronomic and technical qualities of these varieties over a period of four to five years allows the selection of one or more new varieties (F9).

The Yamadanishiki variety was obtained through the single seed descent (SSD) method, a method similar to the bulk method, where only one seed per plant is retained in each generation during the fixation period. The initial crossing, Yamadaho X Tankan Wataribune, was carried out in 1923. In 1928 the pure lines were fixed and the future Yamadanishiki was called "lineage 161". In 1932, after a first selection, it was named "Yama-watari 50-7". A new round of selection took place before it got its definitive name of Yamadanishiki in 1936.

These long and costly methods are now often replaced by modern genetic tools that simplify and accelerate the fixation steps, using haplodiploidy methods, and the selection stages, by searching for genetic markers.

4. Main rice varieties used in sake production

There are now about a hundred varieties of *shuzo-koteki-mai*, to which may be added a dozen table varieties commonly used in sake production. Together they form the *sakamai* or rice used for the production of sake.

This number is constantly changing as new varieties are bred and others forsook, but most of the currently used varieties have been recently obtained, whereas only a few old varieties have survived technical progress.

Here is a broad overview of the main varieties used, presented in alphabetical order with, when available, their region of origin and their registration or market entry date:

Aiyama (Tochigi, 1949) 愛山
The grains and *shinpaku* of the Aiyama are among the most imposing in the *shuzo-koteki-mai* category. Because of this, Aiyama is suitable for *ginjo* production but does not form a satisfactory *kome-koji*, hence a different *kojimai* is sometimes used. Aiyama-based sake have a characteristic depth.

Akinosei (Akita, 1996) 秋の精
Descendant of Miyamanishiki, its technical characteristics are close to the latter, but thanks to its adaptation to lowland cultivation, higher yields can be obtained. Its grains are of satisfactory size (25.5 g per 1000 grains) but have a low *shinpaku* occurrence.

Influence of the rice variety on the final product

By analogy with wine, we tend to consider rice varieties as our grape varieties. However, if any wine professional has a good chance to recognize a particular grape variety (or at least one family of grape varieties) in a blind tasting, this is not the case for sake. Compared to grapes, rice contains very few aromatic compounds and the differences between varieties are minute. Hence, the influence of a variety of rice on the finished product is subtle and depends as much on its physical characteristics as on its chemical composition. For example, rice with a medium grain size that is weak or tends to break during polishing will be less used to produce *ginjo*; the presence of a *shinpaku* will modify the development of the *koji* and the rate of dissolution in the ferment; a higher protein content will lead to a faster and more vigorous fermentation, etc.

Some (misused) cellar practices can easily mask the characteristics of a rice variety: ultra-aromatic yeast for a traditionally rustic Omachi, heavy use of distilled alcohol masking the texture of Yamadanishiki, etc.

For these reasons, the indications given below concerning the style of sake made from each variety remain relatively general. Let us keep in mind that if "wine is made in the vineyard", sake is without question made in the cellar.

Akita-komachi (Akita, 1984) あきたこまち
Popular table rice descendant of Koshihikari, sometimes used in the production of sake.

Akita-saké-komachi (Akita, 2001) 秋田酒こまち
A crossbreeding of local varieties, it is adapted to its northern climate and has good agronomic characteristics. The large size of its grains (27 g per 1000 grains) and its strong *shinpaku* occurrence (both better than the Miyamanishiki) make it a quality rice suitable for *ginjo* production. It was quickly adopted by producers based in Akita prefecture.

Dewanosato (Yamagata, 2004) 出羽の里
Crossbreeding of Ginfubuki and Dewasansan. Intended as a development of the latter, it has better agronomic characteristics, including an increased resistance to cold. Its yield is slightly lower, but at equal grain weight it presents a better occurrence of *shinpaku* and a superior overall quality.

Dewasansan (Yamagata, 1994) 出羽燦々
A Miyamanishiki and Hanafubuki cross that has excellent resistance to cold and lodging, but is relatively susceptible to disease. It has a good occurrence of *shinpaku*, absorbs water homogeneously during cooking and produces deep flavorful sake, with a hint of greenness.

Fukunohana (Hyogo, 1965) フクノハナ
This variety met a brief success between 1967 and 1972 before it virtually disappeared from 1985 onwards. It is now cultivated only in Izushi (Hyogo) and used by the *kura* Fukumitsuya Shuzo (Ishikawa). It is mainly criticized for its sensitivity to deep polishing, high protein levels and poor *koji* cultivation potential, which encourages its use as *kakemai* only.

Fusanomai (Chiba, 2001) 総の舞
Crossbreed of local varieties, Fusanomai has good agronomic characteristics: resistance to cold, lodging and fungi. It presents a good *shinpaku* occurrence and large grains (25.5 g per 1000 grains). Its processing qualities are excellent, close to Yamadanishiki's, and it tends to produce fruity sake.

Ginfubuki (Shiga, 1998) 吟吹雪
This crossing of Yamadanishiki and Tamasakae was made in order to obtain the technical characteristics of the Yamadanishiki while retaining the adaptation of the Tamasakae to the climate of Shiga. With the exception of grain weight, which is lower than that of Tamasakae, Ginfubuki has been a success and is widely used in Shiga.

Gin-ginga (Iwate, 1999) 吟ぎんが
Local variety developed in the early 1990s with the aim of obtaining an early variety adapted to the northern climate of Iwate. It is very resistant to cold and its agronomic and technical characteristics are good (26 g per 1000 grains).

Gin-no-sato (Fukuoka, 2007) 吟のさと
Descendant of Yamadanishiki, developed in order to obtain a local rice adapted to the production of *kome-koji* less sensitive to lodging. A late variety adapted to the southern climate of Kyushu, it retains the technical characteristics of Yamadanishiki (*shinpaku*, grain weight, resistance to polishing, etc.) while offering a better yield (+15%) and a 25 cm shorter straw (for lodging resistance).

Gin-no-sei (Akita, 1993) 吟の精

Developed with the aim of obtaining a variety dedicated to *daiginjo*, bearing large grains and being more resistant to polishing than Miyamanishiki. Unfortunately, the rest of its technical characteristics are disappointing (cold sensitive, low *shinpaku* occurrence, etc.)

Gin-no-yume (Kochi, 2002) 吟の夢

Descendant of Yamadanishiki developed for the production of *ginjo* sake. It has smaller grains (24 g per 1000 grains) but better *shinpaku* occurrence and low protein levels.

Gin-otome (Iwate, 2003) ぎんおとめ

Local variety developed in the same program as Gin-ginga. Its technical characteristics are good, comparable to Miyamanishiki's. It is less resistant to cold but more resistant to certain diseases than Gin-ginga; the two varieties are complementary.

Ginpu (Hokkaido, 2000) 吟風

Crossbreed of Hattannishiki and Kirara 397. Perfectly adapted to the Hokkaido climate by virtue of its cold resistance, it has better processing qualities than Hatsushizuku (a previous local variety), including a better *shinpaku* occurrence. It produces high quality sake with fairly pronounced rice aromas.

Gohyakumangoku (Niigata, 1957) 五百万石

Crossbreeding of Kamenoo and Omachi named in honor of the 1956 exceptional rice crop in Niigata prefecture, which reached 5 million (gohyakuman) *koku* (= 750,000 tons). It produces light, fruity and elegant sake. Being the second most cultivated variety, it is found in many regions, but its low resistance to cold, lodging and diseases limit its development. Moreover, its grains hardly support extreme polishing (*seimaibuai* <50%), limiting its use for high-end sake. However, it has been crossbred many times with other varieties in an attempt to overcome these limitations.

Goriki (Tottori, 1921) 強力

Selected from the native varieties of the region, it disappeared after the war because its high height was no longer adapted to modern cultivation techniques. A group of producers rediscovered it in 1985. It produces powerful and earthy sake, hence its name, which means strength or power.

Haenuki (Yamagata, 1993) はえぬき

Table rice, indirect descendant of Akita-komachi, resistant to cold and lodging, commonly used for sake production.

Hakutsurunishiki (Hyogo, 2007) 白鶴錦

Crossbreeding of Yamadanishiki and Yamadaho developed by Hakutsuru Shuzo, remarkable for the size of its grains (29.2 g for 1000 grains) and its *shinpaku*. It is little used outside its *kura* of origin.

Hanafubuki (Aomori, 1988) 華吹雪

Descendant of Okuhomare, it met a great success thanks to its agronomic qualities (rusticity and yield). Although still abundantly used, Dewasansan, one of its descendants with better transformation skills (notably fewer amino acids) is now preferred.

Hanakagura (Miyazaki, 2000) はなかぐら

Descendant of Yamadanishiki developed in order to obtain a variety more resistant to lodging. It inherited the general characteristics of Yamadanishiki with a lower straw height (shorter by 20cm) and higher yield (greater by 10%). However its relatively low *shinpaku* occurrence and its higher protein level have prompted new selections.

Common rice variety names

A certain recurrence can be observed in the names of rice varieties. Here is the meaning of the main terms used:

Kanji	Pronunciation	Meaning
華	Hana	Flower
誉	Homare	Glory
錦	Nishiki	Brocade
酒	Sake	Sake
雫	Shizuku	Drop
夢	Yume	Dream
舞	Mai	Dance
改良	Kairyo	Improvement

Table 1. Main terms used in rice variety names.

Hanaomoi (Aomori, 2001) 華想い
Crossbreed of Hanafubuki and Yamadanishiki, it inherited very good transformation skills from the latter: low protein content and a high grain hardness that allows for deep polishing.

Hanasayaka (Aomori, 2014) 華さやか
A new kind of strain, whose protein content is altered (rich in indigestible prolamin and low in digestible glutelin), allowing the production of sake poor in amino acids even with a high *seimaibuai*.

Hatsushizuku (Hokkaido, 1998) 初雫
Crossbreed of three local varieties, it has good agronomic qualities, including an excellent resistance to cold, suited to Hokkaido's climate. Its relatively low average grain weight (23.6 g per 1000 grains) and low *shinpaku* occurrence limit its *kome-koji* production qualities. Its processing characteristics are otherwise standard and it gives good quality sake, dry and low in acids and amino acids. This original Hokkaido sake rice has now largely been replaced by Ginpu.

Hattannishiki (Hiroshima, 1962, 1984) 八反錦
There are three main varieties in the Hattan family, all three descended from the historical Hattanso variety: Hattan 35 (1962), Hattannishiki 1 and Hattannishiki 2 (1984). Varieties 1 and 2 have better agronomic characteristics (less susceptible to lodging) and a larger *shinpaku*, but their grains easily break during polishing and are therefore not suitable for *ginjo* making, contrary to Hattan 35. Hattannishiki based sake show an understated aromatic but a rich, earthy flavor and a mild texture.

Hidahomare (Gifu, 1981) 飛騨誉
The only sake rice originating from Gifu region, it is widely used locally but never succeeded farther.

Hinohikari (Miyazaki, 1989) ヒノヒカリ
Popular table variety, descendant of Koshihikari, commonly used in the production of sake.

Hitachinishiki (Ibaraki, 2000) ひたち錦
Original and only recent Ibaraki variety, developed to promote "pure Ibaraki" sake. Widely used locally to produce light and clean *ginjo*, it never succeeded farther despite its overall good agronomic and processing qualities.

Hitogokochi (Nagano, 1997) ひとごこち

Variety with good agronomic and technical characteristics, generally superior to Miyamanishiki: high yield, large grains, strong occurrence of *shinpaku*. Increasingly used, it nevertheless struggles to impose himself against its famous "cousin".

Hitomebore (Miyagi, 1991) ひとめぼれ

Popular table variety descendant of Koshihikari, commonly used in the production of sake.

Hiyori (Miyagi, 2004) ひより

Crossbreeding of Yamadanishiki and Sasashigure developed to obtain a local variety more resistant to deep polishing.

Hohai (Aomori, 1976) 豊盃

An ancient variety, mainly used by the *kura* Miura Shuzo, which sells its sake under the eponymous *meigara* (transcribed "Houhai").

Hokuriku 12 (Niigata, 1935) 北陸12号

Historical variety of Niigata prefecture, also cultivated in Ishikawa, appreciated for its historical importance.

Homarefuji (Shizuoka, 2005) 誉富士

A local selection of Yamadanishiki, its characteristics are very close to the latter. However, its shorter shoots (25 cm shorter), give it a greater resistance to lodging, and its grains are particularly poor in protein. Most Shizuoka *kura* use it because it is the only variety developed in the region.

Hoshiakari (Miyagi, 2001) 星あかり

Descendant of Miyamanishiki and (indirectly) Takanenishiki developed by a private company.

Hyogokitanishiki (Hyogo, 1987) 兵庫北錦

Descendant of Gohyakumangoku appreciated for its resistance to cold and for its large *shinpaku*, which makes it a quality *kojimai*.

Hyogokoinishiki (Hyogo, 1972) 兵庫恋錦

A descendant of Yamadanishiki resistant to lodging, mainly cultivated in the Yokawa district (see "Hyogo-prefecture Yamadanishiki", p.69) and used by the Kikumasamune *kura*. Its large grains are unfortunately very fragile, and therefore require special attention during both polishing and rinsing/steeping.

Hyogonishiki (Hyogo, 2010) 兵庫錦
Crossbreed of Saikai134 and Yamadanishiki (Saikai134/Yamadanishiki// Yamadanishiki), it inherited the main features of the latter while offering a shorter (lodging resistant) straw and a better yield. However, sake produced from Hyogonishiki are comparatively richer in amino acids and less aromatic.

Hyogo-Omachi (Hyogo, 1951) 兵庫雄町
Abandoned variety, ancestor of Hyogoyumenishiki.

Hyogoyumenishiki (Hyogo, 1995) 兵庫夢錦
Indirect descendant of Yamadanishiki, Kikusui and Hyogo-Omachi, developed to diversify the varieties available in the Hyogo area and to obtain a variety more suited to the climate of the western parts of the region (from Ichikawa). It has excellent agronomic and technical characteristics, comparable to Yamadanishiki, except for its shorter straw (more resistant to lodging). Since the seeds have a low germination capacity, the farmer has to compensate by increasing the density of the plantation in the nursery, increasing cultivation costs.

Inishienomai (Hyogo, 2005) いにしえの舞
Descendant of Hyogoyumenishiki developed by the Ozeki *kura* for their own use. Although its technical and agronomic characteristics are satisfactory, it does not attract specific attention from the rest of the industry.

Ipponjime (Niigata, 1993) 一本〆
Descendant of Gohyakumangoku, relatively resistant to cold and lodging, bearing large grains (27 g per 1000 grains) particularly resistant to polishing. Being an early variety, its seeds are often the prey of birds, discouraging many farmers despite high potential yields.

Ishikawamon (Ishikawa, 2008) 石川門
Descendant of Ipponjime and (indirectly) Gohyakumangoku developed in order to obtain an original local variety. It has very satisfactory agronomic and technical characteristics (yields superior to Gohyakumangoku, 26 g per 1000 grains, high occurrence of *shinpaku*) and has been rapidly adopted in the region.

Iwai (Kyoto, 1933) 祝
Descendant of Nojoho, it was abandoned during the war and rediscovered in 1991. Only original rice from the large sake-producing prefecture of Kyoto, it is highly sought after and therefore expensive (more than Yamadanishiki). For this reason and thanks to its huge *shinpaku*, it is mainly used in the production of *ginjo*.

Kairyo-hattan-nagare (Shimane, 1960) 改良八反流
Improvement of Hattan-nagare (historical variety) developed for greater resistance to diseases and lodging. Its technical characteristics are good but this variety remains anecdotal.

Kairyo-omachi (Shimane, 1960) 改良雄町
Improvement of Omachi, adapted to the climate of Shimane. Its grains break during polishing, it is therefore not adapted to the production of *ginjo*. Moreover, its high shoots make it susceptible to lodging.

Kairyo-shinko (Akita, 1959) 改良信交
Improvement of Takanenishiki, adapted to the climate of Akita.

Kamenoo (Yamagata, 1893) 亀の尾
An ancient table variety, which fell into disuse after the war because of its inadequacy for "modern" cultivation methods. The massive use of fertilizers aggravates its sensitivity to diseases and the risk of lodging due to its tall shoots. Many varieties used today were developed through Kamenoo crossbreeding, including: Koshihikari, Sasanishiki, Goyakumangoku, Takanenishiki. Accepted as *shuzo-koteki-mai* since 1951 despite the small size of its grains and its low *shinpaku* occurrence. Driven by enthusiasm for ancient varieties, the Kamenoo has found favor with some fifty *kura* in recent years. Kamenoo sake products are robust and deep with good aging potential.

Kan-no-mai (Shimane, 1996) 神の舞
Crossbreed of Gohyakumangoku and Miyamanishiki developed to obtain Gohyakumangoku's technical characteristics and Miyamanishiki's cold resistance. Thanks to this resistance and its precocity, it is suitable for cultivation in the mountainous areas of Shimane, between 200 and 500 meters above sea level. It offers both good yield and large grains (28 g per 1000 grains).

Kazenaruko (Kochi, 2002) 風鳴子
Second variety of Kochi, developed in the wake of Gin-no-yume. A descendant of Ipponjime, it exhibits better disease resistance and processability, while its other characteristics are comparable.

Kikusui (Niigata, 1937) 菊水
Descendant of Omachi, selected for its shorter straw (more resistant to lodging, one of Omachi's big flaws). Quickly abandoned because of its sensitivity to insects, it was rediscovered by the eponymous *kura*, Kikusui.

Kinmonnishiki (Nagano, 1956) 金紋錦

Crossbreeding of Yamadanishiki and Takanenishiki. Its agronomic characteristics can not compare to recent varieties, but the depth of the sake produced is interesting. For years, only Fukumitsuya *shuzo* in Ishikawa used this variety for their "Kuroobi" sake. Since 2004, it has also been used in the Nagano prefecture.

Kirara 397 (Hokkaido, 1989) きらら397

Historically, the first variety of quality table rice cultivated in Hokkaido. Appreciated for its resistance to cold, it is still widely cultivated for the table. For sake production however, even if still occasionally used, it has been largely replaced by new varieties, better suited for processing.

Kissui (Yamagata, 1993) 亀 粋

Improvement of Kamenoo obtained by the Yonetsuru Shuzo *kura*.

Kitashizuku (Hokkaido, 2014) きたしずく

The latest variety from the Hokkaido Agriculture Experimental Station, a crossbreeding of Hoshinoyume (a Hokkaido table rice, like Kirara 397), Omachi and Ginpu. Due to its newness, we lack experience of its processing qualities.

Koi-omachi (Hiroshima, 1996) こいおまち

Descendant of Kairyo-omachi developed in order to get a variety less susceptible to lodging. Compared to its ancestor, its straws are shorter by 15 cm and it bears larger grains and *shinpaku* (26.3 g per 100 grains).

Kojonishiki (Aomori, 1967) 古城錦

Historical Aomori prefecture rice, descendant of Gohyakumangoku.

Kokuryo-Miyako (Yamaguchi, 1889) 穀良都

Native variety, difficult to grow but historically considered superior to Kamenoo for the quality of sake produced. It disappeared after the war and was rediscovered in 1999 in the form of a few seeds stored in a university.

Koshihikari (Niigata/Fukui, 1956) 越光

Indirect descendant of Kamenoo, it could be labeled the "Yamadanishiki of table rice". Cultivated in almost all of Japan and other parts of the world, it spawned many new varieties. Readily available, it is commonly used in everyday sake production.

Koshikagura (Niigata, 2010) 越神楽

Crossbreeding of Yamadanishiki and a descendant of Hokuriku, developed to obtain a variety adapted to the (precocious) Niigata climate with Yamadanishiki's technical characteristics. Overall, it satisfies these requirements (25.5 g per 1000 grains) but is still little used.

Most common *meigara* characters

Meigara are chosen for their poetic beauty, to attract good fortune or in reference to a place, a legend or even a famous competitor. We thus observe a certain recurrence in the characters used. Some characters used in rice varieties (see "Common rice variety names", p.45) are also used for *meigara*, mainly *hana*, *homare*, *mai* and *yume*, but many others are used too:

Theme	Character	Pronunciation	Meaning
Earth	山	*Yama*	Mountain
	田	*Den*	Rice field
	金	*Kin*	Gold
Water	泉	*Izumi*	Water spring
	川	*Sen*	River
	水	*Mizu*	Water
	雪	*Yuki*	Snow
Sky	天	*Ten*	Sky
	月	*Tsuki*	Moon
	日	*Ni*	Sun
Beings	花 ou 華	*Hana*	Flower
	菊	*Kiku*	Chrysanthemum
	鶴	*Tsuru*	Crane (bird)
	女	*Onna*	Women
	男	*Otoko*	Men
Status	白	*Haku*	White
	誉	*Homare*	Glory
	大	*O*	Big
	正宗	*Masamune*	(Play on words)
	高	*Taka*	High

Table 2. Main terms designating *meigara*.

Please beware, the same character may have several pronunciations in Japanese. Here, we only give one for the sake of simplicity.

Koshinoshizuku (Fukui, 2003) 越の雫

Crossbreeding of Hyogokitanishiki and Miyamanishiki developed to obtain a local variety adapted to *ginjo* production (unlike Okuhomare and Gohyakumangoku the other two most cultivated varieties in the area).

Koshitanrei (Niigata, 2004) 越淡麗

Crossbreeding of Gohyakumangoku and Yamadanishiki developed to provide Niigata producers with a variety capable of withstanding deep polishing (<50%), unlike Gohyakumangoku (the main local variety). Its name comes from the "*tanrei-karakuchi*" style (fresh and light) of Niigata sake. Koshitanrei enjoys the best of both parents: Gohyakumangoku's *koji*-making qualities and dry and fresh sake style, and Yamadanishiki's resistance to polishing, *shinpaku* and profound and noble aroma profile. For these reasons, it is notably used in *ginjo* and *daiginjo* production.

Kuranohana (Miyagi, 2000) 蔵の華

Descendant of Yamadanishiki adapted to the northern climate of Miyagi prefecture, it remains little used despite good technical characteristics, in particular a better resistance to lodging and larger grains than Miyamanishiki.

Kyonohana (Yamagata, 1926) 京の華

Ancient variety with very high straws (hardly shorter than Omachi) and low yield, descendant of Shin-Yamadaho. Despite a strong occurrence of *shinpaku*, its technical characteristics can not compare with modern varieties (notably, its above average protein level). It was rediscovered in 1984 by the Tatsuizumi *kura* which has since produced its eponymous sake: Kyonohana *junmai daiginjo*.

Maikaze (Gunma, 2011) 舞風

First and only local variety, developed under the "Gunma-no-sake" program to allow the production of 100% local Gunma sake. It is an indirect descendant of Yamadanishiki and Wakamizu and possesses good agronomic and technical characteristics, close to the latter.

Misatonishiki (Akita, 2000) 美郷錦

Crossbreeding of Yamadanishiki and Miyamanishiki, its agronomic and technical characteristics are close to the latter, with a better *shinpaku* occurrence but lower yield.

Miyamanishiki (Nagano, 1978) 美山錦

Improvement of Takanenishiki obtained by mutagenesis. It is the third most cultivated *shuzo-koteki-mai* variety. It has excellent agronomic and technical characteristics: medium grains (25 g per 1000 grains), low protein content and high *shinpaku* occurrence. Its good resistance to cold has made it a variety widely used for crossbreeding in the northern regions. It is perfectly suited to the production of *ginjo*. Miyamanishiki-based sake are generally powerful, round and textured.

Mutsuhomare (Aomori, 1985) むつほまれ

Table rice, particularly rich in amylose, sometimes used in sake production.

Nakate-Shinsenbon (Hiroshima, 1950) 中生新千本

A table rice commonly used in sake production.

Nojoho (Hyogo, ancient) 野条穂

Ancient variety, parent of Iwai, rediscovered in 2001.

Okuhomare (Fukui, 1984) おくほまれ

Variety bearing very large grains (29.5 g per 1000 grains) with strong *shinpaku* occurrence (90%), but very brittle at polishing, making it difficult to produce *ginjo*. Okuhomare-based sake are rich in acids and amino acids.

Seed production

When seeds of a cultivated plant are used as seed, there is a risk of "genetic drift": natural mutations accumulating generations after generations within a variety end up modifying its characteristics. Also, although rice is a self-pollinating plant, natural crossbreeding can sometimes occur in the field, via pollen from another variety grown in a nearby field, for example.

For these reasons, farmers buy their seeds from seed growers who preserve and guarantee the purity of their varieties thanks to strict control in each generation:

Seeds are grown in dedicated fields, separated from all other rice crops (in order to limit the risks of cross-pollination), and purified of all weeds and "off-type" plants (plant with an atypical phenotype, indicating a mutation or external pollination). Seed lots are also laboratory-analyzed to confirm varietal purity, absence of contamination by seeds of other species, germinative power, sanitary state, etc. This process guarantees the consumer that his favorite bottle of sake is effectively produced with a given variety.

Omachi (Okayama, ancient) 雄町

This native variety was reduced to a mere 6 hectares in 1970 but redeveloped rapidly in the '90s. Many varieties, including Yamadanishiki, descend from Omachi and many Omachi variations exist in different prefectures. This very tall variety (120-150 cm) is particularly difficult to grow and matures late. Its large grains are adapted to deep polishing. It is one of the most difficult rice varieties to master in fermentation but, skillfully used, it gives magnificent sake, full and deep, with a slight rustic, earthy feeling.

Ooseto (Kagawa, ancient) オオセト

Native variety, generally classified as table rice, it can however, give beautiful, fairly dense, sake.

Oyamanishiki (Toyama, 2001) 雄山錦

Descendant of Hida-Homare and (indirectly) of Miyamanishiki, it has excellent agronomic and technical characteristics and is suitable for *ginjo* production. As an early variety with broad *shinpaku*, it is compared with Gohyakumangoku, but offers superior yields and does not break during polishing.

Saganohana (Saga, 2000) さがの華

First local variety, crossbreeding of Wakamizu and Yamadanishiki. Relatively weak in the field, it has good technical characteristics.

Saikai 134 (Fukuoka, 1971) 西海134号

Descendant of Yamadanishiki, easy to grow but with a high protein content. One of the few varieties adapted to Kyushu island's climate.

Saitonoshizuku (Yamaguchi, 2008) 西都の雫

Descendant of Kokuryo-Miyako and (indirectly) of Yamadanishiki. It represents a marked improvement from Kokuryo-Miyako with greater field hardiness and larger grains (26 g per 1000 grains).

Sakanishiki (Shimane, 2001) 佐香錦

Crossbreeding of Kairyo-hattan-nagare and Kinmonnishiki, it inherited the former's good technical characteristics. Although appreciated for its precocity it is, however, relatively weak in the field.

Sakemirai (Yamagata, 1999) 酒未来

Crossbreeding of Yamasake 4 and Miyamanishiki developed by Takagi Shuzo *kura*, which produces the cult sake "Juyondai". It has good technical characteristics including high yield and large grains (26.5 g per 1000 grains). However, its occurrence of *shinpaku* is medium and its bellied position tends to weaken the grain during polishing.

Sakemusashi (Saitama, 2004) さけ武蔵

Only *shuzo-koteki-mai* variety in the prefecture, despite a sizable sake production. Crossbreeding of Kairyo-hattan-nagare and Wakamizu, it inherited the latter's good agronomic characteristics while exceeding its polishing limitations. Its *shinpaku* size and occurrence are, however, lower.

Sasanishiki (1963, Miyagi) ササニシキ

Popular table rice, descendant of Sasashigure, sometimes used in sake production.

Variety indications on labels

Most sake bottles mention the variety, or varieties, of rice used to produce this sake. This indication is authorized if the variety or varieties represent at least 50% by mass of the rice used. The label must also specify the proportion of each of the varieties indicated. The Japanese transcription of the different varieties name presented here will allow you to recognize them with certainty on your sake bottles. If you do not know where to look for it, technical information is usually displayed on the back of the bottle. The characters "酒米" for "*sakamai*" usually precede the mention of the variety.

Sasashigure (Miyagi, 1952) ササシグレ

Table rice variety, indirect descendant of Kamenoo, very popular in the '50s and '60s, still seldom used in the production of sake.

Senbonnishiki (Hiroshima, 2002) 千本錦

Crossbreeding of Nakate-Shinsenbon and Yamadanishiki developed to obtain a variety with processing qualities similar to the latter while earlier (harvested 8 days earlier) and more resistant to lodging.

Shiga-Wataribune 6 (Shiga, 1916) 滋賀渡船６号

A historical selection of Wataribune adapted to the climate of Shiga, abandoned then rediscovered in 2004. Several varieties come from the same selection, they are differentiated by their number: 2, 4, 6, 26, etc.

Shinriki (Hyogo, ancient) 神力

Selection of Hodoyoshi made in 1877, appreciated as table rice for its high yield. It was rediscovered in the 2000s by the Chiyonosono *kura*.

Shin-yamadaho 1 (Hyogo, 1921) 新山田穂１号

Selection of Yamadaho with a better chemical composition than the latter (lower proteins and fatty acids, higher amylose level) but longer stems. Abandoned and rediscovered in 1991 by the Hakutsuru *kura*.

Shirakabanishiki (Nagano, 1983) しらかば錦

Variety obtained by mutation of the Reimei variety (itself obtained by mutation of the Fujimori variety), developed to provide a variety adapted to high-elevation climate (700-800 m) in Nagano mountains, above the Miyamanishiki cultivation area.

Shirafuji (Niigata, 1893) 白藤

An ancient variety, forgotten in the '30s and rediscovered in 2004. It was considered as the "feminine" counterpart of the "masculine" Kamenoo variety.

Shiragiku (Aichi, 1944) 白菊

Improvement of Kikusui, more resistant to insects and easy to grow but with a low *shinpaku* occurrence. Abandoned quickly and rediscovered in 2007 by the eponymous *kura*.

Shizukuhime (Ehime, 2007) しずく媛

Variety resulting from a natural mutation of Matsuyama-Mitsui, a local table rice commonly used for sake production. Its technical characteristics are good (strong occurrence of *shinpaku*), particularly with regard to its origins, but its agronomic characteristics are average.

Suisei (Hokkaido, 2010) 彗星

Crossbreeding of the two regional flagship varieties: Hatsushizuku and Ginpu. Slightly less resistant to cold than the latter, it has a low protein content and gives fine and elegant sake.

Tajimagoriki (Tottori, 1928) 但馬強力

Historical variety appreciated for its resistance to polishing and its strong occurrence of linear *shinpaku*. Abandoned in 1935, it was rediscovered in 2000 in Hyogo prefecture.

Takanenishiki (Nagano, 1952) たかね錦

Historical variety from which the Miyamanishiki was derived. The latter is preferred because of its superior technical characteristics (superior grain size and *shinpaku* occurrence, lower protein content).

Tamasakae (Shiga, 1954) 玉栄

Descendant of Shiragiku. Difficult to manage in fermentation, it tends to give powerfully aromatic and slightly rustic sake (earthy/animal/green).

Tatsunootoshigo (Yamagata, 1999) 龍の落とし子

Crossbreeding of Miyamanishiki and Yamasake 4 developed by Takagi Shuzo producing the cult sake "Juyondai". Other varieties are generally preferred because of the average size of its grains and its low occurrence of *shinpaku*.

Tochigisake 14 (Tochigi, 2005) とちぎ酒14
Indirect descendant of Hitogokochi, field hardy and high yielding but with a low
shinpaku occurrence. As the only modern local variety, it is widely used in Tochigi
prefecture.

Tojinoyume (Hyogo, 2004) 杜氏の夢
Crossbreeding of Hyogokitanishiki and Gin-no-sei, appreciated for its precocity, its
resistance to cold and its linear *shinpaku*, which allow for deep polishing.

Tominoka (Toyama, 2010) 富の香
Descendant of Yamadanishiki developed to obtain a variety with comparable
technical characteristics, adapted to the climate of Toyama (early). It was quickly
adopted in the region.

Toyokuni (Yamagata, 1903) 豊国
Ancient variety, historically appreciated for its long straws (of 1 m) used in basketry.
Rediscovered in 1994, it remains anecdotal.

Tsuyubakaze (Nara, 1966) 露葉風
First and only local variety of Nara prefecture. Sensitive to lodging, it was
abandoned in 1990 and rediscovered in 2001. Its technical characteristics are good
and it tends to produce sake with a certain depth.

Ushuhomare (Yamagata, 2000) 羽州誉
Descendant of Miyamanishiki, developed by Takagi Shuzo, producer of the cult sake
"Juyondai". High yielding variety with average technical characteristics: average
shinpaku occurrence and relatively small grains (24.5 g per 1000 grains).

Wakamizu (Aichi, 1985) 若水
Historical variety of Aichi prefecture with very good agronomic and technical
characteristics (including 25.7 g per 1000 grains and very strong *shinpaku*
occurrence), it has been and remains widely used. However, as a descendant of
Gohyakumangoku, it inherited its low resistance to polishing, which limits its use.

Wataribune (Ibaraki, 1895) 渡船
Late variety, susceptible to lodging, abandoned then rediscovered in 1988 by the
founder of the eponymous *kura*, Wataribune.

Yamadaho (Hyogo, 1912) 山田穂
An ancient variety, used at least since the 19th century, the mother of Yamadanishiki.
Several theories exist about its discovery. Its extremely hard stems give it excellent
resistance to lodging. Its grains do not have *shinpaku* but they absorb water
particularly well, allowing for effective liquefaction. It is notably poor in protein for
an ancient variety.

Yamadanishiki (Hyogo, 1936) 山田錦

Known as the "king" of sake rice, it is the most cultivated variety. Its agronomic and technical characteristics are excellent, especially for the production of *ginjo*: large grains (28 g per 1000 grains) with high *shinpaku* occurrence and highly resistant to polishing. Obtained in 1923 from a crossbreeding of Yamadaho and Tankanwataribune, it was first marketed in 1936 and spread throughout the country after the war. It has been used in a large number of crossbreedings. Clayey slopes are ideal for its cultivation. Almost every *kura* in the country uses Yamadanishiki for at least one cuvee, usually their most exclusive. It produces powerful sakes that can be distinguished by their balance, their fullness and their noble and complex aromatic profile.

Yamasake 4 (Yamagata, 1983) 山酒４号

Crossbreeding of Kinmonnishiki and Yamadanishiki exhibiting high yield, large grains (26.9 g per 1000 grains) and an acceptable *shinpaku* occurrence. For these reasons, it was used in several later crossbreedings.

Yuinoka (Iwate, 2012) 結の香

Crossbreeding of Hanaomoi and Yamadanishiki carried out to obtain a variety adapted to the production of *daiginjo* sake. Apart from the weight of its grains (26.5 g per 1000 grains) and its central and small *shinpaku*, which allow for deep polishing, the rest of its technical and agronomic characteristics are rather disappointing (including elongated and thin grains, and low *shinpaku* occurrence).

Yumeakari (Aomori, 2002) ゆめあかり

Table rice sometimes used for sake production.

Yumenokaori (Fukushima, 2003) 夢の香

Descendant of Hattannishiki and (indirectly) Dewasansan, developed to replace Gohyakumangoku. Its excellent technical and agronomic characteristics quickly imposed it as a prominent variety. Compared to the "model" on which it was based it offers greater field hardiness and grains of comparable size with a better *shinpaku* occurrence and more resistant to polishing.

Yumesansui (Aichi, 2001) 夢山水

Local descendant of Yamadanishiki with comparable technical characteristics, it was quickly adopted in Aichi and Yamanashi.

5. *Shuzo-koteki-mai* cultivation area

Most rice varieties described in the previous chapter are grown in a limited area, usually centered on their region of origin. This is explained by the variety of climates existing from north to south of Japan, but also by historical reasons or, regional preference.

The table below shows for each region the main cultivated varieties and, for reference, the number of *kura* and their share in the national production of sake.

Prefecture	Main cultivated varieties	Number of *kura*	Production vs. Nat. prod. (vol.)
Hokkaido	Ginpu, Hatsushizuku, Suisei	13	1.0%
Aomori	Hanafubuki, Hanaomoi, Hohai, Kojonishiki, Hanasayaka	21	0.8%
Iwate	Gin-ginga, Gin-otome, Yuinoka	22	0.8%
Miyagi	Hiyori, Hoshiakari, Kuranohana, Miyamanishiki, Yamadanishiki	30	1.3%
Akita	Akinosei, Akita-Sake-Komachi, Gin-no-sei, Hanafubuki, Hoshiakari, Kairyo-shinko, Misatonishiki, Miyamanishiki	34	3.2%
Yamagata	Dewanosato, Dewasansan, Gohyakumangoku, Kairyo-shinko, Kissui, Kyonohana, Miyamanishiki, Sakemirai, Tatsunootoshigo, Toyokuni, Ushuhomare, Yamadanishiki Yamasake 4	50	1.5%
Fukushima	Gohyakumangoku, Hanafubuki, Miyamanishiki, Yumenokaori	59	2.7%
Ibaraki	Gohyakumangoku, Hitachinishiki, Miyamanishiki, Wakamizu, Wataribune, Yamadanishiki	34	1.0%
Tochigi	Gohyakumangoku, Hitogokochi, Miyamanishiki, Tamasakae, Tochigisake 14, Wakamizu, Yamadanishiki	29	1.3%
Gunma	Gohyakumangoku, Maikaze, Wakamizu	23	0.6%

Prefecture	Main cultivated varieties	Number of *kura*	Production vs. Nat. prod. (vol.)
Saitama	Sakemusashi	30	3.8%
Chiba	Fusanomai, Gohyakumangoku	28	1.3%
Tokyo	-	9	0.4%
Kanagawa	Wakamizu	12	0.2%
Niigata	Gohyakumangoku, Hattannishiki 2, Hokuriku 12, Ipponjime, Kikusui, Koshikagura, Koshitanrei, Omachi, Takanenishiki, Yamadanishiki	92	7.9%
Toyama	Gohyakumangoku, Miyamanishiki, Oyamanishiki, Tamasakae, Tominoka, Yamadanishiki	18	1.3%
Ishikawa	Gohyakumangoku, Hokuriku 12, Ishikawamon, Yamadanishiki	33	1.1%
Fukui	Gohyakumangoku, Koshinoshizuku, Okuhomare, Shinriki, Yamadanishiki	36	0.5%
Yamanashi	Hitogokochi, Tamasakae	11	2.6%
Nagano	Hitogokochi, Kinmonnishiki, Miyamanishiki, Shirakabanishiki, Takanenishiki	77	1.8%
Gifu	Gohyakumangoku, Hidahomare	50	0.9%
Shizuoka	Gohyakumangoku, Homarefuji, Wakamizu, Yamadanishiki	28	0.8%
Aichi	Wakamizu, Yumesansui	42	3.9%
Mie	Gohyakumangoku, Isenishiki, Kaminoho, Yamadanishiki	41	0.6%
Shiga	Ginfubuki, Shigawataribune, Tamasakae, Yamadanishiki	33	0.7%
Kyoto	Gohyakumangoku, Iwai, Yamadanishiki	40	15.7%
Osaka	Gohyakumangoku, Omachi, Yamadanishiki	10	0.2%

Prefecture	Main cultivated varieties	Number of *kura*	Production vs. Nat. prod. (vol.)
Hyogo	Aiyama, Fukunohana, Gohyakumangoku, Hakutsurunishiki, Hyogokitanishiki, Hyogokoinishiki, Hyogonishiki, Hyogoyumenishiki, Inishienomai, Nojoho, Shinriki, Shin-yamadaho, Shiragiku, Takanenishiki, Tajimagoriki, Tojinoyume, Wataribune 2, Yamadaho, Yamadanishiki	70	31.7%
Nara	Tsuyubakaze, Yamadanishiki	32	0.9%
Wakayama	Gohyakumangoku, Tamasakae, Yamadanishiki	11	0.8%
Tottori	Gohyakumangoku, Goriki, Tamasakae, Yamadanishiki	19	0.2%
Shimane	Gohyakumangoku, Kairyo-hattan-nagare, Kairyo-omachi, Kan-no-mai, Sakanishiki, Yamadanishiki	29	0.4%
Okayama	Omachi, Yamadanishiki	30	0.9%
Hiroshima	Hattan, Hattannishiki 1, Hattannishiki 2, Koiomachi, Omachi, Senbonnishiki, Yamadanishiki	43	2.3%
Yamaguchi	Gohyakumangoku, Hakutsurunishiki, Saitonoshizuku, Yamadanishiki	20	0.4%
Tokushima	Yamadanishiki	11	0.1%
Kagawa	Omachi, Yamadanishiki	7	0.2%
Ehime	Shizukuhime, Yamadanishiki	32	0.4%
Kochi	Gin-no-yume, Kazenaruko, Yamadanishiki	19	1.0%
Fukuoka	Gin-no-sato, Gohyakumangoku, Omachi, Saikai 134, Yamadanishiki	40	0.7%
Saga	Saganohana, Saikai 134, Yamadanishiki	22	0.7%
Nagasaki	Yamadanishiki	12	0.2%
Kumamoto	Shinriki, Yamadanishiki	9	0.4%
Oita	Gohyakumangoku, Wakamizu, Yamadanishiki	15	0.8%

Prefecture	Main cultivated varieties	Number of kura	Production vs. Nat. prod. (vol.)
Miyazaki	Hanakagura, Yamadanishiki	2	0.0%
Kagoshima	-	0	0.0%
Okinawa	-	1	0.0%
Nara	Tsuyubakaze, Yamadanishiki	32	0.9%
Wakayama	Gohyakumangoku, Tamasakae, Yamadanishiki	11	0.8%
Tottori	Goriki, Gohyakumangoku, Tamasakae, Yamadanishiki	19	0.2%
Shimane	Gohyakumangoku, Kairyo-hattan-nagare, Kan-no-mai, Kairyo-omachi, Sakanishiki, Yamadanishiki	29	0.4%
Okayama	Omachi, Yamadanishiki	30	0.9%

Table 3. Rice and sake production by prefecture, from north to south of Japan.
Source: 2008 (numbers) 2010 (rice), Japanese Sake and Shochu Makers Association.

As we can see, some varieties (such as Yamadanishiki) are cultivated in many regions, well beyond their original agricultural basin. These varieties are so well known and appreciated that most *kura* in the country wish to use them. Some regions specialize in the production of such varieties and distribute them to the four corners of the country. At the same time, research is being carried out in order to adapt them to the climates in other regions.

This kind of research may trigger political tensions between the various regions and research centers. Indeed, obtaining a new successful variety can boost not only agriculture but also the entire regional sake industry. The economic stakes are enormous: the Yamadanishiki market in Japan alone represents about one billion yen.

Thus, some paradoxical situations appear: although no seed of Yamadanishiki has ever officially been exported outside the Hyogo region, this variety is cultivated in almost all the Japanese prefecture.

Seed production, the example of Hyogo's Yamadanishiki

In the case of Yamadanishiki, 14 pure lines from the original lineage obtained in 1928 are preserved in the Hyogo region. The certified seeds of these 14 lines represent the "breeder seeds", retained by the JA.

Three generations separate "breeder seeds" from the "seeds" used by farmers. In each generation, the controls necessary to maintain the variety's purity (and its characteristics) are carried out by the breeder in order to guarantee seeds as pure as possible at the end of the chain.

Only farmers based in Hyogo can obtain Hyogo Yamadanishiki certified seeds. On the other hand, grains intended for the production of sake (whose varietal purity is not controlled) can be sold by farmers to *kura* anywhere in the country.

From these "exported" grains, research institutes from other regions have recreated "pure lines" of Yamadanishiki. This work has generally been coupled with new selections designed to ensure better adaptation to the local climate. These lines are now multiplied according to the model described above, and the seeds obtained are marketed to farmers all over the country.

The original grains having been obtained by these research institutes through diverted routes and these grains having not been certified for their conformity to the variety, Hyogo officials continue to claim that there is no real Yamadanishiki outside Hyogo prefecture.

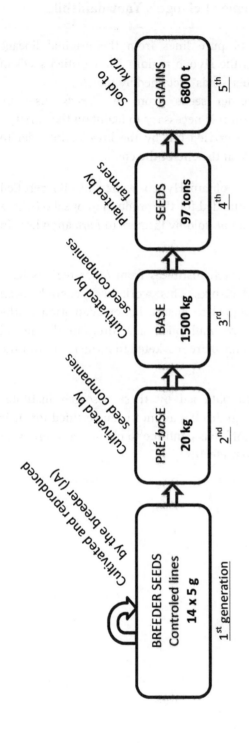

Figure 4. Multiplication and preservation of Yamadanishiki pure lines in Hyogo prefecture.

6. Rice varieties renewal

As mentioned above, most of the rice varieties described have been developed relatively recently, largely because of advances in breeding techniques. This could result in a rapid renewal of varieties used in production.

Variety	2015		2005		Ranking 2015 vs. 2005
	Harvest (t)	%	Cultivated area (ha)	%	
Yamadanishiki	38853	36,5%	4781	32,6%	=
Gohyakumangoku	26247	24,6%	4324	29,5%	=
Miyamanishiki	7838	7,4%	1394	9,5%	=
Omachi	2886	2,7%	358	2,4%	+1
Akita-Sake-Komachi	2367	2,2%	-		+
Dewasansan	2247	2,1%	177	1,2%	+3
Hitogokochi	1741	1,6%	-		+
Hattannishiki	1660	1,6%	237	1,6%	-2
Hanafubuki	1406	1,3%	190	1,3%	-1
Ginpu	1309	1,2%	219	1,5%	-3
Koshitanrei	1221	1,1%	-		+
Hyogoyumenishiki	(542)	(0,5%)	390	2,7%	-14
Tamasakae	(594)	(0,6%)	166	1,1%	-7
Autres	17660	16,6%	2429	16,6%	
Total	106571	100%	14665	100,0%	

Table 4. The 11 most cultivated *shuzo-koteki-mai.*
Source: Japanese Sake and Shochu Makers Association.

Note that the first three places in the ranking are firmly established (1/ Yamadanishiki, 2/ Gohyakumangoku, 3/ Miyamanishiki). On the other hand, the bottom of the ranking is regularly shaken up by the appearance of new varieties or by meteorological events affecting the yield of a variety or a region (typhoons, rain or low temperatures at heading, for example).

The stability and crushing weight (60-70% of the total) of the first three varieties is explained by strong consumer demand for known varieties. This demand creates a large market that encourages farmers to plant these easily sold varieties, reinforcing the supply and visibility of these varieties.

In the bottom part of the table, the small volumes and the high geographical concentration of the local varieties make them susceptible to trends and yield variations. Outside of the "big three", farmers are eager to use new varieties, which are more resistant or offer better yields, and sake producers like idiosyncratic varieties that help them stand out in a competitive market. Combined with the annual character of rice crops, these factors explain the rice market's high volatility: in just a few years after its registration, a new variety can enter the top ten.

iii.   Rice quality assessment systems

1. The official system

The Japanese Ministry of Agriculture (MAFF) classifies table rice produced in Japan into three categories according to quality criteria overlapping those of the codex alimentarius. Two additional categories (*toku-jo* and *toku-to*) are specific to *shuzo-koteki-mai.*

Rice producers who so wish may have their batches of rice inspected by a laboratory approved by the MAFF and thus obtain a classification. More than 98% of the rice produced is thus inspected because the market value of a rice lot is directly correlated to its classification. Moreover, sakes from unregistered rice can only legally be marketed as *futsushu* ("basic" sake, which is not part of the *tokutei-meisho-shu*, see Table 21).

The classification criteria for rice, as defined by MAFF, are presented in Tables 5 and 5 bis.

Two parameters are defined with respect to a minimum:

-The **density** represents the minimum weight in grams of one liter of rice grains (810 g/L for class 1).

-The **standard** represents the minimum percentage of standard grain i.e. that is flawless in terms of size, shape, appearance (texture, luster and transparency), hardness, uniformity, and grain filling. In class 1, at least 70% of the grains must comply with the standard.

The other parameters define the characteristics of the grains that do not conform to the standard. In class 1, of the 30% maximum of non-conforming grains allowed (standard = 70%), up to 15% may be immature grains and 15% maximum may present other defects. Of these other defects, a maximum of 7% chalky grains, 0.1% colored grains, 0.3% paddy (i.e. in which the husk was not properly removed during dehulling, see "Rice polishing (*seimai*)", p.72) and 0.2% foreign materials (such as pebbles or the seeds of other plants) are tolerated.

The immature, paddy or chalky grains, as well as foreign materials, are defined by the codex alimentarius. Colored grains, including red, black, and striated grains, are defined by the same codex. The other types of defective grains are precisely detailed by the MAFF; these include sprouted, sick, cracked, broken, malformed, stained, or insect-damaged grains. In all, MAFF distinguishes 26 sub-categories of defective or immature grains that we will not detail here.

Defective and immature grains tend to break during polishing, causing a greater loss of material. Moreover, their internal structure and chemical composition differ, in particular with respect to starch content, which affects water absorption and therefore steaming, the *koji* development and dissolution in the ferment.

Furthermore, the presence of immature or chalky grains is an indicator of non-optimal growing and maturing conditions. A high rate therefore indicates a globally lower quality of the rice lot.

As no post-assessment sorting is done, the entire lot is used in the production of sake. Most *toji* therefore prefer to work with higher-class rice, prompting a high demand and price for it. Moreover, thanks to their larger grains, such rice is better suited to the production of *ginjo* sake.

Recommended varieties

For each Japanese prefecture there is a catalog of rice varieties (both table rice and sake rice) "recommended" to farmers. New varieties resulting from local research are inscribed there regularly, sometimes even under a provisional name before their official registration in the varieties register.

Other varieties, from neighboring prefecture or nationally recognized (Yamadanishiki and Gohyakumangoku, for example), can also be included in the catalog.

Based on these catalog, the Ministry annually publishes two lists of rice varieties for which the accredited laboratories are respectively obliged or allowed to offer classification services.

Given the importance of this classification for rice marketing, these recommended variety catalogs have a strong influence on locally grown varieties: with the exception of very specific cases (such as contracts with a *kura*), farmers choose their varieties exclusively from within this catalog.

Uruchi-mai	Minimum			Maximum						Harvest declared in 2005	Harvest declared in 2014
	Density (g/l)	Standard	Immature grains	Damaged grains and foreign materials							
				Total	Chalky	Colored	Paddy	Foreign materials			
1	810	70%	15%	15%	7%	0.1%	0.3%	0.2%		75.1%	81.4%
2	790	60%	20%	20%	10%	0.3%	0.5%	0.4%		19.8%	15.3%
3	770	45%	25%	30%	20%	0.7%	1.0%	0.6%		3.3%	1.3%
Not ranked										1.8%	2.0%

Table 5. Quality assessment criteria for table rice.

Source: MAFF.

Shuzo-koteki-mai	Minimum			Maximum					Harvest declared in 2005
	Density (g/l)	Standard	Immature grains	Damaged grains and foreign materials					
				Total	Chalky	Colored	Paddy	Total	
Toku-jo	840	90%	5%	5%	3%	0	0.1%	0	0.9%
Toku-to	830	80%	10%	10%	5%	0	0.2%	0.1%	22.9%
1	810	70%	15%	15%	7%	0.1%	0.3%	0.1%	58.7%
2	790	60%	20%	20%	10%	0.3%	0.5%	0.4%	12.0%
3	770	45%	25%	30%	20%	0.7%	1.0%	0.6%	3.9%
Not ranked									1.7%

Table 5 bis. Quality assessment criteria for *shuzo-koteki-mai*.

Source: MAFF.

2. Hyogo-prefecture Yamadanishiki

Every year, an independent agency, the Japan Grain Inspection Association, classifies table rice produced into 3 grades. For a given variety of rice, an entire prefecture or zone may be classified as Toku-A, A, or A'.

Within the prefecture of Hyogo, an equivalent classification system exists for Yamadanishiki. It distinguishes 4 qualities, depending on the place of production:
- **Toku-A or A**: designated areas of Hyogo prefecture,
- **B**: any other area in Hyogo prefecture,
- **C**: other prefectures.

Muramaiseido

The historical roots of this classification are to be found in the *muramaiseido* (literally "rice system by village") established at the end of the 19th century.

Following an 1873 reform, property tax was no longer levied in rice but in money instead, and its amount was no longer calculated based on yields but fixed at 3% of the plot's "potential". As the surplus was no longer taxed, farmers pushed production to its maximum, thereby reducing the quality of rice. Given the shortage of rice to meet their requirements, Nada's *kuramoto* and Yokawa and Kato growers partnered to ensure a sustainable, high quality supply. This association called *muramaiseido* became more than just a commercial agreement, with each party supporting the other over many crises (droughts, earthquakes, etc.).

The *muramaiseido* determines the price of the rice by village, taking the Yoneda and Kamikume districts of Kato city as reference points. In 1939, a *koku* of rice from these two villages was worth 43.10 ¥. The price for the surrounding villages ranged from 40.10 ¥ to 44.10 ¥.

The Toku-A zones are located exclusively within the "cities" of Miki and Kato, located just north of the large city of Kobe. These two "cities" are in fact rural areas, administrative divisions with respective areas of 176.58 and 157.49 km^2. Areas classified as Toku-A or A are listed by "districts" of 1 to 4 km^2, identified by a single postal code (see the next page for the list of "districts" classified A-a and A-b).

Of course, only rice producers based in the "Toku-A" or "A" area profit from this system, and no rice or sake producer would put a "B" or "C" on their label. Moreover, there is a certain irony in classifying as "C" any rice produced outside the prefecture of origin of this classification.

In addition to this system, local producer associations have chosen to reclassify their plots into three categories: a, b, c. The reading of this system is made complicated by the various territorial reforms that have made the lists obsolete. Here is the updated list of districts classified "A-a" and "A-b", which cover the same area as the "Toku-A" districts.

a. A-a classified districts

-36 districts of **Miki** city, or the totality of **Yokawa** city (formerly 38 districts):

Yoneda, Ooso, Kichiyasu, Inada, Kinkai, Fukuyoshi, Ariyasu, Watase, Yamagami, Nagatani, Uematsu, Taya, Hokoji, Yudani, Nishioku, Kashio, Kajiya, Ohata, Nitta, Kamiarakawa, Hataeda, Fukui, Tomioka, Kaminaka, Furukawa, Jitsuraku, Furuichi, Maeda, Bishamon, Ichinose, Higashida, Kusuhara, Okudani, Toyooka, Kitasuijo and Mizukami.

-15 districts of **Miki** city, or most of **Kuchiyokawa** city (17 districts):

Baba, Higashi, Higashinaka, Hisatsugu, Hoki, Kunugihara, Maki, Minamibata, Momozaka, Nishinaka, Oshima, Rengeji, Sasahara, Satowaki and Tonohata.

-21 districts of **Kato** city, or the totality of **Tojo** city (formerly 27 districts):

Tenjin, Hashikadani, Kurodani, Akitsu, Shobudani, Nagasada, Eifuku, Yokodani, Mori, Okamoto, Iwaya, Morio, Shinjo, Yoshi, Ozawa, Sakae, Atsutoshi, Matsuzawa, Higashitarumi, Ohata and Yabu.

-6 districts of **Kato** city, or the former **Yoneda** town of Yashiro city:

Mawaribuchi, Hata, Ikenouchi, Kamikume, Shimokume and Kume.

-5 districts of **Kato** city, or the former **Kamifukuda** town of Yashiro city:

Kamimikusa, Shimomikusa, Fujita, Yoshima and Makino.

b. A-b classified districts

-3 districts of **Kato** city, or the former **Kamifukuda** town of Yashiro city:

Kinashi, Yamaguchi and Umaze.

-6 districts of **Kita** city, or the totality of **Ozo** town (formerly 9 districts):

Kanzuke, Kamiozo, Nakaozo, Hisaibara, Sudare and Ichihara.

-13 districts of **Kita** city, or the totality of **Ogo** town (formerly 16 districts):

Kizu, Hagiwara, Ogo, Katsuo, Minamisoo, Kitasoo, Nakayama, Nose, Koda, Mikage, Higashita, Gyonohara and Kitahata.

-12 districts of **Miki** city, or the totality of **Hosokawa** town (formerly 22 districts):
Hosokawanaka, Kanaya, Masuda, Mizuho, Momozu, Nakazato, Nishi, Takahata, Takashino, Taruho, Toyochi and Wakigawa.

-4 districts of **Miki** city, or the totality of **Shijimi** town:
Toda, Mitsuda, Misaka and Iwaya.

-2 districts of **Ono** city:
Nakatani and Wakimoto.

3. Rice quality and sake production

The existence of the official and semi-official systems described above does not prevent some producers, cooperatives or associations from having their own quality assessment in parallel. Thus, we see the unregulated terms "premium", "top", "super top", etc., appearing on rice bags.

For Yamadanishiki of Hyogo, a « Toku-A *toku-jo* super top quality » label can hence be found. How then, can we compare the different categories: for example, would it be better to have a *toku-jo*/A or a *toku-to*/Toku-A??

In fact, as shown by the 2005 harvest figures (see Tables 5 and 5 bis, p.68), the *toku-to* and "1" qualities form the bulk of the rice crop. Moreover, Yamadanishiki's own classifications only concern small volumes of very high quality rice and therefore only a few *kura*, mainly in the Nada region. Hence, the importance given to this system is largely due to the publicity given to it by some *kura* (such as sake bearing the mention « premier grand cru classé A » in reference to its "Toku-A" Yamadanishiki and the classification of Saint-Emilion wines).

In terms of quality, the official ranking (*toku-jo, toku-to*, 1, 2, 3) takes precedence over others because of its assessment of the actual quality of a given rice lot. In the end, only 1% of the national production gets the name *toku-jo*.

iv. **Rice transformation: polishing, washing, steeping and steaming**

1. **Rice polishing (*seimai*)**

> **Seimaibuai**
>
> The *seimaibuai* or rice's "polishing rate" (*seimai* = polishing, *buai* = rate) is expressed as the weight of rice after polishing divided by the initial weight of rice. Rice from which 25% of the mass has been removed is therefore 75% polished. 35% polished rice has therefore undergone more polishing than 50% polished rice, which is itself more polished than 75% polished rice. This calculation method is used irrespective of the method of polishing and is recognized legally, specifically for classification of sake as *ginjo* or *daiginjo*.
>
> In order to facilitate understanding, values and comparisons of polishing rate will always be expressed in *seimaibuai*. For a small value of *seimaibuai* (<50%), we will therefore speak of "deep polishing".

a. **Rice grain structure**

The grains of rice obtained after harvesting are called paddy. They consist of a protective envelope (the husk which constitutes about 20% of the weight of the grain) and a fruit called husked or cargo rice. This fruit, generally beige in appearance (the bran is still present) is often commercially referred to as brown rice. The rice received and processed by the *kura* is in the form of cargo rice. When a polishing rate is calculated, cargo rice is used as the reference.

The cargo rice comprises from the outside towards the inside:

-The outer layers of the **pericarp**. Pigmented and rich in fiber, they form the bran and give cargo rice its color.

-The **seed coat**, a protective envelope of the fruit, rich in fiber.

-The **nucellus**, a residue of the ovary that formed the grain, rich in fiber.

-The **aleurone layer**, rich in proteins.

-The **subaleurone layer**, rich in lipids and proteins.

-The **starchy endosperm**, extremely rich in starch.

The subaleurone layer and starchy endosperm constitute the endosperm: the embryo's reserve tissue that allows it to grow and form a seedling before it is able to produce its own energy through photosynthesis. The embryo itself or germ, rich in proteins, is also situated under the aleurone layer.

For making sake, only the endosperm is used, i.e. a maximum *seimaibuai* of 90%, except in the very rare case of "*genmaishu*" (i.e. sakes made from unpolished rice).

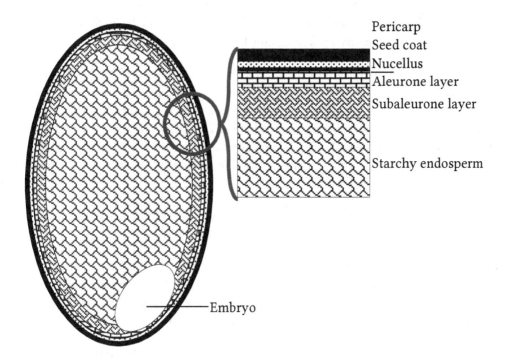

Figure 5. Structure of rice grain outer layers.

Table 6 below summarizes these different elements:

	Function	Composition	Weight
Pericarp	Protection	Fibers, pigments	1-2%
Seed coat	Protection	Fibers, minerals	
Nucellus	Residue/protection	Fibers	5-6%
Aleurone layer	Protection/reserves	Proteins	
Embryo	Future rice plant	Proteins, lipids	3%
Subaleurone layer	Reserves	Proteins, lipids	90%
Starchy endosperm	Reserves	Starch	

Table 6. Structure of a grain of cargo rice: function, composition and relative masses of the different cellular layers.

b. Polishing techniques and their history

Unlike other cereals, rice husks adhere to their grains and hulling is always necessary to make paddy rice suitable for consumption.

To do this, a mortar and pestle was traditionally used: the movement of the pestle in a large quantity of rice produces friction of grains against each other and separates the husks from the grains. However, this rudimentary system is inefficient, time consuming and produces many broken or non-husked grains.

In the 17th century, the invention of the mechanical pestle, operated by foot then by hydraulic force (at the end of the 18th century), improved the process and offered the possibility of lowering the *seimaibuai* down to 90%. It was then found that white rice is more digestible, has better taste and keeps better. The latter phenomenon is due to the fatty acids, present especially in the subaleurone layer, that get removed during polishing. These fatty acids oxidize during storage, giving old brown rice a rancid taste (*komai*, literally "old rice").

Unfortunately, polishing also eliminates vitamin B1, the deficit of which caused beriberi to affect many people of the time (poets, *daimyo*, and even an emperor).

Thus, at the end of the 17th/beginning of the 18th century, *hakumai* or polished rice (as opposed to "*genmai*", brown rice) appeared, initially just for the elite. Continuous improvement of polishing methods, especially the switch from pestles to millstones, made rice polishing trivial by the second half of the 19th century.

The rice used in sake production followed the same trajectory. Originally produced from brown rice, white rice became the norm, initially for *kakemai* and then for all rice. The success of the *morohaku* sakes of the Itami region, pioneers in this matter, did much for the adoption of the method.

Kojimai	Kakemai	Sake	Translation
brown	brown	*Namizake*	Common sake
brown	white	*Katahaku*	Half-white
white	white	*Morohaku*	All-white

Table 7. Sake based on white or brown rice during the 17th century.

In 1896, the Satake company marketed the first electric rice polishing machine, and, for the first time ever, rice polished to 75% could be obtained.

Vertical polishers, which appeared in 1930, now make it possible to obtain advanced polishing beyond technical requirements (see "Extreme polishing", p.82). However, these machines represent a heavy investment and only a handful of *kura* are equipped with their own polisher. Most of them therefore rely on specialized service providers who own these machines.

Here's how they work:

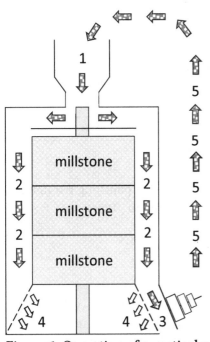

1/ The polisher is fed at its top by a noria system.

2/ The rice goes down into the polishing chamber where it is polished between a rotating millestone and a fixed cage.

3/ The rice leaves the polishing chamber through a door whose opening is regulated by a weight system, thus limiting the descending speed of the rice in the chamber.

4 / Rice flour (*nuka*) is removed from the polishing chamber through a sieve.

5 / The noria system brings the polished grain at the top of the machine. Many repetitions are necessary in order to achieve the desired polishing rate.

Figure 6. Operation of a vertical polisher.
Standard capacity: 1.8 t of rice per lot.

During polishing, the grain warms up and loses moisture, making it brittle. At the same time, the internal layers of the grain, more delicate than the outer layers, are exposed. Thus, as polishing progresses, the grain becomes increasingly fragile.

The rotation speed must therefore be lowered in order to limit the risk of breakage: from an initial 500 revolutions per minute to 350 revolutions per minute for a 35% *seimaibuai*. For this reason, the polishing time required to obtain a deep polishing is exponential. The most extreme example of that is Tatenokawa Zenith, for which 1% polished Dewasansan rice was obtained after 1800 hours, giving a polishing rate of 0.055% per hour.

Seimaibuai	Standard polishing time (h)	Polishing rate (%/h)	Rotations (/min.)
70%	12	2.5	395
67%	17	1.9	395
60%	33	1.2	390
55%	40	1.1	380
45%	55	1.0	370
35%	63	1.0	350

Table 8. Polishing time examples, for Yamadanishiki.

Some varieties, more or less fragile or brittle, require suitable polishing parameters. Gohyakumangoku for example, may be polished up to twice as fast as Yamadanishiki. Its grains however, break much more.

c. Assessing polishing quality

The *seimaibuai* is an apparent polishing rate (initial weight/final weight) that aggregates all parameters and can therefore cover a set of very disparate realities. However, to evaluate the quality of a polishing, it is necessary to use finer indicators:

Net polishing rate

This indicator is used to eliminate the bias of broken kernels that cause *seimaibuai* to decline but are a net loss: internal kernel layers are eliminated, smaller residues are removed with polishing flour, and the remaining broken kernels disrupt the development of the *koji* during the production of *kome-koji*.

$$\textbf{Net polishing rate} = \frac{\text{Weight of 1000 (unbroken) kernels}}{\text{Initial weight of 1000 kernels}}$$

An "ineffective polishing rate" can be deducted from this value, i.e. the percentage of broken kernels:

Ineffective polishing rate = net polishing rate − *seimaibuai*

For a *seimaibuai* of 70%, an inefficient polishing rate of 10% means that 10% of the grains have been broken during the polishing and that the actual polishing rate of the remaining kernels is 80%.

Heterogeneity of polished kernels

It is illusory to think that a macroscopic process such as polishing produces thousands of perfectly calibrated grains. Depending on their position in the millstone, their initial size and their specific characteristics, the actual polishing rate of each grain is heterogeneous.

The quality of the polishing is estimated by measuring the weight of each grain in a sample of the assessed lot. A tight distribution around the targeted *seimaibuai* indicates a satisfactory polishing while a wide distribution indicates heterogeneous polishing (see graphic below).

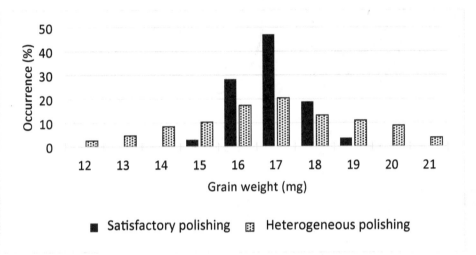

Chart 5. Examples of grain weight distribution after polishing.
Lots of Yamadanishiki, initial 1000-grain weight: 28 g, 60% seimaibuai.

Shape of the kernels

During polishing, the grains rotate, which favors a more rounded shape and therefore a greater polishing along the length of the grains. Exterior layers of the grain are thus retained over the width of the grain while internal layers are removed along its length.

In 1998, Tomio Saito solved this challenge by implementing new polishing parameters that allowed a flat polishing, along the cellular layers of the grain. A more advanced method of ultra-flat polishing has since been introduced by the Daishichi *kura*.

For a given polishing ratio, flat polishing allows a material gain of about 10% (18% for ultra-flat polishing): a 70% polished flat rice will have technical characteristics (protein and lipids ratio, in particular) close to a traditional 60% polished rice.

This allows for qualitative gains and saving of material but does not call into question the official classifications, with only the apparent ratio (see "*Seimaibuai*", p.72) being taken into account.

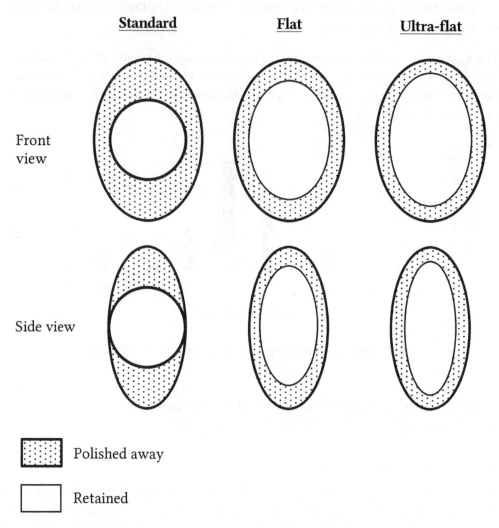

Figure 7. Modeling the influence of polishing methods on the removal of the grain's internal layers.

40% seimaibuai (white volume = 40% of the gray volume); grain of rice considered as a homogeneous ellipsoid; polishing standard spherical, polishing flat proportional in all three axes (-26.3%), ultra-flat polishing equal in all three axes.

To achieve this, it is necessary to reduce the rotation speed of the millstone (by half for flat polishing) and to increase the pressure in the polishing chamber. The rotation (and therefore polishing) is thus maximized on the long axis of the grain. The polishing time for ultra-flat rice is about 50% higher than for a conventional polishing.

d. Purpose of polishing

The main official quality criterion of sake as defined by the Japanese government (*ginjo, daiginjo,* etc.) is the polishing rate. Let's see why.

As detailed above (see "Rice grain structure", p.72), the chemical composition of the various cell layers of rice differs. The external layers are richer in protein, minerals and lipids, while the inner layers are richer in starch.

Thus, the chemical composition of polished rice depends directly on the polishing rate:

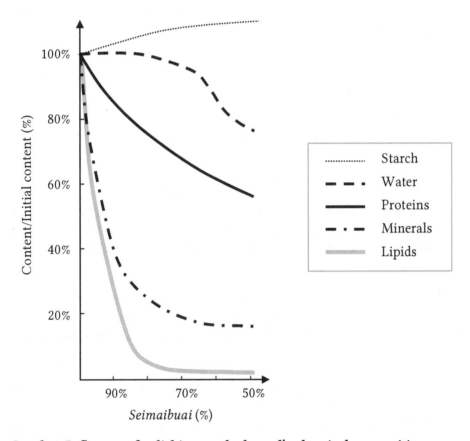

Graph 6. Influence of polishing on the kernel's chemical composition.
Source: NRIB.

As can be seen from Graph 6, above, rice polishing makes it possible to rapidly eliminate the vast majority of rice lipids and minerals, which are mainly contained in the outer layers of the grain.

Minerals

The main minerals contained in rice (phosphate, potassium, calcium) are useful as yeast and *koji* nutrients. However, iron is highly undesirable. Indeed, during its development, the *koji* produces delta-N-acetyl-delta-N-hydroxy-L-ornithine, which can react during fermentation with the amino acids of rice (glycine and serine) to form deferriferrichrysin.

This molecule can bind to an Fe(III) ion to form a red-brown complex, called ferrichrysin. This pigment is one of three sources of color in sake and can radically alter its appearance at a concentration of a few parts per million (ppm). Moreover, iron has a catalytic effect on the reaction between sugar and amino acids, which leads to Maillard reactions (browning and aromatic transformations generally considered negative, see "Aging", p.198).

Minerals	Phosphate	Potassium	Calcium	Sodium	Zinc	Iron
Concentration (mg/kg of rice)	94	92	24	5	0.12	0.08

Table 9. Main minerals in milled rice (90% *seimaibuai*) (mg/kg).

Lipids

Rice lipids account for 1.5 to 1.7% of the grain mass for sake rice and 1 to 4% for table rice. They are mainly present in the bran, embryo and subaleurone layer (18-23% lipid in mass), in the form of 3 categories of simple (glycerolipids, sterols) and complex (sphingolipids) lipids. These lipids are in the vast majority of cases eliminated by polishing.

The albumen contains very few lipids (0.3-0.8% by mass), mainly lipids with a single carbon chain (monoacyl): fatty acids and lysophosphoglycerides, associated with amylose. Of these, the most represented fatty acids are linoleic, oleic and palmitic acids.

The presence of these lipids in the wort greatly reduces the production of aromatic esters during fermentation. Since esters are the main source of fruity flavors in sake (see "Fermentation aromas", p.172), low levels of lipids (and therefore deep polishing) are desirable.

Although it represents only 3% of the grain mass, the lipid-rich embryo tends to adhere to the grain during polishing, up to a *seimaibuai* of 80%. This partly explains the strong inflection of the "lipid" curve observed in Graph 6 around this value.

Proteins

The main proteins in milled rice (90% *seimaibuai*) are: gluteline (80%), albumin (1-5%), globulin (4-15%), prolamin (2-8%). In the wort, these proteins are hydrolyzed into amino acids under the action of *koji* enzymes.

The main amino acids released are the following:

Amino acids (3c code)	Glu	Asp	Leu Arg	Val	Phe Ala Ser Tyr Ile Gly	Lys Pro Thr	Met Cys
Content (g/(16g N))	18	9	8	6	5	4	2

Table 10. Main amino acids of milled rice (g/(16 g N)).
g/16g N = gram per 16 grams of nitrogen, a standardized unit used for comparing the amino acid content of different proteins, equivalent to a "gram per 100 grams of protein".

Among these, alanine, glutamic acid, aspartic acid and arginine contribute to the umami taste (the "savory" fifth basic flavor, along with acid, salty, sweet, bitter) of sake. However, too high a concentration of amino acids gives heavy, bitter and unbalanced sake, and increases the risk of aging deterioration.

Structure

Polishing exposes the core of the grain in which the starch granules, more loosely packed compared to the outer section of the grain, contain higher amylose levels (even in the absence of *shinpaku*). This structure promotes fast water absorption during soaking (see "Cleaning, washing and steeping (*senmai* and *shinseki*)", p.84) and accelerates the dissolution of the grain in the wort. It also modifies the *koji* development on the grain by facilitating its implantation (see "*Koji*", p.93).

In conclusion, polishing has a direct qualitative impact on the sake's aroma (via lipids), color (via iron) and structure (via amino acids). Moreover, we will see in the chapter devoted to the *koji* that the polishing modifies deeply its development and its activity, also affecting the style of the sake produced.

A deep polishing allows one to obtain a fine, elegant and aromatic sake, the main characteristics of a *ginjo*.

> **Extreme polishing**
> **1. Deep polishing**

Recently, a few *kura* have become famous for producing very high-end sake (30,000-60,000 ¥ and more) made with extremly polished rice. Asahi Shuzo *kura* paved the way with its "Dassai 23" sake, made from 23% polished rice, and until recently the most extreme examples originated from Niizawa *kura* with its "Super 8" and "Prize" sakes of 8% and 7% polished rice, respectively. Tatenokawa *kura* seem to have put an end to this game of "who has the smallest" in October 2017 with its 1% *seimaibuai* "Komyo" sake.

But, beyond the obvious marketing implications, are there any technical interests in such polishing rates?

Those *kura* generally argue for the "purity" of the grain's core, stripped of its lipids, minerals and proteins. In fact, beyond a *seimaibuai* of 60%, only the rate of proteins decreases significantly. But then, how is it possible that "Prize" has an amino-*sando* of 0.9, a value certainly low, but quite comparable to, or even greater than, other *junmai daiginjo* polished to 40% or 50%?!

Quite simply, because yeasts can not grow and survive without a minimum amount of assimilable nitrogen (ammoniacal nitrogen or amino acids), which is an essential nutrient. It can be considered that a *moromi* is deficient in nitrogen when its assimilable nitrogen content is less than 140 mg/L or an amino-*sando* equivalent of 0.75. The fermentation is then very difficult to maintain and the *toji* can be forced to complement the *moromi* with assimilable nitrogen which, whatever its form, will provide protein, and thus amino acids to the sake. Note that Tatenokawa's 7% and 1% polished sakes boast an amino-*sando* of 0.5, which shows some mastery.

Focusing on another aspect of sake making, producing a quality *koji* based on tiny pearls of rice is an almost impossible mission and many adjustments to the conditions of cultivation must be made: ultimately, the use of industrial enzymes may be necessary to complement the *koji*.

As we see, there are not strong technical arguments in favor of these "super-polished" sake. Nevertheless, sake produced in this way receives great attention from producers and is of an extremely high quality: they are challenging to make and require great experience. On the other hand, you can probably find comparably good sake for a fraction of the price.

> **Extreme polishing**
> ## 2. Minimal polishing

At the other extreme, more and more sake made from rice very lightly polished (88%, 90% or even more) have started to appear. They are usually produced by *kuramoto* involved in "natural", "organic" or historical approaches. The economic value of such polishing rates is fairly obvious: all things being equal, an 88% polished rice gives 17.3% more sake than a 75% polished rice, and 46.7% more than a 60% polished rice.

The high *seimaibuai* also keep most of the aromatic characteristics of the rice and thus produce sakes with pronounced rice aromas, earthy and rich in umami. In addition, technical advances in terms of polishing (flat and ultra flat), *koji* cultivation and fermentation control have contributed to being able to greatly mitigate the usually negative consequences of low polishing.

These sake are particularly interesting for those wishing to better understand the characteristics of the different rice varieties and offer great results for old rice varieties with a strong personality (such as Omachi).

e. Storage after polishing: *karashi*

Once polished, the rice is too dry to be used immediately; if used so, it could become waterlogged during steeping and break (see "Cleaning, washing and steeping (*senmai* and *shinseki*)", p.84). It is therefore necessary to let it rest until it regains a moisture content close to what it was before polishing (13-15%). The longer the polishing process, the longer the rest period (*karashi*): from a few days to several weeks.

However, rice should not be stored for long periods, either before or after polishing. In fact, a rice used after one year or more of storage, called "*komai*" (old rice), will produce a defective sake with a high concentration of dimethyl sulphide (DMS). The resulting aroma (cabbage, onion) and sake are called "*komaishu*".

This phenomenon is due to oxidation of rice lipids and can be prevented by cold storage (<15 °C / 59 °F). However, the use of *komai* is discouraged due to the migration of potassium to the heart of the grain, which stimulates the development of *koji* and yeast, hindering the production of a quality *kome-koji* and accelerating fermentation.

f. Polishing flour: *nuka*

Two types of flour (*nuka*) originate from polishing: a brown flour, rich in fiber and minerals, corresponding to the first 10% of polishing, and then a white flour rich in starch.

Rice

The first is used in animal feed. The second is used by the agri-food industry for the production of biscuits or distilled rice alcohol.

2. Cleaning, washing and steeping (*senmai* and *shinseki*)

After polishing, the grain must be cleaned of residual flours present on its surface. Traditionally, it is placed in a bag, net or sieve and then stirred manually in clear water for one minute. The cleaning water rapidly loads with starch particles and takes on a milky white appearance. The rice is then rinsed for a few seconds in running water, until a clear water is obtained, indicating that all the polishing residues have been eliminated.

This cleaning (*senmai*) must be quick and the excess water drained immediately to prevent the rice from absorbing too much water before soaking. Today, machines can perform this task (using a whirlpool system) and the manual method is only retained for high-end sake.

Steeping rice (*shinseki*) is a necessary step to obtain homogeneous cooking. Indeed, dry rice tends to become waterlogged during steam cooking, while wet rice reacts more consistently. It is for this reason that rice cannot be used directly after polishing (see "Storage after polishing: *karashi*", p.83).

Steeping is done directly after rinsing with the aim of achieving a moisture content of rice of around 30%.

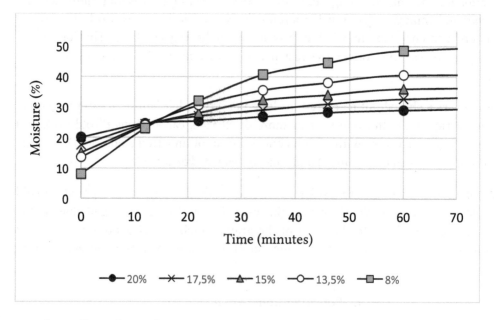

Graph 7. Effect of initial moisture on rice water absorption kinetics during steeping.

A 1% decrease in the initial moisture content increases the final moisture content by about 3%. This justifies the *karashi* period (see "Storage after polishing: *karashi*", p.83) which allows the rice to regain a moisture content of about 10-15% after polishing.

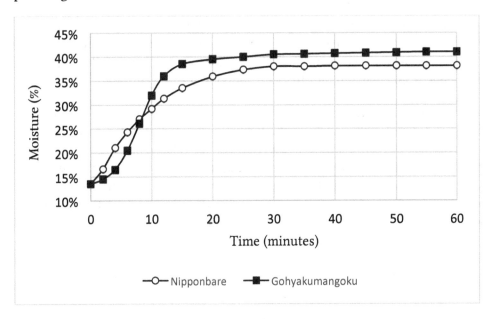

Graph 8. Effect of the rice variety on rice water absorption kinetics during steeping. *Nipponbare: a model table rice variety.*

As can be seen from Graph 8, the soaking time required to achieve a 25-30% moisture level on a 50% polished Gohyakumangoku is about 8-12 minutes.

In this range, it takes 10 seconds to change the moisture content by 0.2%. This time can be considerably reduced for deeper polishing or other varieties. The soaking time must therefore be determined and followed precisely.

The water absorption rate is mainly correlated with *seimaibuai* (+), rice variety, temperature (+) and initial moisture content (-). The water absorption curves versus polishing rate or temperature have similar profiles, a higher temperature or a lower *seimaibuai* resulting in a higher absorption rate and a higher final moisture content.

The *toji* knows the range of moisture content that suits him depending on the variety and type of sake he wishes to obtain. However, each batch of rice is unique because the internal structure of the grain depends strongly on the growing conditions and therefore on the year. In order to know exactly the soaking time required for a given batch, the *toji* carries out a test.

This test consists of observing some grains in a black cup during soaking.

The same type of cup is used for all operations related to rice quality, the contrast of the white rice on a black background allowing a precise view of the grain.

The soaking time is determined by the appearance of the grain: it is satisfactory when the grain takes on a slightly translucent and pearly appearance. This highly intuitive and empirical test requires extensive experience in working with rice. However, it cannot be replaced by a simple measurement of the moisture content that does not take into account other characteristics of the grain. Determining a steeping time (from a few minutes to a few hours) is one aspect of the *toji* art.

Once the steeping time has been determined, the batch is steeped. For small lots (such as rice for high-end sake *koji*), the typically very fast steeping can be done in small sieves. For larger quantities, the rice can be placed in large fabric bags, equipped with straps to move them through a system of rails and hooks installed in the *kura*. The bottoms of these bags are pierced in order to allow the evacuation of the rice after drainage (the bags are tied up during the manipulations). Pick-up trolleys of suitable sizes, i.e. about 1 cubic meter, can be used for soaking.

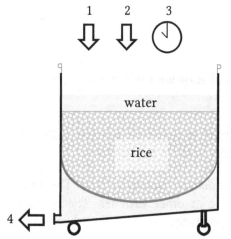

The soaking process is described in Figure 8.
1 / The trolley is filled with water.
2 / The rice-filled bag is placed in the trolley.
3 / The steeping time is controlled.
4 / The water is evacuated quickly through the trolley's drain.

Figure 8. Rice steeping trolley.

Other equivalent systems exist, the only constraint being to be able to evacuate the water very quickly in order to precisely observe the soaking time. The largest *kura* use automated soaking chambers.

Depending on requirements, the water can be stagnant during steeping or renewed sequentially (*tsuke-kaye*) or continually (*kake-nagashi*) via water circulation. Depending on water renewal, an exchange takes place between the grain and the water: certain soluble elements of the grain such as potassium and phosphate are partially washed away while the grain absorbs minerals.

It is assumed that for a standard process, about 20-40% of potassium and 20% of phosphate are removed. Since these elements are necessary nutrients for fermentation (see "Water minerals and their impact on sake", p.113), soaking time and water renewal must be determined while taking this parameter into account to not deplete the grain too much.

Less polished or old rice ("*komai*", see "Storage after polishing: *karashi*", p.83) requires a long steeping or high water renewal, whereas the loss must be limited for nutrient-poor rices (with low *seimaibuai*) to avoid a difficult fermentation.

Furthermore, the composition of the washing water must be rigorously controlled so that it does not contain undesirable elements that the grain could absorb, such as iron (see "Water minerals and their impact on sake", p.113).

After steeping, the rice is left to stand for several hours to drain excess water and to homogenize the moisture within the grains before steaming. Rice steaming often takes place at dawn, with the grains having rested during the night.

3. Rice steaming (*mushimai*)

When the excess water has been drained and the rice has been rested, it has a reached a homogeneous moisture content and is ready to steam. Rice steaming is traditionally done at dawn and is the first task of the day for *kurabito*.

The purpose of steaming is to obtain a rice grain that is soft inside (gelatinized) and firm outside, homogeneous in appearance and free from uncooked (whitish and opaque) starch granules.

Gelatinization is the process of solubilization of the starch granules at the heart of the kernel, which gives rise to an irreversible swelling of the grain. The gelatinization of the starch makes it more accessible to enzymes, allowing a good development of the *koji* (see "*Koji* cultivation (*seikiku*)", p.97) and a better solubilization of the grain in the wort. It is obtained by steaming the rice for 45 to 60 minutes.

Just like steeping, steaming rice requires adaptions for each batch: the *toji* tests the result of each cooking in order to adjust, if necessary, the following. The most standard test consists of forming a small ball of cooked rice in one's hand. The rice is kneaded to form a dough called *hineri-mochi* (*mochi* is a rice dough cake, very common in Japan). The ease with which the rice crushes, the elasticity, the color and the transparency of the dough are all indications of the quality of the cooking.

The traditional Japanese rice cooking tool is called *koshiki*. It consists of two terra-cotta containers. The first contains water, while the second, pierced and placed above, contains the rice to be steamed. This model has been adapted to steaming the large quantities of rice needed to produce sake.

The *koshiki* of traditional *kura* consists of a *sugi* tank into which the rice is transferred. This tank is placed on a cast-iron receptacle filled with water, heated by wood fire. The lower part of the *koshiki* is generally buried so that only the opening of the vat, from which the steam comes out, emerges from the ground. This makes it easier to handle the tank containing the rice. Moreover, this arrangement makes it possible to heat the cast iron tank on all its sides, accelerating the rise in temperature of the water and thus limiting the production of cold steam, which moistens the rice without cooking it. Cooking the rice with a *koshiki* is described in Figure 9 below:

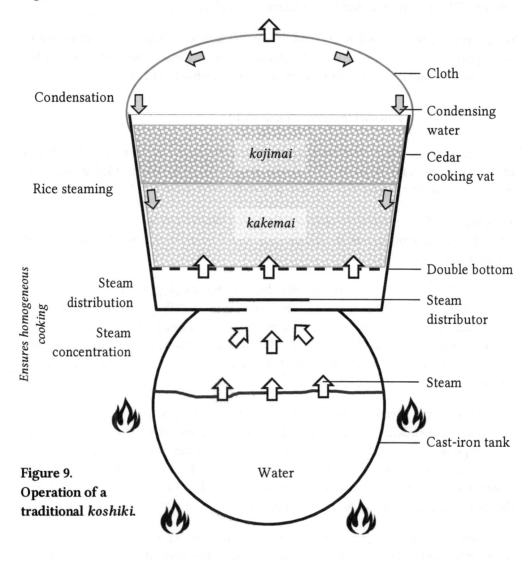

Figure 9. Operation of a traditional *koshiki*.

By construction, *koshiki* steaming is a source of cooking heterogeneities, both vertical and axial:

- **Vertically**, the lower layers of rice, closer to the arrival of steam tend to be cooked more and wetter. For this reason, *kakemai*, for which the grain integrity and the final moisture content are less crucial is loaded first into the *koshiki*. Similarly, the most polished rice, which absorbs water faster, is loaded last.

- **Axially**, the rice in the center of the *koshiki* tends to receive more steam and cooks faster. For this reason, special attention is paid to homogeneous distribution of the vapor, via a concentration and distribution system. Moreover, the water condensing at the top of the *koshiki* and along its walls moistens the peripheral grains, forming soggy grains called "*koshiki-hada*". If *kome-koji* is produced from this type of grain, it will form clusters called "*konpeito*" in reference to a Japanese candy in the shape of a spiked ball. Thus, the walls of the tank must be insulated in order to limit the condensation (especially if the *koshiki* is made of metal that conducts heat better than cedar).

These two types of heterogeneity justify the extended duration of *koshiki* rice steaming. Indeed, if theoretically 15 minutes are enough to obtain the gelatinization of the starch, cooking in a *koshiki* lasts between one hour and one hour and a quarter (20 to 25 minutes for the steam to penetrate to the heart of the rice mass and 40 to 50 minutes of actual cooking). This duration ensures that all the grains are sufficiently cooked.

Moreover, during the steaming, some of the volatile fatty acids of the rice volatilize and get eliminated. The disappearance of these lipids favors the production of aromatic sake, and is therefore desirable (see "Purpose of polishing", p.79). Moreover, the prolonging of the cooking process promotes the denaturation of rice proteins, decreasing the level of amino acids of the wort and the final sake.

Only a few *kura* retain a traditional *koshiki*, with stainless steel and gas having advantageously replaced wood for greater ease of handling and cleaning. However, the   principles   remain   unchanged.

Koshiki-daoshi

At the end of the season, when spring arrives and the *kurabito* must soon return to the fields, the last batch of rice is cooked. The "*koshiki*" (traditional rice steaming tool, see "Rice steaming", p.87) is reversed ("*taoshi*") to clean it before storing it for several months.

This *koshiki-daoshi*, which signals the imminent end of the production season, is celebrated by a banquet and offerings to the *kami*.

Today, even if the *kurabito* do not return to the fields and even if the *koshiki* is replaced by automated machines, *koshiki-daoshi* is still celebrated as one of the important events that mark the rhythm of the sake-making season.

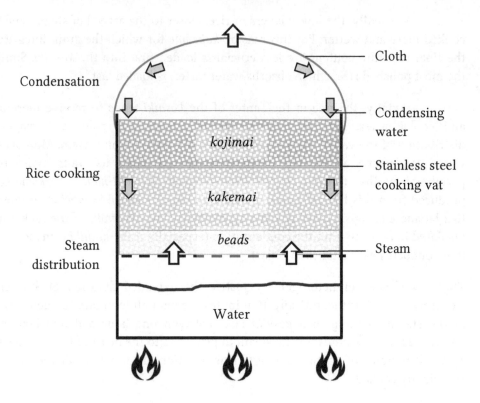

Condensation

Rice cooking

Steam
distribution

Cloth

Condensing
water

Stainless steel
cooking vat

Steam

kojimai

kakemai

beads

Water

Figure 10. Operation of a modern *koshiki*.

With the heating power of modern systems (using gas) far exceeding that of wood, the rise in temperature is rapid despite the fact that only the base of the tank is being heated. This also makes it possible to simplify the steam distribution system, which is replaced by a bed of beads that distributes the steam and condenses the cold vapors.

The rice is loaded into the *koshiki* directly from the bags used for steeping and draining, which have been brought over the *koshiki* by a system of rails and then untied so that their contents can be poured into the *koshiki*.

The rice can be loaded in several layers (the *nukegake* method), separated by jute (or synthetic) fabrics. These canvases can be equipped with the same strap system as the bags used for steeping and draining to facilitate unloading after steaming.

Several lots of rice thus separated can be cooked at the same time in the *koshiki*. Once all the rice is loaded, it is covered with another cloth in order to trap the steam and to offer the most homogeneous cooking possible.

The *koshiki* is loaded and unloaded manually (even with the help of canvases) and its capacity is limited. Also, in order to increase their productivity, the largest *kura* use continuous cooking systems originating from the agri-food industry, which consist of a conveyor belt circulating above a steam source.

This system allows rapid and homogeneous processing of large volumes of rice. In addition, it fits perfectly into a highly mechanized production line (soaking in automated chambers, cooling on conveyor belt, etc.). However, these methods are less suited to small batches and to the fine control parameters required in high-end production. Most *kura* therefore retain at least one *koshiki*.

Recently, new technologies originating from the bioethanol industry have been adapted to sake making. These machines cook the rice in three stages, with the addition of enzymes (α-amylase), resulting in liquefaction of the rice.

Liquefaction facilitates the transport of rice by allowing pumping. It also facilitates fermentation, since starch is already partially degraded, with the downside that a fast fermentation is generally not very qualitative. However, this method does not allow the production of *kome-koji* and deviates very far from a traditional production. It is reserved for entry-level products of the largest *kura* and, more generally, cooking sake.

Apart from this last particular case, the rice moisture content reaches about 40% after cooking. A slightly higher rate is targeted for *kojimai* (41-43%) while a slightly lower rate is desired for *kakemai* (39%). These rates can be considerably lower in some cases, for the production of *ginjo* for example. It should be noted that this absorption of water cannot be directly compared to that of steeping seen in the previous chapter, as the starch structure itself is modified.

4. Cooling and drying (*horei*)

Once the rice is cooked, it must be cooled before use. Depending on the expected use of the rice (*kojimai* or *kakemai*), the objectives and conditions of cooling differ considerably.

The *kakemai* is cooled to at least the temperature of the tank to which it will be added. Since cooling requirements are relatively strict during fermentation, a colder rice is usually introduced to cool the wort (see "*San-dan shikomi*", p.156).

The *kojimai* must, according to the characteristics of the *kome-koji* to be produced, be cooled to around 40 °C / 104 °F (see " *Koji* cultivation (*seikiku*)", p.97). But more than its cooling, it is the drying of the outside of the grain that will make it possible to obtain a quality *koji*. We shall see in the next chapter how the difference between a firm and dry exterior and a soft and humid interior determines a specific development of the mycelium.

The rice must therefore be cooled with not only cold, but also dry air. Traditionally, the ambient air of the *kura*, open to winter winds, is sufficient, but in year-round operating *kura*, cold and dry air must be generated by air conditioners.

Whether the air comes from the outside or air conditioners, it is necessary to ensure a rapid cooling in order to stop the cooking and to retain the properties of the grains. Traditionally steamed rice is spread on mats and left to cool in a windy area of the *kura*. Today, air blowers can be used to cool rice on conveyor belts. This type of machine is particularly suitable following the use of continuous steamers.

Once polished, rinsed, steeped, drained, steamed and cooled, the rice is ready to be used.

Rice transportation in the *kura*

Whether from delivery to polishing, polishing to cleaning, baking to cooking, cooking to cooling, cooling to tank, and so on, many production steps require moving the rice within the *kura*. Depending on the step and on the rice state, several options are available:

Dry rice (delivery/polishing/*karashi*): Depending on the quantity, "dry" rice can be transported in a "big bag" (one-cubic-meter soft bags with 4 straps) or in traditional 50 kg paper bags.

Wet rice (cleaning/rinsing/steeping): Once moistened, rice is transported in bags suspended from rails, or in trolleys. For small quantities (e.g. for *koji*), pierced baskets carried by workers on their backs can be used.

Cooked Rice: An ingenious compressed air propulsion system is used in most *kura* to transport large quantities of cooled rice to tanks. This system consists of a pump that blows compressed air into a wide, flexible pipe. It is fed via a mixer that breaks any clumps of rice that could block the system. In order to slip into the pipe, the rice must be sufficiently cold and dry, so this method is not suitable for *koji* rice. Sometimes, in larger *kura*, additives are used to help lubricate the rice. The latter is transported by trolleys or on workers' backs in pierced baskets.

b. *Koji*

Just like beer, sake comes from the fermentation of a cereal. Since cereals do not contain fermentable sugars but starch, it is necessary to go through a step of converting the starch into sugar to obtain a fermentation. This step is always carried out by enzymes that naturally possess this function.

> ### Technical vocabulary
>
> **Fermentable sugar**
> Fermentable sugars are sugars that can be used as a source of energy by microorganisms (yeasts or bacteria) according to processes called fermentation or respiration (see "Bacteria, fermentations and respiration", p.120). The fermentation we are interested in is the alcoholic fermentation by which the yeasts transform certain sugars into alcohol and carbon dioxide (CO_2), while releasing energy.
>
> **Starch**
> Starch is a large molecule made up of sugar units (D-glucose) joined together. Since these sugars can be released by the action of specialized enzymes in order to be used as an energy source, the starch acts as an energy reserve molecule for plants. This explains its presence in seeds (and therefore in rice) as it is starch that provides the energy needed during germination, until the first leaves take over via photosynthesis.
>
> **Enzymes**
> An enzyme is a protein, catalysing (≈favoring) certain biochemical reactions. Each enzyme is specialized in a particular reaction. The main reactions that concern us are hydrolysis reactions, that is, decomposition of a molecule by water. Amylases promote the degradation of starch into simple sugars and peptidases favor the degradation of proteins into amino acids.
>
> **Proteins**
> Proteins are a family of large molecules. Consisting of a chain of amino acids, they are ubiquitous in the cell and play very diverse roles.

In the case of beer, "malting", which consists of germinating barley (or other cereal) in order to release the enzymes contained in the seed, is used. In the case of sake, a fungus named "*koji*" (*Aspergillus oryzae*), produces and releases these enzymes (and others, see "Cultivation methods and enzymatic activity", p.102) while growing on rice. The *koji* is therefore cultivated on a part of the rice (about 20%) intended for sake that consequently contains the enzymes necessary for fermentation. This rice on which the *koji* has developed is called *kome-koji*.

The central role of the *koji* is illustrated by a famous saying that ranks the three most important stages of sake production: "*Ichi koji, ni moto, san zukuri.*" One *koji*, two *moto*, three fermentation". This saying is also illustrated by the hierarchy of roles within the *kura*.

The *kura* hierarchy

Kuramoto: The owner of the *kura*. Their involvement in the business is very variable. Historically, the *kuramoto*, rich landowners and aristocrats, were mainly occupied with "asset management", but increasingly they are getting involved directly in the *kura*. A growing number of *kuramoto* or their heirs (future *kuramoto*) are now managing production as *toji*.

Toji: The head of production. They manage all the *kura* activities according to the *kuramoto* directives and objectives, assisted by his/her *kashira*. Only a very small, but growing, number of *toji* are female.

Kashira: Literally "the head". Seconding the *toji*, he is his eyes and ears and transmits his instructions. (S)He is part of the *sannyaku* and manage one of the three crucial phases of production (*moto*, *koji* and *moromi*).

Sannyaku: Three highly skilled *kurabito*, each in charge of a crucial phase of production (*moto*, *koji* and *moromi*). The term "*sannyaku*" refers to the three most important ranks in sumo after the *yokozuna*.

Taishi: One of the three *sannyaku*, responsible for the koji, assisted by the *aikoji*.

Motomawashi: One of the three *sannyaku*, responsible for the *moto*.

Kamaya: responsible for rice steaming, assisted by an *aikama* or *oimawashi*.

Dougumawashi: responsible for hygiene and tool cleaning.

Meshitaki: "Cook", usually a woman, (s)he does not necessarily take part in the work of the *kura*.

Jounin, chunin, genin: *kurabito* without special attributions, ranked from the most experienced (*jounin*) to the most rookie (*genin*).

i. *Aspergillus oryzae* origins and history

1. Genetic history

Aspergillus oryzae is a fungus involved in the production of a large number of traditional Japanese foods: sake, *shochu*, *miso*, *mirin* and soy sauce. Because of this importance, it is the subject of numerous research and publications. Its genome was published in 2005 by a team of Japanese researchers, revealing its close proximity to another fungus, *Aspergillus flavus*.

There are, however, two fundamental differences between these fungi:

-*A. flavus* produces a carcinogenic aflatoxin during its development.

-*A. oryzae* has an overexpression of the genes involved in fermentation (secretion of hydrolytic enzymes and transport of sugars and amino acids).

Thus, while *A. flavus* is unusable in food production, *A. oryzae* has ideal characteristics for fermentation. This, however, is not a coincidence. Indeed, it is the progressive selection by humans of the *Aspergillus* strains best adapted to their desired use (fermentation) that has made *A. oryzae* a "super mold". To simplify, we can say that *A. oryzae* is a "domesticated" version of *A. flavus*.

2. Discovery and use of *koji*

The first written mention of the use of the *koji* was found in China, in the "Zhouli", a collection of rites of the Zhou dynasty dated to about 300 BC. Considering the scarcity of documents from this period, we can assume that its domestication in China occurred several centuries earlier.

In Japan, it was only a millennium later, around 725 AD, that the first mention of *koji* use appear in the "Harima no kuni fudoki" ("geography and culture of Harima province"). This delay may be surprising in view of the many exchanges existing within the continent: for example, a foreigner by the name of Nim-pan (Susukori in Japanese) had already produced sake at the court of Emperor O-Jin (supposed reign: 270 to 310). In reality, other techniques have preceded the use of *koji* in the strictest sense.

In another ethnographic collection of the early 8th century, we find the story of a sake produced from the mold found after the rain on rice offerings dedicated to the *kami* (gods) of a Shinto temple. This type of mold used as *kome-koji* is called "*mochi-koji*" as opposed to modern "*bara-koji*". The term "*mochi*" refers to a dough whereas "*bara*" refers to the fact that the grains are detached from each other. In both cases, the rice on which the *koji* develops is called *kome-koji*.

The difference, however, lies not so much in the texture as in the method of obtaining it. If the *bara-koji* is derived from a mastered and controlled process, the *mochi-koji* is derived from the natural development of a set of microorganisms on a substrate. The main differences are described in Table 11, below.

	Bara-koji	*Mochi-koji*
Form	Grains	Block/paste
Substrate	Steamed rice	Raw grain and nuts (rice, millet, acorns...)
Cultivation time	1-3 days	4-30 days
Microorganisms	*Aspergillus*	Filamentous fungi (*Rhizopus, Mucor...*)
Origin	Inoculated	Naturally present in the medium

Table 11. Main characteristics of *bara-koji* and *mochi-koji*.

The development of the *bara-koji* requires the domestication of the *koji* fungus through specific cultivation and the production and conservation of spores. The appearance of such processes seems to date back to the 10th century. At first, each *kura* produced its own *koji*. The first commercial *koji* crops appeared in the 13th century.

However, these crops remained unstable, subject to all kinds of contamination and thus had to be regularly renewed. It was not until the 14th and 15th centuries, thanks to new techniques developed by *koji*-making professionals organized into monopolistic *koji* guilds (together with *toji, shoyu, mirin*, etc. guilds) that healthy and stable *koji* crops were achieved.

The oldest technique of stabilization of *A. oryzae* uses wood ashes: mixed with *kojimai*, they inhibit the development of acidophilic bacteria by alkalizing the medium. They also contain nutrients (including potassium and phosphoric acid), which promote the development of *A. oryzae*. It is interesting to note that the repeated use of ash in the culture media has led to its effectiveness: the *koji* strains most suitable for cultivation in an alkaline medium were selected.

Ashes are also added to the *koji* spores obtained, because their desiccant effect prevents them from rotting. This technique favors the conservation and therefore the transport and commercialization of *koji*.

ii. *Koji* cultivation (*seikiku*)

A. oryzae consists of a mycelium (a set of filaments made of end-to-end cells), partitioned (between cells) and branched. Conidiophores develop on this mycelium: branched asexual reproductive organs carrying green conidia (spores).

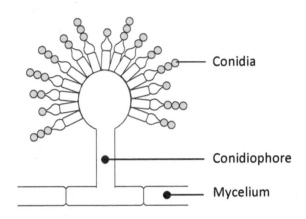

Figure 11. Structure of *A. oryzae* conidiophore.

Koji is marketed in Japan in the form of *tane-koji* or *koji-kin*, "seeds" of *koji*. These are grains of rice on which *koji* has been cultivated until the appearance of conidia, giving them a fluffy green appearance.

In the context of sake production, the appearance of conidia is undesirable because the objective is the production of enzymes by the *koji* and the formation of conidia would divert some of the fungus energy from this task. The *kome-koji* thus appears as rice grains covered with a white down: the mycelium.

1. Traditional method for *kome-koji* preparation

First, steamed rice cooled to 40 °C / 104 °F (see "Rice steaming", p.87) is transferred to the *koji-muro*. The *koji-muro*, literally "*koji* room", is a room in the *kura* with walls made of *sugi* (Japanese cedar) and a controllable temperature and humidity. A *koji-muro* may comprise several chambers to maintain different temperatures and humidity depending on the type of *kome-koji* desired (see "Which *kome-koji* for which sake?", p.107). The control of temperature and humidity can be done using modern methods or simple hatches that the *toji* open and close to control exchanges with the cold and dry air outside.

Traditionally, rice is carried on a man's back, in baskets of 15 kg. If the rice has been cooled after steaming (in a continuous blower for example) it is placed directly in the *koji-muro*. Otherwise, it is manually cooled outside the *koji-muro*.

In this second case, each basket is poured into a burlap of about 70 cm by 150 cm. The rice is spread out and then left to rest in the cold air of the *kura*. It is then regularly mixed by hand until it reaches the desired temperature. During the mixing, any clumps formed during cooking are crumbled to ensure a homogeneous temperature of the rice. The rice must, however, be gently mixed so as not to crush the grains.

When the rice reaches about 40 °C / 104 °F, it is transported in the *koji-muro* where the *koji* cultivation, which can be split into 8 stages, begins:

1- **Hikikomi**: Once in the *koji-muro*, the rice is placed on a canvas, in a wooden box called a "*toko*". The size of the *toko* varies greatly depending on the amount of *koji* to be produced. Classically, it is a table, often with edges about 20 cm high and a system of boards and wedges to adjust the length.

   The rice is mixed ("*te-ire*") in order to obtain a constant thickness in the *toko* and to break up any clumps. As with the following mixing operations, this is done by hand, pushing the rice clumps towards the center of the table with the palms. The rice is then left to stand so that its temperature homogenizes and reaches 30 °C / 86 °F.

   For some *kome-koji*, especially when the *koji-muro* is very hot (see "*Tsuki-haze*", p.107), the process is accelerated with fans. The moisture of the rice after cooking is allowed to reach 30 °C / 86 °F through evaporation, even if the temperature of the *koji-muro* is higher (evaporation consumes energy and lowers the temperature of the rice).

2- **Toko-momi (inoculation)**: Inoculation is carried out when the rice reaches the ideal temperature for *koji* development, i.e. approximately 30 °C / 86 °F. The *tane-koji* are placed in a seeder consisting of a reservoir for the grains and a filter whose mesh allow the passage of the conidia of *A. oryzae* (measuring about 5 micrometers, or 0.005 mm). 0.6-1.0 g of *tane-koji* are used per kg of rice to be inoculated.

   The simplest seeders are metal boxes with a wire mesh bottom. However, their overly wide meshes allow the spores to pass through in blocks, reducing the dispersion. Hence, a tighter filter made of tight fabric (silk) or a simple tissue placed on any container is sometimes preferred.

Koji

The first type of seeder, solid and convenient, is used for most production. The second, when one wants to limit the amount of *tane-koji*, which is particularly the case for the production of *ginjo* (see "Cultivation methods and enzymatic activity", p.102).

Whatever the type of seeder, it is shaken (filter down for the first, filter up for the second) over the rice to release the spores. When the cloud of *koji* spores has fallen, the rice is mixed in order to distribute them well.

Once the rice is perfectly homogeneous, it is gathered in the center of the *toko*, and wrapped with the sides of the fabric on which it rests. Several layers of cotton fabric are added, forming a bud shape and isolating the rice (from external changes in temperature and humidity) while allowing a thermometer probe to be placed in the middle of the pile.

3- **Kirikaeshi:** 8 to 12 hours after inoculation, *koji* has begun to grow, producing heat and carbon dioxide (CO_2). The rice has agglutinated and it is necessary to break up the block of coalesced rice to allow a homogeneous development of the fungus.

The rice is released from its fabric envelope and the rice block is cut into slices using *bunji*. The *bunji* are wooden tools, similar to small, elongated paddles, that are soaked before use to bring a little moisture to the rice while cutting.

The slices are crumbled and mixed in order to separate the rice grains, and then the bud shape is reformed. From this stage, the characteristic smell of *koji* begins to appear: a blend of warm chestnut and fresh mushroom.

4- **Mori:** 24 hours after inoculation, the first powdery white spots (named "*haze*") appear on the grains, revealing the presence of the mycelium. The development of the fungus accelerates and the bud must be opened in order to release the heat and CO_2 produced.

Again, the rice has clumped together and the pile has to be cut and mixed to separate the grains individually. However, the grains, drier than during *kirikaeshi*, separate much more easily.

Once the grains are separated, the bud should not be reformed because the development of the fungus is now rapid and the heat produced must be able to escape quickly. To do this, several methods exist:

Futa-koji
This very labor-intensive traditional method is only used for the production of high quality *kome-koji* intended for high-end sake. The rice is distributed in *kojibuta* or small-sized *toko* (about 30x40 cm) using a *kakioke* (measuring scoop). These are then stacked on several columns. Subsequent operations take place in these *kojibuta*.

Toko-koji

This modern method is used for most *kome-koji*. The rice is spread on the surface of the *toko* to form a 5-10 cm thick layer. Subsequent operations take place on the *toko*.

Hako-koji

This intermediate method, while relatively labor-saving, can offer good qualitative results. The rice is distributed in *kojibako* or medium-sized *toko* (about 150x85 cm) using a *kakioke*. Subsequent operations take place in these *kojibako*.

Whatever the container used, the rice is then covered with a fabric to limit exchanges of CO_2, heat and moisture with the outside air.

4'- **Tsumikae:** In the case of the *futa-koji* method, the temperature of each *kojibuta* evolves differently according to its position in the stack. They are therefore regularly rearranged into a precise order to ensure that each *toko* spends time both at the periphery (colder) and the heart (warmer) of the stack. This operation, named *tsumikae* is repeated every 3 hours until *dekoji*.

5- **Nakashigoto:** 30 hours after inoculation, the rice contained in each *toko* is mixed in order to release the heat and CO_2 produced.

In the case of the *futa-koji* method, the rice is then piled up in the center of the *kojibuta* to form a small volcano. This can be done easily with a wooden ring into which the rice is poured. However, some people believe that rice should not be touched at this stage. In this case, the rice is shaped by twitching the *kojibuta* back and forth.

6- **Shimaishigoto:** 36 hours after inoculation, the rice contained in each *toko* is mixed in order to release the heat and CO_2 produced. In the case of *toko-koji* and *hako-koji* methods, the rice pile is then streaked, by hand (*futa-koji*) or with a large serrated comb. This operation forms small mountains (triangular prisms) of rice, a few centimeters wide and high, along the *toko*.

The objective of this operation is to increase the contact area the rice has with air to facilitate the evacuation of carbon dioxide and heat.

7- **Dekoji:** 42 hours or more after inoculation, when the *toji* considers the *koji* has reached the desired appearance, it is mixed one last time, then placed on jute cloths outside the *koji-muro*, in the *karashi-ba*.

8- **Karashi:** The *kome-koji* is left to rest for a few hours to a day in the cool and dry *karashi-ba*. During this storage, the *koji* activity is slowed by cold but its enzymes continue to work, allowing the maturation of *kome-koji*. When the *toji* needs *kome-koji*, he picks it from the *karashi-ba*.

Sanitary requirements inside the *koji-muro*

The cultivation of the *kome-koji*, which is rich in sugar, offers a favorable substrate for a large number of microorganisms. Some, such as veil-forming yeasts (see "*Ki-moto*", p.125), do not pose undue difficulty, but others can easily spoil a batch of *kome-koji* or, more maliciously, go unnoticed and ruin the final sake. The main known contaminations are due to bacilli, lactic acid bacteria or indigenous ubiquitous yeasts.

For this reason, the sanitary requirements within the *koji-muro* are strict: the room is swept after each operation to remove loose grains, the *kurabito* systematically wash their hands and change shoes before entering the room, etc.

Traditionally, the consumption of fermented products, including *natto* (fermented soy), is prohibited within the *kura* to avoid importing external microorganisms. Moreover, the various parameters likely to indicate contamination of *kome-koji* are carefully monitored and culturing tests can be performed in case a contamination is suspected.

---

2. Modern method for *kome-koji* preparation

The preparation of *koji* can be broken down into a few operations with simple parameters: control of temperature and humidity, mixing, etc. Modern materials and techniques help simplify most of these steps, and thus only a few *kura* scrupulously follow the traditional method for their most high-end sake. Here are some examples of modern methods:

Inoculation: traditionally carried out within the *koji-muro*, it can, in the context of machine-cooled rice, be carried out on the air blower conveyor belt (cooler).

Canvases: traditionally made of cotton, they can be made of synthetic material, better retaining moisture. Sometimes both are used in the same *kura*, depending on needs.

Controlling the temperature and humidity: thermometers, heaters, fans and air conditioners more and more frequently help *toji* in the management of *koji* development parameters.

Larger *toko*: the traditionally small *toko* requires many manipulations (*tsumikae*). In order to facilitate the operations of *naka* and *shimaishigoto*, one can use a big *toko* whose bottom mesh allows good aeration of the mass of rice.

Koji-muro: building or renovating a *sugi koji-muro* is expensive. In addition, it takes several years before the smell of cedar disperses. Instead, synthetic coatings, aromatically neutral and easy to clean, are now often preferred.

Mixing machines: During *mori*, the grains are easily detached from each other and it is possible to facilitate this operation by using a kind of mixer. It may simply consist of a helix separating the grains, fed by a rice-loading funnel.

Koji automata: The ultimate mechanization step for *koji* production is the use of fully automatic machines. The cooked rice and the *tane-koji* are placed in the machine and it performs all the steps through a mixing tool, in compartments whose temperature and humidity are controlled.

These modern methods generate real gains in time and manpower. However, while highly automated methods are suitable for producing *kome-koji* in large quantities for entry-level products, the *toji*'s hand and experience remain irreplaceable for small batches of high quality product.

Indeed, such machines follow a protocol according to predetermined parameters while an experienced *toji* can adapt to each situation. The development of living *koji* on rice is a highly dynamic process and each new batch of *kome-koji* is a special case, with minute variations.

3. Cultivation methods and enzymatic activity

The *koji* produces a cocktail of about 50 enzymes, including α-amylases, glucoamylases, proteases, carboxypeptidase, aminopeptidase, xylanases, glutaminases, lactases, cutinases and lipases.

We will focus mainly on activities directly related to fermentation: amylase (which hydrolyze starch into simple sugars) and protease/peptidase (which hydrolyze proteins into peptides and peptides into amino acids).

The *koji*'s enzymatic activity depends on its growing conditions. However, we can consider the general numbers given in Table 12, below, as standard.

α-Amylases	250 U/g
Glucoamylases	1000 U/g
Protease	3500 U/g
Carboxypeptidase	5000 U/g

Table 12. Standard enzymatic activity of a *kome-koji*.
Enzymatic unit per gram of kome-koji.

Depending on the intended use of a given *kome-koji*, the *toji* seeks a different enzymatic profile and must therefore adjust the *koji*'s growing conditions to produce the ideal cocktail of enzymes.

It is generally preferred to promote amylase activities and to limit protease activities in order to minimize the final amount of amino acids present in sake (see "Purpose of polishing", p.79).

a. Temperature

The hyphae (vegetative part) of *Aspergillus oryzae* survive in a temperature range of 8-45 °C (46-113 °F) and can develop between 25 °C and 37 °C (77-99 °F), with optimum growth at 32-37 °C (90-99 °F).

In addition to its influence on growth rate, temperature plays a major role in determining the ratio of enzymes produced. Overall, a low culture temperature (30 °C / 86 °F) will favor protease and peptidase activities, while a high development temperature (40 °C / 104 °F) will favor amylase activities.

b. Humidity

The initial moisture content of rice affects the *koji*'s development and enzymatic profile. An ideal initial rate is considered to be 35-40%, which is slightly lower than that of the rice at the end of cooking (40%). This rate also limits the risk of crop contamination by other microorganisms, less resistant than *Aspergillus oryzae* to dry growing conditions.

The *kojimai* can therefore be slightly dried during its cooling. Rapid drying in the atmosphere of the *kura* will tend to produce grains that are both moist inside and dry on the outside. This will modify the *koji*'s development and enzymatic balance (see "Which *kome-koji* for which sake?", p.107).

Extreme humidity levels, below 35% or above 40%, favor (by different mechanisms) the production of proteases.

c. Carbon dioxide (CO_2)

Like any aerobic organism, *koji* consumes oxygen (O_2) and releases carbon dioxide (CO_2). The mixing operations carried out during the culture renew the atmosphere and avoid asphyxiation of the fungus.

They also impact the enzymatic equilibrium: a high level of CO_2 (2-5%, versus 0.04% in the air we breathe), due to a low air turnover, favors the production of proteases.

d. Nutrients

There is a correlation between the substrate carbohydrate/protein ratio and the enzymatic equilibrium of *koji*. The production of proteases is maximized for a ratio of 6 to 7 (6 to 7 times more protein than carbohydrate in mass).

White rice has a carbohydrate/protein ratio of 10 to 15 (depending on the variety). Any decrease in the protein content (see "Rice polishing (*seimai*)", p.72) in the *kojimai* increases this ratio and reduces the production of proteases accordingly.

This causes some *kura* to use a *kojimai* more polished than *kakemai*, especially when the latter has a *seimaibuai* greater than 70%:

A strong polishing of *kojimai* implies a low level of proteins and therefore a low protease activity of *kome-koji*. Thus, even if the *kakemai* has a high protein content (high *seimaibuai*), only a small portion of these proteins will be converted to amino acids and it will be possible to produce a low-amino acid sake from a high-protein rice. Of course, all the other parameters presented in this chapter can also be used.

Koji

e. *Koji* species

As explained above, the *koji* used in the production of sake is the fungus *Aspergillus oryzae*, called yellow *koji*. However, the term "*koji*" includes other types of fungi used in agri-food, especially for alcoholic beverages.

-***Aspergillus kawachii*** known as "white *koji*" is used in the production of *shochu*, a distilled alcohol, mainly produced from sweet potatoes, rice, barley, sake *kasu* (sake lees, see "*Kasu*", p.185) or cane sugar.

-***Aspergillus awamori*** known as "black *koji*" is used in the production of *awamorishu*, a 40 to 90 proof distilled alcohol produced from Indica rice.

In China, another family of fungi, *Rhizopus*, with similar properties and roles can be found. Called "qu", the fungi of the *Rhizopus* family are used in the production of baijiu (distilled cereal alcohol) and huangjiu (fermented rice alcohol).

All these fungi can, theoretically, be used in sake production: however examples of their use are limited to outside-the-box thinking *toji*.

The most used of these atypical fungi is *Aspergillus awamori*. Its use in *awamorishu* production is justified by its high citric acid production, which makes it possible to avoid contamination of *koji* and wort despite the high temperatures of Okinawa (the island in southern Japan where *awamorishu* is produced). Use of this fungus gives sake a particular "citric" style.

f. *Koji* varietals

Beyond the different species of *koji* described above (yellow, white, black), there is, after centuries of industrial use and selection, a variety of available *Aspergillus oryzae* phenotypes.

Each *koji* producer offers a range of strains with a general profile more suited to the production of a certain type of sake, or to a particular variety of rice. The characteristics evaluated for each are: the variability of the enzymatic activity, the speed of development, the hardiness, the ease of use, the aromatic profile and the production of acids (citric acid in particular).

For standard culture conditions, the main enzymatic activities can vary by a factor of 1 to 5 depending on the variety of *koji* used.

g. Rice varietals

If most of the time the same variety of rice is used for *kojimai* and *kakemai*, it is perfectly possible to use different varieties, especially when the *kakemai* is unsuitable for *koji* cultivation: absence of *shinpaku*, low resistance to polishing (especially if you want a lower *seimaibuai* for the *kojimai*, see "Nutrients", p.104), high protein levels, etc.

It is thus possible to optimize production costs by using an economical rice (local variety or table rice) in *kakemai* while maintaining a *kome-koji* of high quality.

For standard culture conditions, the main enzymatic activities can vary by a factor of 1 to 2 depending on the rice variety used.

h. Inoculation

An increase by a factor of 10 of the quantity of spores inoculated can increase the protease activity of *koji* twofold. This is why, for high quality *koji*, we try to inoculate all the grains with a minimum of *tane-koji*.

Here is a table summarizing the different parameters and their influence:

Parameter	Value	Favored activity
Temperature	High (40 °C / 104 °F)	Amylase
	Low (30 °C / 86 °F)	Protease
Humidity	Extreme: <35%-40%<	Protease
CO_2	High (2-5%)	Protease
$\dfrac{Carbohydrates}{Proteins}$	High ratio	Amylase
Koji species	Species	Others
Koji variety	Variety	Coefficient 1-5
Rice variety	Variety	Coefficient 1-2
Inoculation	Spores (x10)	Protease (x2)

Table 13. Culture parameters and enzymatic activity of *kome-koji*.

iii.   Which *kome-koji* for which sake ?

All the parameters described in the previous chapter are used in the production of *kome-koji* in order to obtain the ideal enzyme profile for the production of a given sake.

Each *kura*, each *toji*, has their own recipe and sensitivity, making each *kome-koji* unique. However, we can group the different *kome-koji* into 3 major types that we will describe here.

1. *Nuri-haze*

When the *kojimai* is too wet (>40%) or the heart of the grain is not gelatinized (and therefore hard) *koji* develops on the surface of the grain. The outer layers of the grain, rich in protein provide a fertile culture medium and *koji* covers the grain very quickly. As we have seen above, by developing in a high protein medium, *nuri-haze koji* has a high protease activity.

Because of their high protein content, *kojimai* with *seimaibuai* greater than 70% are likely to give *nuri-haze koji*.

2. *Tsuki-haze*

Unlike *nuri-haze, tsuki-haze koji* is a *kome-koji* in which the fungus has developed in the depth of the grain and not on the surface. This atypical development is obtained when the heart of the grain (gelatinized and moist) offers a more favorable culture medium than its surface (dry).

To obtain this result, the *kojimai* can be cooled in the cold and dry atmosphere of the *kura*. However, the rice should not dry too much, at the risk of preventing the implantation of *Aspergillus* spores on the grain. A relatively moist atmosphere is maintained around the grain during inoculation and during the first day. When the *koji* is well established, the *koji-muro*'s atmosphere is dried in order to favor a development of the hyphae in the (wet) depth of the grain.

By developing in the heart of the grain, the fungus finds a low protein environment. As a result, *tsuki-haze koji* has a low protease activity.

This type of *kome-koji* is considered to be the most difficult to obtain and the highest quality: it is used in the production of *ginjo*.

3. So-haze

So-haze koji represents a compromise between the two types of kome-koji described above. In this case, the fungus completely covers the grain and develops into the grain too. However, the penetration of koji in so-haze is two to three times less deep than in tsuki-haze. As a result, so-haze koji protease activity is intermediary between tsuki-haze and nuri-haze. So-haze can be considered the "standard" kome-koji.

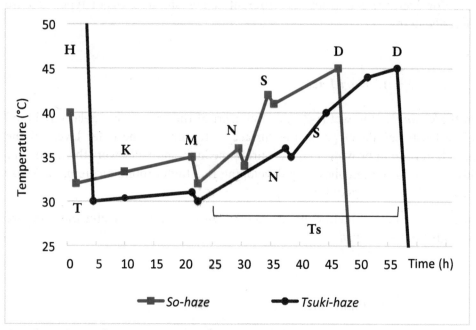

Graph 9. *Kome-koji* temperature during *seikiku.*
H: *Hikikomi,* T: *Toko-momi,* K: *Kirikaeshi,* M: *Mori,* Ts: *Tsumikae,* N: *Nakashigoto,*
S: *Shimaishigoto,* D: *Dekoji.*

4. Using several *kome-koji* for a single sake

During the production of a tank of sake, kome-koji is used four times during shubo and moromi (see "San-dan shikomi", p.153). The result is four batches of kome-koji, named after these four additions: moto-koji, zoe-koji, naka-koji and tome-koji. It is perfectly possible to produce a sake using exactly the same type of kome-koji for each operation. However, most toji choose to slightly modify the culture parameters of each of these koji in order to obtain an enzymatic activity more adapted to the specific stage's necessities.

In the moto, the goal is not to produce alcohol but to grow yeasts. To do this, a rich environment is more favorable. A kome-koji capable of producing a wide range of nutrients, in particular via a high protease activity, is then preferable. Thus for moto-koji, a so-haze-type kome-koji is generally more suitable than a tsuki-haze.

Koji

During the main fermentation, it is the opposite; we want a maximum of amylase activity to provide the sugar that will be converted into alcohol by the yeasts. Thus, for *tome-koji*, a *tsuki-haze*-type *kome-koji* is preferable.

Regarding the two intermediate *kome-koji* (*zoe-koji* and *naka-koji*), it all depends on the style of sake that you want to produce. By using a *so-haze*, the yeast will have a large amount of available nutrients and the fermentation will proceed quickly, producing a powerful sake rich in umami. Using a *tsuki-haze*, the yeast will have few nutrients other than the sugar available, and the fermentation will proceed slowly. The first case is ideal for an entry-level sake, whereas the second is preferable for producing a *ginjo*.

If one pushes this reasoning, it is also possible to adapt slightly the type of *tsuki-haze* produced for the different additions. When producing *ginjo* or *daiginjo*, every effort is made to create a product of the highest quality possible, so this type of adjustment is common.

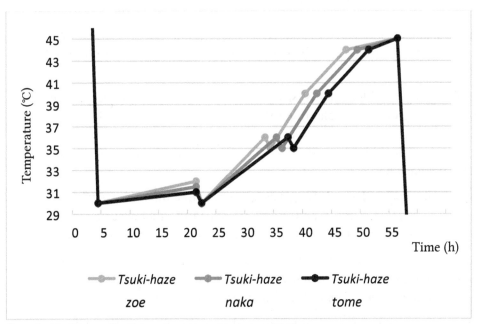

Graph 10. *Kome-koji* temperature during *seikiku*.

Note that this variation of the fermentation rate due to the type of *koji* used will require an adaptation of all the fermentation parameters (see "Fermentation management", p.156).

iv.   *Koji* aroma

The smell of ready-to-use *kome-koji* is a characteristic blend of fresh mushroom and warm chestnut, particularly detectable when the still-warm *koji* is just out of the *koji-muro*.

The main aromatic compounds found in *kome-koji* are: 1-octen-3-one (mushroom), 2-methyl-2-hepten-6-one (citrus), methional (potato), phenylacetaldehyde (rose), (Z)-1,5-octadien-3-one (geranium), isobutanal (spices), 3-methylbutanal (aldehyde), and 1-octen-3-ol (earthy). Some of these compounds are transformed during fermentation but they contribute to the aromatic complexity of sake, especially for *zenkoji* sake (sake made exclusively from *kome-koji* rice).

Sake and seasonal celebrations

Life in Japan is punctuated by numerous festivals and celebrations related to kami, nature, seasons and fieldwork, all of which are opportunities to consume sake.

In the spring, the blooming of *sakura* (Japanese cherry blossoms) indicates the beginning of the rice planting season. This concomitance is at the origin of a belief linking the *sakura* to the *kami* of rice and agriculture. Thus, during the *sakura* blooming season, sake offerings were made to the *kami* in hope of a good harvest.

In the same way, sake and *dango* (sweet *mochi* dumplings whose whiteness and shape evoke the full moon) were offered to the moon during the full moon of September or October, in gratitude for an abundant rice harvest.

Like all offerings, these were later consumed, and these celebrations gave birth to the traditions of *hanamizake* and *tsukimizake*, sake consumed while contemplating *sakura* (*hanami*) or full moon, respectively.

Other types of sake are related to seasonal events or festivals (including the five *sekku* or seasonal festivals): *amazake* or peach flavored *tokashu* for Momo-no-sekku (March 3), iris root flavored *shobuzake* for Tango-no-sekku (May 5), chrysanthemum petals *kikuzake* for Choyo-no-sekku (September 9), herbs and spices *toshizake* for New Year, snowflake *yukimizake* when snow falls or *unagizake* poured on grilled eel for Doyo-no-Ushi-no-hi during summertime (see "Doyo-no-Ushi-no-Hi", p.119).

c. Water

A bottle of sake contains on average 80% water. If we consider the water required for rinsing rice and instruments, steaming, etc., then 30 to 40 liters of water are needed to produce 1 liter of sake.

Despite this, the role of water as the main ingredient of sake is often neglected. We will see how water plays a fundamental qualitative role in sake production.

i.   On the importance of water: Miyamizu discovery

The fundamental importance of water for sake quality was brilliantly highlighted for the first time by Yamamura Tozaemon in 1840.

The sixth head of the Yamamura family (whose sakes are marketed today under the name "Sakura Masamune"), Tozaemon owned two *kura*, 8 kilometers apart, one in Nishinomiya, the other in Uozaki (today part of Kobe).

Despite all his efforts, the Uozaki sakes were never as good as those of Nishinomiya. He tried using the same rice, exchanging personnel, performing the same operations exactly at the same time, but nothing worked until he tried using the water from his Ume-no-ki well from Nishinomiya to produce sake in Uozaki. After having the well water transported in oxen-drawn wooden tanks, the sake produced at Uozaki was as good as that at Nishinomiya.

The quality of his sake quickly made Yamamura Tozaemon, and the water from his Ume-no-ki well, famous. Other *kuramoto* wanted to obtain this magic water, renamed Miyamizu ("Miya water" short for Nishinomiya), which became a traded commodity and spawned water vendors.

Today, Miyamizu springs from about 50 sources, spread over a 700-meter-long area covering two contiguous villages (Nishinomiya and Imazu). It is still a regional treasure and is highly protected by the ten *kura* who have access to it.

Before discovering what makes the Miyamizu exceptional, we will detail the parameters of water that affect the quality of sake.

ii.   Soft water or hard water?

Source waters have variable mineral compositions depending on the nature of the rocks they go through on their watershed. The main ions and dissolved minerals that they contain (from a few to a few dozen milligrams per liter for each mineral) are calcium, magnesium, sodium, potassium, silicates, carbonates and bicarbonates, sulphates, chlorides and nitrates. Spring water also contains, to a lesser extent (of the order of a microgram per liter), nitrogen, phosphorus, iron and manganese, to which we will pay special attention.

Waters are usually classified according to their "hardness", an indicator of their richness in mineral salts calculated as the sum of the calcium and magnesium ion concentrations.

If we consider exclusively water suitable for food production, that is to say free of chemical pollutants (such as heavy metals) or organic matter (such as residues or microorganisms), the water used changes the character of the sake produced in two main ways,

1.   Water texture and taste

From an organoleptic point of view, not all waters are equal. Tasting very hard "mineral" water sourced from a limestone region, such as the French Vosges or Allier, the American Southwest or South East England, compared to that from a traditional spring or filtered water is enough to be convinced. The waters rich in mineral salts have a texture, a thickness and give an angular sensation in the mouth while the so-called "soft" waters are refreshing and almost sweet.

These characteristics are easily transposed to sake: sakes from "hard" waters tend to be textured and almost tannic whereas sakes from "soft" waters are fine and refreshing.

2.   Nutrients and fermentation

Mineral salts are essential nutrients for all life, including microorganisms. Thus, hard water promotes the development of microorganisms and therefore a fast and vigorous fermentation. In contrast, soft water tends to generate difficult, slow and incomplete fermentations. Soft water sakes are therefore generally sweeter (incomplete fermentation) and more aromatic (slow and difficult fermentation) than hard water sakes.

iii.   Water minerals and their impact on sake

Although hardness is a good general indicator, it is necessary to refine our analysis concerning certain mineral salts having a strong impact in sake making. We will treat them in the order of their average concentration:

Bicarbonates (HCO_3^-): they stabilize the pH. In excess, they may maintain too high a pH, with a negative impact on enzyme activity and yeast development.

Chlorine (Cl): Together with sulfur, it contributes to the texture in the mouth: the chlorine/sulfur ratio directs the sake texture toward a crisp and dry aromatic style: slightly bitter when sulfur dominates and a round, textured, sweet style when chlorine prevails.

Sodium (Na): It contributes to the texture in the mouth. In excessive quantity, it brings a bitterness and undesirable salinity.

Calcium (Ca): Essential for yeast development, it has an acidifying effect (via the presence of phosphate in the wort) that promotes enzymatic and yeast activity.

Sulfur (S): Essential for yeast development, necessary for the synthesis of sulfur amino acids: cysteine and methionine. The chlorine/sulfur ratio influences the sake's texture (see "Chlorine", above). In excess, it promotes the appearance of negative sulfur aromas including dimethyl sulfate (an onion-like smell).

Potassium (K): Essential nutrient for the development of microorganisms. In excess, it gives a salty taste.

Silica (Si): Required in small quantities for the development of microorganisms. In excess, it may cause a colloidal haze (turbidity due to suspended particles).

Magnesium (Mg): Necessary for the development of microorganisms and especially for the production of enzymes by the *koji*. In excess (>20 mg/L, normally not naturally reached) it confers an unpleasant bitterness.

Nitrate (NO_3^-): Necessary for the development of microorganisms, and in traditional methods for the selection of yeasts via the action of denitrifying bacteria (see "*Kimoto*", p.125). Levels above 50 mg/L due to agricultural pollution (fertilizer) are undesirable.

Phosphate (H_3PO_4): Necessary for the development of microorganisms. However, it has an alkalizing effect, potentially problematic in excess.

Manganese (Mn): Highly undesirable. In its presence, sakes exposed to ultraviolet light become cloudy and discolored. Water containing more than 0.02 mg/L is considered unsuitable for sake production. However, methods of rectification exist and allow the use of water with a higher rate (see "Modern and atypical techniques for obtaining water", p.116).

Iron (Fe): Highly undesirable, it negatively affects the color and taste of sake (see "Rice polishing (*seimai*)", p.72). Water containing more than 0.02 mg/L of iron is considered unsuitable for sake production.

iv.   Miyamizu, the truth uncovered

Knowing the impact of all these mineral salts, let's see what makes Miyamizu an ideal water. The table below gives the analysis data for the mineral salts mentioned above from different series of waters.

	Miyamizu [1]	Sake-making waters [2]	Japanese waters [3]	Bottled waters [4]
pH	7.0	6.5	7.2	7.3
Composition (mg/L)				
TDS* (180°C / 356°F)	300	240	unk.	268
Bicarbonate	50	25	140	246
Cl	32	42	45	16
Na	32	29	55	10
Ca	37	26	14	66
SO_3	24	27	7	20
K	20	10	6	2
Si	11	11	23	unk.
Mg	6	6	6	11
P	2.28	0.15	unk.	0.1
Mn	0.04	0.07	unk.	nc
Fe	0.002	0.006	unk.	0.01

Table 14. Comparing the mineral profile of different water types.

(1) *Averages of an 11 sample series taken from 4 Nishinomiya sources.*
(2) *Averages of a 43 sample series taken from sources used by kura in 11 prefectures across Japan.*
(3) *Medians from a series of 15,000 Japanese groundwater samples.*
(4) *Medians of a series of 339 mineral waters commercially available in the world.*
TDS: Total dissolved solids

We can see that Miyamizu is a hard water (rich in mineral salts) compared to the average Japanese water. The microorganisms necessary for the production of sake (*koji*, lactic acid bacteria and yeasts, mainly) thus find in Miyamizu the nutrients essential for their development.

It is worth noting the high concentration of phosphate, which is often a limiting element, whose potential undesirable (alkalinizing) effects are neutralized by the presence of calcium. Moreover, there is very low concentration of two undesirable elements: manganese and iron. Miyamizu thus favors a vigorous, rapid and complete fermentation, a quality particularly sought after until the beginning of the 20th century when modern techniques of monitoring and controlling fermentations were developed.

Miyamizu's unique characteristics and scarcity (just 700 m of wells exist) can be explained by its origin: it comes from the meeting of two distinct underground water sources whose mixture creates the Miyamizu.

v.   Soft water fermentation

As we have just seen, Miyamizu is a hard water, ideal for fermentation. However, Japanese waters are generally quite soft, especially because of the low presence of limestone in the archipelago, and rather rich in less desirable elements, namely salt (NaCl) due to the presence of the sea, and silicates due to the volcanic origin of many bedrocks.

Faced with the difficulties of fermentation posed by the lack of nutrients in the (very soft) waters of Hokkaido, new brewing techniques were invented by Senzaburo Miura.

In 1878, he founded a *kura*, hoping to extract some value from the unsold table rice left by ships departing for Osaka from the port of Hiroshima. Then, after studying sake production in Nada he tried to apply the methods he had learned at home. Unfortunately, the sake deteriorated regularly and after four years of unsaleable production, the company went bankrupt.

It was only in 1892, after exploring many other possibilities and following a study trip to Fushimi (Kyoto), that he discovered that the source of the problem was the water. The methods he observed being used in the area (which has softer water than Nada) put him on the right track, and in 1898 he published a booklet on the production of soft water sake.

His method can be succinctly summarized in two points:

- the production of a particular *kome-koji* (*tsuki-haze koji*),
- a slower fermentation, at low temperature.

He dedicated himself to spreading his technique throughout Hiroshima's *kura*, and success meet by resulting regional sakes in 1907 and 1911 national competitions highlighted his work throughout Japan. Subsequently, his technique was gradually exported and laid the foundation for the *ginjo* sake that we know today. Indeed, the style became so popular that *ginjo* sake is now produced with all kinds of water.

vi.   Modern and atypical techniques for obtaining water

Since the chemistry of sake-making water is now well known, it is possible to use modern methods to obtain the desired characteristics from any water.

1. Subtractive methods

As we have seen above, some elements (such as iron) are undesirable in sake-making waters. It may thus be necessary to use subtractive methods to obtain clean water to produce quality sake.

The first of these methods is filtration, which eliminates any macroscopic particles (usually organic residues and microorganisms). Iron and manganese, the two most undesirable ions, can be removed by precipitation and filtration through the oxidation of dissolved $Fe(II)$ ions in solid $Fe(III)$, and dissolved $Mn(II)$ in solid $Mn(IV)$. The oxidation of iron can be done by simple aeration of water, but the oxidation of manganese requires the use of stronger oxidants such as ozone or chlorine. In the first case, the operation can be carried out simply by spraying the water to be treated over a "collection and filtration" tank (earth filtration). Other methods of removing iron include adsorption or flocculation. Traditionally, activated carbon or persimmon tannins were used (see "Fining", p.192), but today ion-exchange resins or stabilized tannin gels are often preferred.

In the case of overly ionic water, it is also possible to use a wide range of water purification methods (such as osmosis or ion exchange resins) and to then restore a balance by additive methods.

2. Additive methods

One of the first additive methods known is the use of potassium nitrate (or saltpeter) for *shubo* (see "*Ki-moto*", p.125). Today, *toji* have at their disposal all the necessary elements to transform any water into "Miyamizu" (see p.114 for the details of these characteristics). Here is an example of a "recipe" for the correction of fresh water: 100 L of water, 120 g of potassium, 40 g of sodium chloride ("salt"), 40 g of calcium and 6 g of magnesium.

The ability to rectify brewing waters has paved the way for the use of atypical waters, often for marketing purposes, claiming greater purity or "health" benefits: there are sakes produced from melted water harvested from glaciers or snow (especially in the north, Hokkaido), surface or deep sea water (desalted or not), etc.

Processing rice

Sake rice is generally described as either shuzo koteki-mai or table rice, however the Japanese government separates table rice in two categories: "staple food rice" and "processing rice".

Processing rice is a category of rice that can only be purchased by companies who process rice into other food products such as sake, miso, mirin, rice crackers, etc. and it cannot be purchase or resell for direct human consumption. To enforce this regulation, processing rice is always sold already polished and companies that use it must keep a clear traceability.

Processing rice is produced in fields that cannot legally produce staple food rice (the Japanese government manage the surfaces allowed to produce staple food rice to control the staple food rice market). Processing rice quality is equivalent to that of standard staple food rice, however as it cannot be sold for direct human consumption, it is cheaper. Processing rice can be classified through the official assessment system. Hence, it can be used to produce tokutei-meisho-shu.

Other sources of starch such as rice flour can legally be used to produce sake. They are mainly used to produce cooking sake but still represent a far-from-negligible part of sake production.

In recent years, due to the decline in sake production, less and less staple food rice has been used to make sake see annex 1.

Chapter II

Sake Fermentation

Chapter II: Sake fermentation

As we have seen, the three main ingredients of sake are rice, *koji* and water. Assembled, they constitute the raw material of sake. However, without the action of microorganisms, we would only obtain a sweet, non-alcoholic drink: *amazake*. It is the yeasts that, through alcoholic fermentation, transform the sugar into alcohol and, at the same time, produce the aromas we like.

In reference to this alcoholic fermentation, we will examine the major steps that allow the transformation of the basic ingredients to raw sake and will see in this chapter that this so-called "fermentation" consists of a variety of biochemical reactions, carried out by a complex ecosystem of microorganisms.

a. Yeasts, bacteria and fermentations

Yeasts and bacteria are tiny unicellular living organisms, measuring 0.2 to 2 micrometers for bacteria and 6 to 50 micrometers for yeasts. They are ubiquitous, active or dormant, and develop rapidly as soon as a favorable environment is available.

There are many families and species of yeasts and bacteria. Some are useful for humans, especially in the food industry. The yeast most used by humans for millennia, whether in the production of bread or alcoholic beverages, is *Saccharomyces cerevisiae*. It is also responsible for the alcoholic fermentation of sake.

Doyo-no-Ushi-no-Hi

"Doyo" refers to the 18 days preceding a change of season in the Chinese calendar (at the beginning of February, May, August and November). For modern Japanese, this term refers to late July/early August, the most torrid period of the hot and humid Japanese summer.

In Japan, each day is associated with one of the twelve signs of the Chinese zodiac, Ushi-no-hi being the day of the ox. So there are one or two "Doyo-no-Ushi-no-hi" during which it is recommended to eat dishes starting with "u" (like "ushi") "to fight against summer fatigue".

Today the Japanese consume mostly grilled eel (*unagi*), on which they can pour sake. They then eat the eel and drink the *unagizake*.

i.   Yeast metabolism

Like humans, yeasts use sugar (glucose) as a source of energy. Degrading it totally or partially in a series of biochemical reactions, they produce ATP (adenosine triphosphate), a molecule used as a functional source of energy. Yeasts have two different ways to produce energy by degrading sugar:

- In the presence of oxygen, they "**respire**": yeasts completely oxidize glucose in water and carbon dioxide with the following simplified result:

$$\text{Glucose} + 6\ O_2 \rightarrow 6\ CO_2 + 6\ H_2O + 36\ ATP$$

- In the absence of oxygen, they "**ferment**": yeasts partially degrade glucose with the following simplified result:

$$\text{Glucose} \rightarrow 2\ \text{ethanol} + 2\ CO_2 + 2\ ATP$$

It is immediately apparent that the second reaction is much less efficient (18 times less ATP produced per molecule of glucose) but produces alcohol (ethanol). It is therefore this operation, called "anaerobic" (in the absence of oxygen), which mainly interests us in the production of sake.

We will see, however, that "aerobic" mechanisms (in the presence of oxygen) are also at work during "fermentation" (here the term is used in the general, macroscopic sense), especially during the yeast multiplication phases.

ii.   Bacteria, fermentations and respiration

Just like yeasts, bacteria use sugar as a source of energy. On the other hand, their metabolic pathways differ. In the context of sake, we will retain three main reactions that are the result of various families of bacteria:

- **Homolactic fermentation** carried out by bacteria of the *Lactobacillus* genus:

$$\text{Glucose} \rightarrow 2\ \text{lactic acid} + 2\ ATP$$

- **Heterolactic fermentation** carried out by bacteria of the *Leuconostoc* genus:

$$\text{Glucose} \rightarrow 1\ \text{lactic acid} + 1\ \text{ethanol} + 1\ CO_2 + 2\ ATP$$

These two fermentations are generally grouped under the term "lactic fermentation". The lactic acid produced acidifies the medium, allowing the development of yeasts. In addition, it plays a fundamental role in the taste of sake (see "*Ki-moto*", p.125).

- **Aerobic nitrate respiration** carried out by denitrifying bacteria:

$$\text{Glucose} + 12 \text{ nitrate} \longrightarrow 6 \text{ H}_2\text{O} + 6 \text{ CO}_2 + 12 \text{ nitrite} + 36 \text{ ATP}$$

This is a type of respiration in which nitrate replaces the oxygen that yeasts, animals and plants use.

Other types of fermentations and other groups of secondary bacteria are present during sake fermentation, but their impact is (for us) negligible.

iii.   Fermentation, secondary metabolites and sake

In all living beings, all the biochemical reactions linked to survival or reproduction constitute the primary metabolism. The molecules resulting from primary metabolism are called primary metabolites. Together with this primary metabolism, a secondary, non-vital metabolism exists, whose products are named secondary metabolites.

Metabolism (primary and secondary), works by cascading reactions, producing a large number of molecules. For example, the fermentation or cellular respiration reactions described above are only balances of chemical equations. Several sets of reactions, such as glycolysis or the Krebs cycle, are involved. Many molecules are thus formed, including pyruvate, succinate, fumarate and malate.

Among these are molecules having an impact on sake's organoleptic qualities, including organic acids, flavor compound and their precursors. Pyruvate is, for example, a precursor of diacetyl (which has a buttery odor) whereas succinate is a precursor of succinic acid.

The conditions of the fermentation, the types of yeasts and bacteria present, therefore condition the metabolic activity, the metabolites produced, and ultimately, the taste of the sake.

We will see the different methods developed to select yeasts and put them in conditions of fermentation adapted to the production of quality sake.

b. The "*shubo*" or yeast starter

Of all the existing yeast and bacteria species, only a few are able to produce quality sake. On the other hand, there are many that can grow in the wort. If an unwanted bacteria or yeast develops, it is called "contamination". It is sometimes possible to remedy a contamination during fermentation, however a contamination usually leads to sake of low quality or unfit for consumption.

The art of sake fermentation is therefore to create a favorable environment for the development of "desired" microorganisms, to the exclusion of all others. The constitution of such a medium is the goal of the *shubo*. It is a "yeast starter": a first fermentation step, carried out on a reduced volume and whose objective is to obtain a large quantity of yeasts, able to ferment and produce quality sake.

i.   *Shubo* history

As stated above, the ancestor of sake is probably a mixture of rice and water macerated for several days. In this original process, there was no guarantee that the naturally occurring yeast was suitable for sake production and the quality of the final product could be extremely variable (or even unfit for consumption).

The "ancestor" of *shubo* consisted of collecting a small amount of wort from a satisfactory tank to seed additional tanks. However, this method does not give consistent results due to the low amount of leaven transferred. In addition, it is not usable at the beginning of the season or in the case of small isolated productions (since no pre-existing tank is available).

The invention of the yeast starter, of which we find the first written traces in the 14th century, optimizes and systematizes this seeding process. It allows the producer to evaluate the qualities of the yeast before fermentation and to avoid contaminations. Practically, the *toji* creates several yeast starters (fermentations in small quantities), judges their respective qualities, and selects the best as bases for fermentations. We can therefore consider that in its ancestral form, the yeast starter is a kind of "yeast catcher".

With the development and specialization of production, cellar's atmosphere became filled with quality yeasts (descending from the fermentation yeasts of previous vats), making this selection role less and less critical, and, ultimately, obsolete in 1906 with the creation of readily available "selected" yeasts.

We speak of "selected" yeast as opposed to "native" yeasts when they are deliberately chosen for their qualities and brought from the outside. This is the case

Shubo

for yeasts selected by the government or by private institutes, and sold to sake producers (see "Indigenous and selected yeasts", p.142).

The methods of *shubo* thus quickly evolved to focus on the multiplication of selected yeasts before fermentation.

Indeed, the second major interest in the preparation of a yeast starter is to find one that produces a large population of yeasts ready to ferment to ensure that no other microorganism can overrun the chosen yeast when the main fermentation (*moromi*) begins. Two effects combine in that regard: the large number of present yeasts makes it more difficult for other microorganisms to implant themselves (competition for resources, toxin production, etc.), and, in the event that a second microorganism would develop, its importance would be minimal in relation to the chosen yeast. The principle of *san-dan shikomi* (passage from the yeast starter to the main fermentation in three stages, see "*San-dan shikomi*", p.153) is also part of the same objective.

The different methods developed over time by *toji* to create an effective yeast starter are described below.

ii.   *Bodai-moto* or *mizu-moto*

1. History

The *bodai-moto* is the original yeast starter technique, formalized in the 14th century by the monks of Shoryaku-ji temple in Nara. Since the 12th century, temples had become the main brewing centers of sake and many of the technical innovations developed were born between their walls. The sake-making diaries of the time are to this day a source of relevant information.

2. Method

Information differs on the exact form of the original *bodai-moto*, however the different authors agree on its main features. The goal of the *bodai-moto* is to produce an acidic liquid rich in lactic acid bacteria called *soyashimizu* (*soyashi* = praised, *mizu* = water), hence its other name of *mizu-moto*.

To do this, the *toji* macerates for 3 to 8 days a mixture of rice and water. Some of the rice can be steamed, but traditionally no *koji* is used.

During this maceration, indigenous amylolitic lactic acid bacteria develop and perform a heterolactic fermentation. These bacteria have the ability to transform rice starch into sugar by producing amylolitic enzymes similar to *koji* amylases. Among these bacteria, the most represented belong to the *Leuconostoc* genus, in particular *Leuconostoc mesenteroides.*

When the brewer notices the beginning of the fermentation by the appearance of a release of gas (CO_2) and the acidification of the mixture, the wort is filtered to extract the *soyashimizu* water.

Cooked rice and *kome-koji* are then added to *soyashimizu.* It is possible to reuse the rice macerated during the first stage by cooking it after filtration.

By hydrolyzing starch and rice proteins, *koji* enzymes release amino acids and sugar. The resulting acid-rich, nutrient-rich fluid is an ideal substrate for *Saccharomyces cerevisiae* yeasts. These indigenous yeasts multiply in the medium and carry out an alcoholic fermentation. After 6 days of fermentation, the *bodai-moto* contains a large number of yeasts and is ready to use.

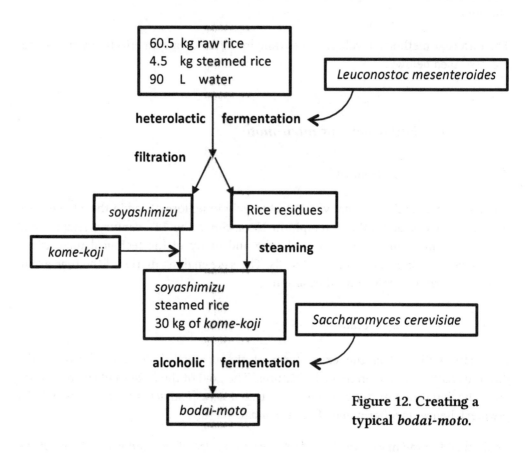

Figure 12. Creating a typical *bodai-moto.*

iii.   *Ki-moto*

1. History

We find the first traces of the existence of the "*ki*"-*moto* (later "*kimoto*") in writing of the late 17th century, which, given the reasonable amount of information available on the sake-making methods of the time probably dates quite precisely its formalization. The "*ki*" of *kimoto* can be translated as "pure". One can see here an allusion to the quality of the sake produced by this method, as opposed to the, then classic, *bodai-moto.*

More than three centuries separate these two methods as described here. In this interval, many technical innovations (polishing, *koji,* etc.) emerged, radically modifying the technical constraints. Additionally, it seems likely that intermediate methods emerged before the formalization of the *kimoto* method.

2. Method

We will describe in this chapter the traditional process of producing a *kimoto*. Note that each *kura* has its own method, varying the main parameters. However, the mechanisms described below remain valid.

1st day: combining

In a *hangiri* (low stainless steel or traditionally wooden container) steamed rice, *koji* and water are placed in the following approximate proportions (by mass): 15% *kome-koji*, 45% rice, 40% water. The ingredients are then mixed by hand.

Depending on the method, rice or *koji* is allowed to macerate in water before placing the third ingredient. The goal is to start extracting either rice starch or *koji* enzymes. The second method is more widespread but the choice is often limited by the availability of the elements: according to the *kura* organization, the *dekoji* and the rice steaming do not generally take place at the same time.

Mixing is carried out at low temperature (6-8°C / 43-46 °F) to avoid the development of undesirable microorganisms. Several *hangiri* are prepared at the same time to cover the *shubo* needs of the *kura.*

2nd day: *motosuri,* grinding

After a few hours of rest (classically, the next morning) the mixture is crushed with a kind of pole-handled wooden masher (*kabura-gai*). In two or three stages of a few minutes spread over the day, three men per *hangiri* transform the mixture into a lumpy paste.

This grinding is indiscriminately called *yamaoroshi* or *motosuri*: *motosuri* is the literal term for the "*suri*" grinding of the *moto*, *yamaoroshi* is a more pictorial and poetic version that conveys the idea of the destruction ("*oroshi*") of a rice mountain ("*yama*"), by the action of the *kabura-gai*.

The *motosuri* is done rhythmically to ensure that the rods do not interfere with each other. The rhythm is given by a traditional song that the workers sing in chorus. This song is also used to time the mixing. For the same reasons, there are traditional songs ("*sake zukuri uta*" literally "songs for sake work") for almost all *kura* operations, from cleaning tools or rice to homogenizing tanks.

Historically, the first mixing step was done with the feet because of the hardness of the rice grains (the low polished grains absorb water very slowly, see "Cleaning, washing and steeping (*senmai* and *shinseki*)", p.84). Today, some continue this tradition but the lower *seimaibuai* allows mixing directly with a *kabura-gai*.

3rd day: blending

The contents of several *hangiri* are then transferred to a *tsubodai*: a small tank enameled steel of 500 to 650 L. This step is called "*orikomi*". The number of *hangiri* and the size of the *tsubodai* depend on the amount of sake to be produced for that batch.

During this first 3-day long cold phase, the rice liquefies, progressively releasing starch and protein while the *kome-koji* releases its enzymes (amylase and protease) that will transform them respectively into sugar and amino acids (see "*Koji*", p.93). Then begins a resting phase of 2 to 3 days at low temperature, called *utase*.

This "rest" is however only apparent as strong microbial activity is in progress throughout. During its cultivation, the *kome-koji*, which offers a nutrient-rich environment, has been contaminated by a large number of microorganisms other than *Aspergillus oryzae*. These microorganisms are released in the *shubo* and meet various fates as a consequence of the environment change (aerial to liquid):

Amylolitic lactic acid bacteria (*lactobacilli*, mainly *Leuconostoc mesenteroides*) develop rapidly, just as in the *bodai-moto*.

Aerobic yeasts (*Candida* and *Pichia* genus) develop on the surface, forming a thin veil, while native anaerobic yeasts develop in the *shubo*.

Ubiquitous denitrifying bacteria (see "Bacteria, fermentations and respiration", p.120), mainly of *Micrococcus*, *Escherichia*, *Pseudomonas*, *Enterobacter*, *Aerobacter*, *Achromobacter* and *Flavobacterium* genus are also present.

At this stage, the nitrate level of the mixture is adjusted by the addition of potassium nitrate. Denitrifying bacteria transform nitrates into nitrites, toxic for yeasts and for themselves.

It is difficult to date precisely the occurrence of this practice but it is unlikely that the water used historically was naturally rich in nitrates. In addition, potassium nitrate, formerly known as saltpeter, is easy to obtain from urine, and its use is ancient, especially in China for gunpowder.

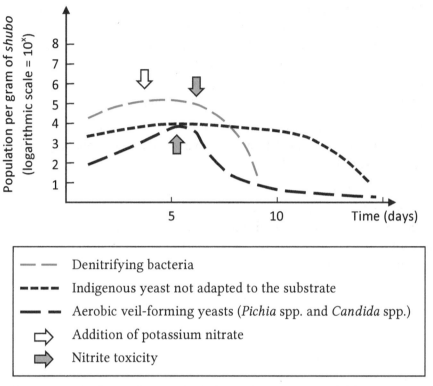

Graph 11. Microbial population of *shubo* in *kimoto* method (1).
Note: in the literature, mention can be made of nitrous acid in place of nitrite: this is the acid form of the acid/base pair: nitrous acid/nitrite.

From 5-6th to 15th day: *maedaki* (first warming)

During this phase, the *shubo* is slowly warmed from 6 °C to 22 °C (43-72 °F) by the use of "*daki*": small sealed, stainless steel, or traditionally wooden, buckets. This method is named "*daki-daru*". Every day, a *daki* filled with hot water (65 °C / 149 °F) is placed in the center of the tank. The presence of the *daki* in the tank creates a temperature gradient that offers a range of media adapted to different enzymes and microorganisms according to their temperature optima.

After a few days of fermentation, the *shubo* liquefies. It is then possible to heat the tank homogeneously. To do this, the *daki* is rotated, in a spiraling rising and falling movement. A *daki* of more than 10 kg is easily actioned thanks to the *shubo*'s lift (remember that the *shubo* is a dense and viscous liquid).

When the temperature difference between the tank and the room becomes too great, the *daki* can be combined with small electric heaters. This method is called "*anka*" and sometimes completely replaces the *daki-daru* method.

This long phase is very active at the microscopic level (see Graph 12, next page):

Amylolitic lactic acid bacteria continue their development but are rapidly replaced by *lactobacilli*, mainly *Lactobacillus sakei*. These non-amylolitic bacteria need *koji* enzymes to develop and are therefore not present in the *bodai-moto*. They are nevertheless more efficient in their use of nutrients and more resistant to the acidity of *shubo*, which quickly becomes toxic for *lactobacilli*. Selected bacteria can be brought into the medium. However, they have few advantages and are rarely used, the appropriate indigenous lactic acid bacteria being very common.

The continuous acidification of the *shubo* by lactic fermentation eliminates the microorganisms least adapted to acidic environments: indigenous yeasts, then *leuconostoc*, and finally *lactobacilli*.

On the other hand, yeasts of the *Saccharomyces cerevisiae* type are perfectly tolerant to acidity. Whether native or exogenous (selected), they grow rapidly. In the second case, they must be introduced into the *shubo* between the 10th and 15th day: early enough to take the lead over the other yeasts but late enough for the medium to suit them (acidity and nutrients).

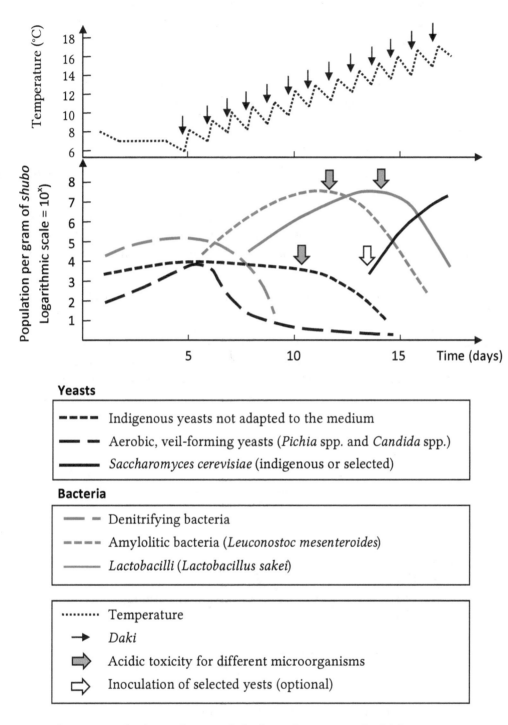

Yeasts

-----	Indigenous yeasts not adapted to the medium
— —	Aerobic, veil-forming yeasts (*Pichia* spp. and *Candida* spp.)
———	*Saccharomyces cerevisiae* (indigenous or selected)

Bacteria

— —	Denitrifying bacteria
-----	Amylolitic bacteria (*Leuconostoc mesenteroides*)
———	Lactobacilli (*Lactobacillus sakei*)

·········	Temperature
➜	*Daki*
⇨	Acidic toxicity for different microorganisms
⇨	Inoculation of selected yests (optional)

Graph 12. Microbial population of *shubo* in *kimoto* method (2).

During the *maedaki*, the *shubo* liquefies completely and takes on yoghurt-like aromas. Around the 13-14th day, CO_2 gas starts to cover the tank. This is the sign of a significant presence of yeasts in the *shubo* (about 10^7 yeasts/mL, i.e. $1/10^{th}$ of the final count). This stage is named "*fukure*".

The next day, the *shubo* is covered with foam. This is considered to be the sign of the fermentation's actual beginning. This stage is named "*wakitsuki*".

16th to 19th day: *atodaki* (second warming)

The *shubo* is now almost completely liquid and the fruity aromas of alcoholic fermentation take precedence over milky notes.

It warms up naturally thanks to the energy released by fermentation, and the volume of foam increases (more or less, depending on the type of yeast used) until it requires the addition of a collar (a plastic cylinder placed on the tank that prevents the foam from overflowing).

The rice starch is almost completely consumed and the *shubo* sugar level and yeast concentration peak.

The last *daki* used is called *nukumitori-daki* and contains boiling water. The thermal shock it causes kills the weakest yeasts, thus selecting the best yeasts for the main fermentation. It has been proven that this method selects the most aromatic yeasts, favoring in particular isoamyl acetate and ethyl caproate (see "Fermentation aromas", p.172).

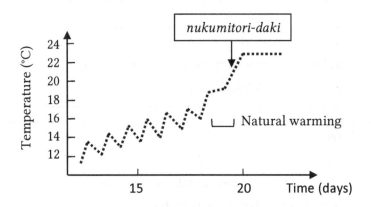

Graph 13. *Shubo* temperature in *kimoto* method (3).

20th day and following: cooling and maturation

The *shubo* enters a maturation phase, the sugar concentration drops rapidly while the amount of yeast reaches its maximum. The yeast activity decreases accordingly, no longer allowing the *shubo* to maintain its temperature which drops to around 6 °C / 43 °F.

The first stage of cooling can be accelerated by dividing the *shubo* into *hangiri*. This is called "*moto-wake*" (*moto* division).

The maturation of the *moto* (or "*karashi*") lasts from 3 to 7 days and presents several points of interest: it avoids a thermal shock to the yeasts during the transition towards the main, low temperature fermentation, and it places the yeasts in a dormant phase from which they will wake up more apt to multiply.

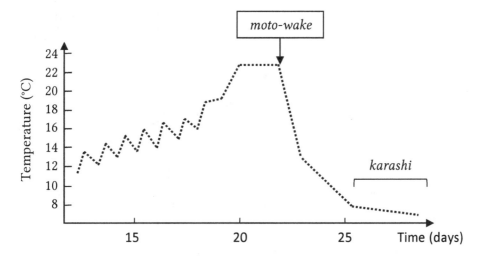

Graph 14. *Shubo* temperature in *kimoto* method (4).

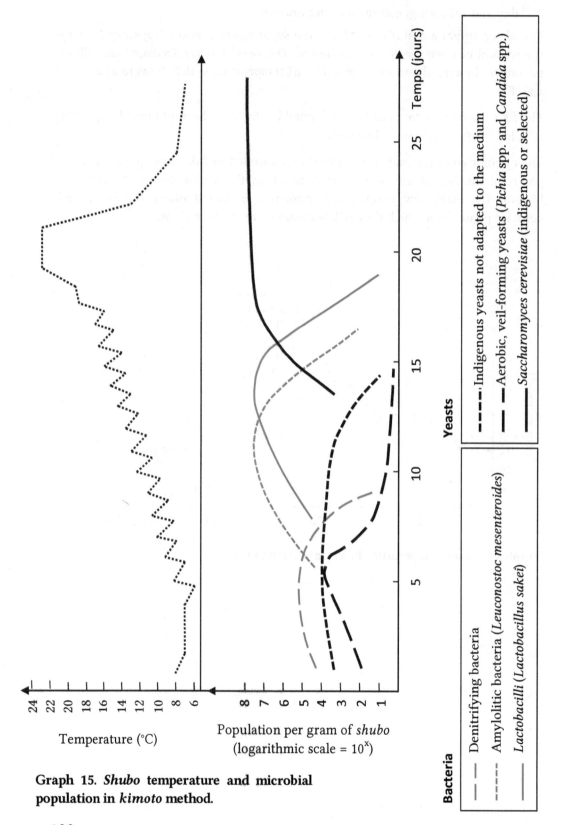

Graph 15. *Shubo* temperature and microbial population in *kimoto* method.

Temperature (°C)

Population per gram of *shubo*
(logarithmic scale = 10^x)

Temps (jours)

Yeasts

······ Indigenous yeasts not adapted to the medium

– – Aerobic, veil-forming yeasts (*Pichia* spp. and *Candida* spp.)

—— *Saccharomyces cerevisiae* (indigenous or selected)

Bacteria

– – Denitrifying bacteria

······ Amylolitic bacteria (*Leuconostoc mesenteroides*)

—— Lactobacilli (*Lactobacillus sakei*)

iv. *Yamahai-moto*

1. History

In 1909, in the wake of the creation of the NRIB, Professor Kinichiro Kagi conducted research on *shubo* and discovered that *yamaoroshi* was not necessary for the development of yeasts. The replacement method he invented, then called *yamaoroshi hai-shi* ("stop *yamaoroshi*"), quickly became simplified to "*yamahai*".

This is at least the story as it is told. Even considering the immutability of the techniques specific to Japan, it seems perfectly unlikely that an exhausting and useless practice lasted for more than 300 years. So, why is the *yamahai* method so recent?

Until the early 1900s, although 70% polished rice could be obtained through existing methods (use of a water mill), the vast majority of commercially available sake had an 85% *seimaibuai*. A pamphlet of the time specifically criticizes sake with low *seimaibuai* for the waste of rice they represent.

However, the invention of the first motorized polishing machine and the success of Hiroshima sakes (see "Soft water fermentation", p.115) promoted the development of *ginjo* sake and completely changed the outlook: quality sake of the 20th century all, or almost all, have a *seimaibuai* under or equal to 70%.

However, whereas low polished rice requires significant mechanical work to dissolve in water, this is not the case for highly polished rice. As explained above (see "*Ki-moto*", p.125), the first grinding of *kimoto* was historically done with feet because of the hardness of low polished rice grains. But, under a *seimaibuai* of about 70% (variable, depending on the variety and vintage), the grains of rice dissolve in water under the effect of *koji* enzymes even without mechanical action.

It was thus the democratization of the low *seimaibuai* that allowed the abandonment of *yamaoroshi* and the invention of the *yamahai* method.

For the same reason, there is almost no *futsushu* produced according to the *yamahai* method and even these have *seimaibuai* of 70% or less. Further research would probably have made it possible to circumvent this limitation, via the addition of enzymes for example, but the quasi-concomitant discovery of the *sokujyo* method (described on the next page) quickly and advantageously occupied the field.

2. Method

The *yamahai* method proceeds with the same steps as the *kimoto* method described above, with a few minor differences.

The mixing of rice (*yamaoroshi* or *motosuri*) does not take place. It is therefore necessary to promote the dissolution of rice grains by another method. To do this, a little more water is used in the *shubo* and the initial temperature is higher by a few degrees. In addition, a mixture of *kome-koji* and water called "*mizu-koji*" is systematically constituted 2 to 3 hours before the addition of rice, to extract *koji* enzymes.

The difference in environment resulting from these modifications is not without consequences on the microbial flora. Denitrifying bacteria have been shown to play a lesser role than in the *yamahai* method, partially replaced as a pioneering species by a lactic acid bacterium, *Lactobacillus acidipiscis*.

v. *Sokujyo-moto*

1. History

In 1899, Mr. Eda Kamajiro demonstrated that the key element of *shubo* is obtaining an acidic solution. He then had the idea of bypassing traditional methods by directly using an industrial lactic acid solution. He presented this new method, called *sokujyo* ("quick method"), in a publication dated 1909.

The *sokujyo* method, which saves two weeks on *shubo* production, was promptly adopted and now accounts for almost all (99%) of sake production.

2. Method

In this method, the complex ecosystem that we studied in the previous chapters is replaced by an addition of industrial lactic acid.

A mixture of water, *kome-koji*, and steamed rice is made, in the same proportions as for traditional methods. Then, a solution of lactic acid is added, thereby lowering the pH to 3.5-3.8; for a 75% standard lactic acid solution in water, an addition corresponding to 0.65% of the total volume of the *shubo* is necessary.

This sudden lowering of pH eliminates most microorganisms from water and *koji*. However, a medium rich in sugars and acids such as *shubo* remains highly favorable to the development of many acidophilic microorganisms. Also, the *sokujyo* method does not allow the natural selection of yeasts, unlike the traditional methods described above.

It is therefore necessary to inoculate immediately and in large quantities (10^5-10^6 cells/gram) selected yeast to avoid contamination of the *shubo*.

The enzymatic activity must also start immediately to provide nutrients to the seeded yeast. The heat of the just-steamed rice is used to initially warm up the *shubo* to 18-20 °C (65-68 °F) during *shikomi*. Once the mixture is done, it is placed in a cold room (8-10 °C / 46-50 °F) to favor the implantation of the yeast while limiting the risk of contamination.

The *shubo* remains at low temperature for 1 to 2 days (*utase*), during which the mixture is regularly homogenized. To do this, it can be stirred with a *kai* (pole-handled wooden masher) but the rice grains are not yet digested and the mixture is particularly hard.

A metal chimney, pierced at its base, can then be placed in the tank to access the liquid present at the bottom of the tank and regularly water the mixture with it (see Figure 13).

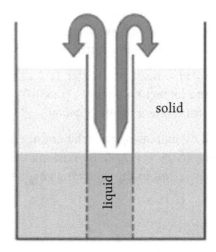

This method called *kumikake* homogenizes the enzymatic action and the development of yeasts in the tank. It also prevents the upper part of the rice from remaining dry, which would effectively exclude it from the *shubo* and could promote the development of undesirable microorganisms. It is also possible to use this system to hasten the *shubo* cooling by placing cold *daki*, filled with ice, in the chimney.

Figure. 13. *Kumikake* (homogenization).

After the *utase*, the chimney is removed and then begins a warming process similar to the *kimoto* method. Using *daki* and heaters (*anka* method) the *shubo* reaches a temperature of 20 °C / 68 °F in 5 to 8 days.

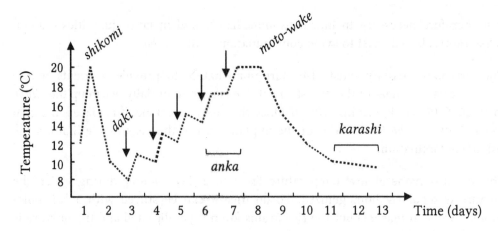

Graph 16. *Shubo* temperature in *sokujyo* method.

Just like in the case of the *kimoto* method, the *shubo* is then cooled thanks to the *moto-wake* method.

The alcohol content of the *sokujyo moto* rises rapidly due to high temperature and high concentration of inoculated yeasts. However, it must not exceed 15%, to not cause toxicity to the yeast: water additions are sometimes used to control this.

Because of these kinetics, the *karashi* period of *sokujyo* must be shorter (1-2 days only) than in the *kimoto* method (see "Shubo use and impact on quality", p.138). The *sokujyo-moto* is ready to be used in less than 2 weeks (versus 4 for the *kimoto*).

It is possible to further shorten the *sokujyo* method by increasing the temperature of the *shubo* to 18-20 °C (65-68 °F) at the coldest and up to 25 °C (77 °F). By pushing this reasoning to the extreme one obtains the method described in the following chapter: the *ko-on-toka moto*.

vi.   *Ko-on-toka moto*

This method, an immediate derivative of the *sokujyo* method, appeared with the industrialization of production methods. It consists in heating the mixture for 5 to 6 hours at 55-60 °C / 130-140 °F, before the addition of lactic acid. This both stimulates the action of *koji* enzymes in order to rapidly obtain a wort rich in sugars and amino acids, and kills the microorganisms originating from the *koji*.

The following steps may be the same as in the conventional *sokujyo* method, or a higher temperature method may be used. In this second case, the mixture is cooled to 25 °C / 77 °F. before being inoculated. Thanks to this ideal development temperature, the desired concentration of yeasts can be reached in 2 days.

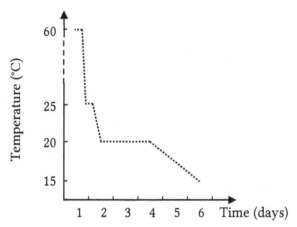

Graph 17. *Shubo* temperature, *ko-on-toka* method, high temperature.

Note that in addition to the pasteurization of *koji*, incubation at high temperature also has an impact on its enzymatic activity. Indeed, *koji*'s enzymes react differently to temperature, thus *ko-on-toka* and *sokujyo moto* differ in their nutrient composition.

The *ko-on-toka*-type *shubo* is fast to produce, which reduces costs. Moreover, thanks to the initial pasteurization, very few microorganisms other than the selected yeast develop there. This provides guarantees for food safety and reproducibility, qualities particularly appreciated by large companies for their entry-level sake.

vii.   *Kobo-shikomi*

Some companies have pushed even further the modernization of their production techniques by purely abolishing the *shubo* stage. In this method a large quantity of commercial yeasts and lactic acid are directly added at the beginning of the main fermentation, during *hatsu-zoe* (first addition, see "*San-dan shikomi*", p.153).

This method finds its main interest at the beginning of the season, when most *kura* have to wait several weeks for a *shubo* to be ready before starting the first *moromi*. However, the existence of the previously described rapid methods, the additional cost of purchasing larger quantities of commercial yeasts and finally the deseasonalization of production make this method a last resort.

viii.   *Shubo* use and impact on quality

1. Traditional methods

Traditional methods (*bodai, kimoto* and *yamahai* as opposed to *sokujyo* or *ko-on-toka* methods) have several specific features.

Lactic activity: The lactic fermentation of traditional *shubo* sows the *moromi* with lactic acid bacteria. These are then more active during the main fermentation (about 30% more bacteria during the *moromi*) with a consequent higher acidity, but also lactic aromas (such as diacetyl, butarate, etc.) that bring a greater aromatic complexity to the sake.

The lactic fermentation of *bodai-moto* is entirely ensured by heterolactic bacteria while that of other traditional *shubo* also involves homolactic bacteria. The sakes derived from *bodai-moto* method are therefore less rich in lactic acid than *kimoto* or *yamahai* sakes and perceived as slightly less acidic. In addition, heterolactic fermentation tends to produce a relatively high concentration of acetic acid (instead of ethanol, see "Bacteria, fermentations and respiration", p.122). The sakes from the *bodai-moto* method therefore have stronger acetic notes (vinegar).

Indigenous microorganisms: Traditional methods are the only ones that allow the use of indigenous yeasts, as they offer a perfectly adapted but nutrient-poor environment, limiting the risks of contamination. However, the vast majority of sakes produced today use selected yeasts.

Lactic and denitrifying bacteria, on the other hand, are most often indigenous. These indigenous microorganisms, specific to each *kura* can constitute a differentiating element, or even an element of "terroir" (see "Sake and terroir", p.215).

Microorganism diversity: The diversity of microorganisms involved in the production of traditional sake widens their aromatic palette (for better or for worse). These sakes are therefore generally richer, more complex and present, in a less unequivocal way, the aromatic characteristics of the selected yeasts.

Yeast resistance: Traditional methods make it possible to obtain and select yeasts that are more resistant to end-of-fermentation conditions (few nutrients and a lot of alcohol). They thus avoid the production of undesirable aromas, resulting from metabolic pathways activated by yeast under stressful conditions in extreme environments, while allowing the fermentation to be prolonged to obtain drier sakes with a higher alcohol content.

This resistance can be explained in particular by the lower alcohol content of traditional *shubo* and its more gradual increase. These conditions are favorable for the synthesis by yeasts of palmitic acid (a fatty acid), which limits the diffusion of ethanol through the yeast membranes, while *sokujyo* conditions promote the production of another fatty acid, linoleic acid.

Enzyme activity: Environmental conditions, including acidity or temperature, influence the activity of *koji* enzymes. The progressive acidity of traditional *shubo* promotes proteolytic activity, producing sakes that are richer in amino acids and thus in umami.

More precisely, the proteolytic activity of *koji* can be divided into two main groups: proteases, which cut down proteins into peptides (chains of amino acids), and carboxypeptidase, which cuts down peptides into amino acids. While different type of protease with different optimum range of pH exists, from alkaline (10.5) to semialkaline (8.3) neutral (6-7) and acidic (3), the three types of carboxypeptidase all have an acidic optimum pH of 3-4. It has be found that when working together at low pH, acid protease (AP) and acid carboxypeptidase (ACP) produce small peptides (2-3 amino acids long) that can not be hydrolyzed further by the *koji* enzyme. On the other hand, when AP are allowed to work beforehand (specifically around the 7-10 days of the *kimoto* method), they release large peptides (75+ amino acids) that can be latter hydrolyzed into free amino acids by ACP. Both those peptides and free amino acids accumulate in the wort and can be found in the final sake. However, while free amino acids impart a positive umami to sake, small peptides can bring negative bitter tastes. Furthermore, free amino acids being more easily used as nutrients by yeasts, *kimoto* methods offer a more favorable environment for yeast development.

Sakes made through traditional methods tend to be drier, acidic, deep and complex.

With respect to the market, the commercial use of *bodai-moto* died out at the beginning of the 20th century. However, in 1988, the temple at the origin of the creation of *bodai-moto* joined a group of sake producers to revive this technique. Today, its use remains totally anecdotal and most of the sake produced generally has other atypical characteristics (*nigorizake, genmaishu*, etc.). They are therefore quite difficult to characterize but generally have a significantly acidic, acescent and lactic profile.

The *yamahai* sakes have more marked aromatic characteristics (lactic, earthy), and are generally richer in sugars and acids than *kimoto* sakes. The latter are often more "clean", aromatically, as opposed to the more "wild" or "rustic" *yamahai*.

Today the *kimoto* method is the most recognized of traditional methods, especially because of the folklore that accompanies it around *yamaoroshi*. However, many *kura* prefer the labor-saving *yamahai* method. Purists point out, however, that the *kimoto* method gives slightly higher qualitative results, especially for aromatic purity.

2. Modern methods

Modern methods (*sokujyo* mainly) have quickly gained popularity as they are convenient, greatly predictable and reproducible, and save time and space (in terms of tanks and, thus, cellar space), but also due to the style of sake obtained.

Today they represent the vast majority of sake produced (99%), so it is difficult to define their general characteristics, which are the norm. However, their profile emerges from the description we made above of traditional sake. In contrast to these, they are aromatically pure, very marked by the characteristics of the selected yeast used, and poor in acids and umami.

This "crystalline" profile was much sought after from the early 1900s with the appearance and development of *ginjo* sake.

Life in the *kura* (1/2)

Historically, *kurabito* were peasants who accompanied a *toji* to spend the winter months working in a *kura*, sometimes far from home. They worked and lived in their community, away from their families, 4 to 6 months a year, returning only a few days, if they could, for New Year celebrations.

Today, things have changed. Some *kurabito* are permanent employees, most of them locals and when they come from far away, modern means of transport allow them to return regularly to their families. This welcomed improvement in the living conditions of *kurabito*, however, signals the death knell of community life and a certain organization of work. Indeed, it is increasingly rare to see *kura* offering housing and food to its employees, as they generally prefer to return home.

Life in the *kura* (2/2)

Here is the example of a day's work in a traditional *kura*.

5:30 am: The team gathers for a short briefing, then everyone washes their hands before entering the *kura* and greet Matsuo-sama (see "Matsuo-sama, Shinto, and sake production", p. 33).

6 am: The *kome-koji* is taken out of the *karashi-ba* and the *mizu-koji* is prepared while the *kamaya* starts cooking the rice.

7 am: The rice is steamed while the team is having breakfast: a bowl of rice and a *miso* soup, with a side of pickled vegetables, an egg or a little fish.

8 am: The rice is unloaded from the *koshiki* and cooled. Then, depending on the type of cooling (natural or in a wind blower), the *taishi*, assisted by his assistants, proceeds to the first rice mixing in the *koji-muro*.

10 am: Break.

10:30 am: The *kojimai* is inoculated and the *kakemai* is added to the *mizu-koji* and to the vats, which are then homogenized. The *motomawashi* does his analysis.

12:00: Lunch.

1:30 pm: Depending on the season, the *dougumawashi* scrapes the dried foam off the vats, the sake pressing is prepared, sake is pasteurized or filtered, *kasu* is cleaned and packed for selling, etc.

3:00 pm: Break.

3:30 pm: The rice to be used on the next day is rinsed, steeped and drained. At the end of the day, it is loaded into the *koshiki*, ready for the next morning.

5 pm: "End" of work.

5:30 pm: Dinner prepared by the *meshitaki*, washed down with sake!

6 pm: A well-deserved, warm and comforting bath. In Japan the bath water is not changed between two users as they shower themself before entering. However, out of respect, baths are taken in hierarchical order.

7 pm+: According to the needs of the *kome-koji*, the *taishi* returns nightly to the *koji-muro*, sometimes every 90 minutes for *tsumikae*.

Shubo

c. Indigenous and selected yeasts

i.   Indigenous yeasts

Yeasts, like bacteria, have the ability to survive in a dehydrated state as spores. It is in this form that they move, carried by air currents, towards new environments to colonize. The air around us contains thousands of spores, ready to develop if they reach a suitable environment, that is to say containing at least water and a source of energy (such as sugar). This is especially true in places where significant amounts of yeast are or have been present, such as fermentation cellars.

For centuries, it is these yeasts ("native" yeasts) that have been used in the production of sake. It suffices to produce a favorable environment for the development of these yeasts, and to wait for spores to settle there. This is the principle of the traditional *moto* described in the previous chapter.

However, whatever the technical refinements, there is no guarantee that the fermentation is carried out by a suitable yeast. This is an important risk factor for the producer. The main consequences for users of indigenous yeasts are: low resistance to *moromi* conditions resulting in fermentation stoppages, production of undesirable compounds (volatile acidity for example), and development of contamination yeasts.

These prospects, combined with the low volumes potentially involved (about 1% of sake is produced through traditional *shubo*) and in the absence of significant potential gains, discourage most producers. Today sakes produced using indigenous yeasts can be counted on the fingers of one hand. Their producers generally justify their choice by considerations of patrimonial order (not to say marketing).

The point can be made, however, that in a cellar that has been used for decades or centuries to produce sake and is full of fermentation yeasts, or even selected yeasts used in adjacent vats, the very notion of indigenous yeasts is unclear.

However, even if selected yeasts eventually take over, the use of indigenous yeasts leaves more room, at least at the beginning of fermentation, for a certain variety of yeasts that can bring more complexity to sake. We will come back to this in the discussion on the notion of terroir in sake (see "Sake and terroir", p.215).

ii.   Origins of yeast selection

Risks related to the variability of indigenous yeasts have been known for a long time and are at the origin of the *shubo* technique. However, if the *shubo* allows for the judgement of a yeast's qualities (by checking its fermentation kinetics, aroma and so on), thus preventing the development of harmful indigenous yeasts in the main fermentation (a shubo containing such yeasts would be discarded), the actual development of a quality yeast is fortuitous. Hence, techniques meant to favor the implantation of quality yeasts "a priori" developed in parallel to the *shubo*.

A 12th-century Chinese book, "Beishan jiujing" offers two methods: seeding via a tank already in fermentation, or harvesting and drying the foam of a fermenting tank, which could be done by steeping a wool cloth in the tank's foam.

This second solution has the distinct advantage of providing a yeast in storable form (thus usable from one year to another) but also transportable and therefore marketable. Year after year reuse of dried yeasts from the best vats of the previous year is the starting point for yeast selection.

This method has made it possible to obtain, after decades or even centuries, yeasts that are perfectly adapted to the production of quality sake.

Each *kura* then had its own "proprietary" yeast, well established in its cellars, fruit of its selection work and with characteristics adapted to its ingredients, its methods and its style. The only thing left to do was to collect these yeasts and spread them, and this is what the Japanese government did.

iii.   The "Kyokai" yeasts

It was in 1906 that the Japanese government launched the first national project for the selection and diffusion of yeasts for sake production. This is one of the first missions attributed to the brand new NRIB (see "A short history of sake", p.16).

A selection campaign was therefore conducted throughout Japan to collect the "proprietary" yeasts of each *kura*. It resulted in the collection of 60 strains, among which the Sakura Masamune *kura* yeast was distinguished. It was reproduced then marketed under the name "Kyokai #1", the diminutive of Nihon Jozo Kyokai, the NRIB.

Subsequently, NRIB continued to conduct selection campaigns to respond to changing techniques, needs and trends. The NRIB catalog has expanded to contain 14 Kyokai yeasts, of which we describe the main characteristics below.

Even today, the *kura* from which these yeasts originate are proud of this paternity. They create special cuvees (Ichigo #1 for Sakura Masamune, Rokugo #6 for Aramasa, or Nanago #7 for Masumi) and are often considered the only source of authentic yeasts. Purists who believe that yeasts marketed by the association are only lesser quality copies source their yeast directly from the *kura*.

Kyokai #1

Selected in 1906 in the prefecture of Hyogo within the Sakura Masamune *kura*. Abandoned for more than 60 years, this yeast was recently put back into service by its *kura* of origin for the creation of its "Yakimare Kyokai Ichigo Kobo" sake. Its optimal fermentation temperature (20 °C / 68 °F) and acid production, both high, no longer meet today's quality criteria.

Kyokai #2

Selected in Kyoto in 1908-1911, in the Gekkeikan *kura*. It is distinguished by a round cell shape observable under the microscope (the other varieties being oval). This yeast is no longer used.

Kyokai #3

Selected in 1914 in the prefecture of Hiroshima within the Suishin *kura*. This yeast has not been used since the 1930s.

Kyokai #4

Selected in 1924 in Hiroshima prefecture in an unknown *kura*. Appreciated for its rich aromatic profile. This yeast has not been used since the 1930s.

Kyokai #5

Selected in 1923 in Hiroshima prefecture within Kamotsuru *kura*. Appreciated for its fruity aromatic profile. Fallen into disuse because of its high acid production.

Kyokai #6

Selected in 1930 in the prefecture of Akita, within the Aramasa *kura*. Very robust, it develops and ferments effectively even at low temperatures, making it a good candidate for traditional *shubo*. Its aromatic qualities are more noticeable on the palate than on the nose. It was a great success before falling into disuse after the war. Today it is mainly used by its original *kura*, Aramasa, which produces a special sake from this yeast: "Rokugo".

Kyokai #7

Selected in 1946 in the prefecture of Nagano, in Masumi *kura*. Very reliable and effective in fermentation even at low temperatures, it has a rich aromatic profile. This yeast was for a long time, undoubtedly, the most used. Today, more aromatic yeasts have replaced it for the production of *ginjo*, but it remains the most common standard yeast. Many selected yeasts are descended from it. The *kura* of origin, Masumi, continues to produce a *junmai daiginjo* with this yeast: "Nanago".

Kyokai #8

Mutant of the #6 strain obtained in 1978 by the NRIB. It was quickly abandoned because of its high acid production, especially at high fermentation temperatures. In 2003, a group of *kura* started using this yeast again.

Kyokai #9

Discovered in 1953 in the prefecture of Kumamoto, within Kouro *kura*, then developed within the prefecture's fermentation research institute. It is also known as Kumamoto yeast. Several yeasts close or derived from #9 exist, including KA-1 and KA-4. Fermenting quickly, even at low temperature, and offering a fresh aromatic profile (melon/apple, especially, thanks to ethyl caproate) it was for a long time the most used yeast in the production of *ginjo*. It remains today a standard for the production of aromatic sake but has been surpassed by the most recent ultra-aromatic yeasts (see "Ultra-aromatic yeasts", p.149).

Kyokai #10

Selected in 1952 in the prefecture of Ibaraki, in the Meiri Shurui *kura*. It ferments slowly, preferably at low temperatures and produces fewer acids (especially malic) than other yeasts. Sensitive to alcohol, its fermentation finish can be difficult. It is atypical in its production of higher alcohols (alcohol flavors, spirits) with high concentrations of propanol and very little butanol. It is still widely used in the greater Tohoku region, north of Honshu, where the temperature is suitable.

Kyokai #11

Mutant of #7 discovered in 1975, it is more tolerant to alcohol and can therefore produce very dry sakes, low in amino acids. While doing so, it produces a lot of malic acid and has fallen into disuse for this reason.

Kyokai #12

Selected in 1965 in Miyagi prefecture, within the Urakasumi *kura*. It ferments slowly, both at low and high temperatures and is suitable for traditional *shubo*. Not very aromatic compared to modern yeasts, it is now little used outside Miyagi even if it remains at the origin of a classic sake, Urakasumi Zen.

Kyokai #13

Discovered in 1979 at the Experimental Research Station of the Ministry of Economy by crossing strains #9 and #10. It is known for its very aromatic, fresh and crunchy character as well as its low acidity. It is no longer distributed.

<u>Kyokai #14</u>

Selected in 1996 from the Kanazawa Research Institute in Ishikawa Prefecture, it is also known as Kanazawa Yeast. It offers an original aromatic profile, juicy and ripe (pear and banana) thanks to its production of isoamyl acetate. It is still widely used.

This catalog may give the impression of yeast strains fixed since their selection; however, this is not so. Despite predominantly asexual reproduction by mitosis, which *a priori* maintains the characteristics of a yeast year after year, it is difficult to maintain a pure industrial strain. Also, new selections are regularly made to rejuvenate a strain or improve it.

iv.   Obtaining new yeast strains

There are two main methods for obtaining yeasts: selection and improvement.

Selection consists of collecting indigenous yeasts and selecting the most suitable for fermentation. This is achieved by carrying out model fermentations, which make it possible to appreciate the qualities of each collected yeast.

In the case of Kyokai yeasts, harvesting within *kura* favors the selection of yeasts that are already highly adapted to fermentation. However, it is also possible to collect yeasts in all types of places. The chances of getting a quality yeast are however much lower.

Improvement consists of trying to optimize certain existing yeast characteristics. To do this, the characteristics of the concerned yeast are varied in a more or less controlled manner. Then, as described above, the most suitable yeasts are selected. There are different methods to obtain genetic diversity from a yeast strain:

- By **natural mutation**: the pace of yeasts reproduction allows for obtaining a certain variability of characters over a relatively short time (see the example of non-foaming yeasts on the following page).

- By **mutagenesis**: the phenomenon of natural mutation is promoted by means of a mutagenic agent, either physical or chemical, such as UV rays.

- By **sexual reproduction**: under particular conditions, especially of high stress, the yeasts produce spores which, when fused, carry out a genetic mixing. It is possible to obtain natural sexual reproduction by placing the strains under adequate conditions, however the success rate is low. Current hybridization methods can reproduce this natural phenomenon in vitro. It is thus possible to combine several strains hoping to get the best of each.

- By **genetic engineering**: it is possible to introduce one or more genes in a yeast in order to confer it a particular character. This simplest and most effective method is now confronted with ethical controversies over GMOs. However, it opens a wide range of possibilities, desirable or not.

Many improvements have been made, either within the NRIB, or within its local branches or private companies, such that there are now dozens of #7 or #9 yeasts, for example. These yeasts are referred to as belonging to the "family" of the yeast from which they are derived.

A yeast whose characteristics are significantly different from its family will be named independently, but this is not the case for all selections. Thus, many *kura* use #7 yeasts that are sourced from different companies (or different regions), such that they actually use different yeasts, although with very similar characteristics.

While Kyokai yeasts still make up a large portion of the yeasts used in sake production, many local and private selections have been made. Among these, several research topics have been particularly popular because of the technical advances they have allowed. Here are a few:

v.   Non-foaming yeasts

During fermentation, an abundant foam ("*awa*") is formed above the tank. Traditionally, the appearance of this foam is used by *toji* to follow the progress and quality of the fermentation. Each stage is named according to the aspect of the foam, starting from the appearance of the first bubbles (*suji-awa*) at the end of the 2nd or 3rd day of fermentation.

Japanese name	Translation
Suji-awa	Muscles
Mizu-awa	Water
Kani-awa	Crab
Iwa-awa	Rock
Taka-awa	High
Ochi-awa	Falling
Tama-awa	Ball
Ji	Ground

Table 15. Names and meanings of the fermentation foams aspects.

Although these terms are still commonly used in *kura*, modern methods of analysis and especially the determination of ethanol now allow a more accurate monitoring of fermentations. Moreover, the presence of large amounts of foam, especially during the *taka-awa* stage, which lasts about 10 days, poses sanitary difficulties and tank capacity shortages.

Indeed, at this stage, the volume of foam corresponds more or less to the volume of the wort. It is therefore necessary to provide tanks twice as large to contain the foam and this oversizing is expensive. In addition, when falling, some of the foam adheres to the walls, creating areas conducive to the development of contaminating microorganisms.

In the natural state, the yeasts used for sake systematically produce foam. However, thanks to their genetic diversity, yeasts can lose this character and ferment without foaming. The archives mention several occurrences of this type of fermentation, generally to the surprise of the concerned *toji*. In 1963, Professor Akiyama became interested in the subject and undertook research that would produce commercially available non-foaming yeasts (from 1971).

The formation of foam during fermentation is explained by the hydrophobic nature of the yeast walls: they "cling" to gas bubbles that rise to the wort's surface and prevent them from bursting on the surface, creating a thick foam. This hydrophobic character is due to the presence on the walls of a protein: Awa-1.

During a yeast culture, because of the rapid reproduction of microorganisms, a large number of generations succeed one another. Among these, natural mutations may appear at random, yeasts for which the Awa-1 gene is non-functional, thus not producing the Awa-1 protein and having a hydrophilic wall. These yeasts no longer cling to gas bubbles, the bubbles burst on the surface and the amount of foam produced is minimal.

The method for obtaining non-foaming yeasts from a foaming yeast culture consists of placing a bubbler in the culture while skimming regularly the hydrophobic yeasts that rise to the surface. After 7 or 8 repetitions, the population of hydrophilic yeasts dramatically increases, and then a pure culture is obtained.

With this technique, non-foaming yeasts were selected on the basis of strains #6, #7, #9, #10 and #14, and respectively named #601, #701, #901, #1001, and #1401. Their characteristics are in all respects similar to those of the mother strains, apart from the formation of foam. For non-foaming yeasts, the maximum volume increase of the tank during fermentation is 20-30% (versus 100% for foaming yeasts).

Some consider that these non-foaming yeasts do not give the same qualitative results as the parent strains and prefer to continue using foaming yeasts. Indeed, even if the characteristics of the two types of yeasts are identical, the presence or absence of foam has an impact on the fermentation environment: the foam constitutes a barrier with the outside air and a fermentation medium in its own right. At constant parameters, the use of non-foaming strains results in a slightly faster fermentation.

However, non-foaming yeasts have been adopted by the vast majority of the profession and now represent 80% of the yeast market. Today, research focuses primarily on non-foaming yeasts and most of the new strains are non-foaming. The non-foaming yeasts constitute a considerable progress in terms of ease of use, for a close, if not similar, qualitative result to their foaming, parent strains.

vi.   Ultra-aromatic yeasts

The ultimate recognition for a *toji* is to receive a gold medal (or many, year after year) at the "Zenkoku Shinsu Kanpyokai", or National New Sake Competition. Founded in 1910 as one of NRIB's first projects, this national competition sees about three-quarters of the profession present at least one sake. Sakes are evaluated in two rounds rated 1 to 5 in the first and 1 to 3 in the second (1 being the best score). Top-rated sakes move to the second round and win a gold medal. There are also other regional, less prestigious, competitions operating with the same system.

However, contrary to what is generally known in Europe with agricultural product competitions, the sake presented is not the sake usually marketed by each *kura*. Rather, it is an exercise in style to demonstrate the skill of a *kura* and a *toji* rather than evaluating the quality of its standard products.

Thus each *kura* produces for these events a small amount of high-end sake, specially prepared for the competition. The goal is to get the most aromatic sake possible so that it stands out on the tired palate of the judges.

The sake presented are therefore generally *daiginjo* called "competition *daiginjo*", rarely *junmai* because of the richer character of these (see "Benefits and impact of alcohol addition", p.180). For years, the classic recipe for competition *daiginjo* was nicknamed "YK35": Y for Yamadanishiki, K for Kumamoto (yeast #9) and 35 for the *seimaibuai*.

Competition sakes are not usually marketed but rather offered to distinguished guests or events. If you have the chance to own a bottle, do not wait to open it, these prized specimens are made to appear at their best during the contest, that is to say very young.

The importance of these medals pushed the sector towards the selection of ever more aromatic yeasts in order to help the *kura* distinguish themselves. A major area of research concerns the production of high concentrations of ethyl caproate, an aroma of fresh apple and melon (see "Fermentation aromas", p.172).

The main, so-called "ultra-aromatic" yeasts are described below:

Kyokai #1501

Marketed under this name since 1996, it comes from a selection made by the research institute of Akita prefecture, which has marketed it under the name AK-1 since 1990. Very aromatic, it ferments slowly, at low temperature and produces few acids.

Kyokai #1601
Crossbreeding of #7 and #1001 developed by Gekkeikan *kura* (see "Kyokai #2", p.146) under the name "No. 86", this ultra-aromatic yeast produces large amounts of ethyl caproate and a low acidity.

Kyokai #1701

Recent yeast, it ferments well and produces large quantities of esters: isoamyl acetate and ethyl caproate. Due to its more complex aromatic profile, better adapted to *junmai*, it is used less than #1601 or #1801. It also produces more acidity than the latter, at a level comparable to #7.

Kyokai #1801

Recent crossbreeding between #1601 and #9. Very aromatic and low in acidity, it is adapted to the production of *ginjo* and has gained popularity very quickly.

vii.   Local or private yeasts

NRIB no longer has a monopoly on the research and commercialization of selected yeasts. The local research stations of the Ministry of Finance (on which sake production depends) or the Ministry of Agriculture, as well as private biotechnology companies, now offer a wide range of yeasts. The main lines of research are the same as those of Kyokai but also cover adaptation to specific local conditions such as fermentation temperature or certain varieties of rice. Some projects are exercises in poetry or marketing, such as the selection of yeasts on wild flowers or in high mountain lakes. Here are some examples of these yeasts:

Komachi

Developed in Akita prefecture for its adaptation to local rice: Akita-Sake-Komachi.

M-310

Developed in Ibaraki prefecture, in the Meiri Shurui *kura* (see #10), this ultra-aromatic yeast has distinguished itself in national competitions.

#28 and #77

Yeasts developed from #7, producing large quantities of malic acid and adapted to the production of *koshu*, *kijoshu* and low-alcohol sake.

viii.   Other lines of research

Other types of yeast have been developed according to specific needs, and the democratization of selection and genetic engineering techniques should further broaden the range of yeasts available on the market.

We can mention the existence of yeasts that do not produce urea, a molecule involved in the formation of ethyl carbamate, a potential carcinogen, during sake storage (yeasts Karg701, Karg901 and Karg1001 respectively derived from #701, #901 and #1001).

There are also yeasts producing lesser amounts of pyruvate, a compound that forms diacetyl, responsible for aromatic deviations (cheese, perspiration), a yeast producing pink sake (hard to use as these yeasts can not synthesize an amino acid, adenine, which must be added to the wort), antibiotic-resistant yeasts to regain control over a contaminated fermentation, etc.

The use of these yeasts is extremely marginal.

ix.   Using selected yeasts

Today, the selected yeasts can be sold in several forms: they are cultivated in liquid medium and a fraction of this yeast-rich liquid is called *ekijo-kobo* or "liquid yeast". In the cultures, some of the yeasts sediment, creating a solid phase. This fraction can also be marketed under the name *deijo-kobo* or "yeast mud".

The *deijo-kobo* can be dehydrated by pressing or centrifugation to give a "solid yeast" or *kokei-kobo*. Among *kokei-kobo*, dehydration to less than 10% moisture gives an active "dry yeast" or *kanso-kobo* that can be stored for long periods. Less dehydration gives a stick of "raw yeast" or *nama-kobo* that must be used quickly.

Whatever the form in which the *toji* buys its yeasts (*ekijo-kobo* bulb, *nama-kobo* stick or *kanso-kobo* pack), it can make a first multiplication before use in the *shubo*. To do this, he places the yeasts in a liquid medium, rich in nutrients, which can be simply obtained by macerating *kome-koji* for 24 hours in water.

This first multiplication phase has the advantage of reducing the volume of yeast to be purchased, and in the case of solid yeasts, rehydrating them and preparing them for fermentation.

d. *Moromi*

When the yeast has been chosen and multiplied in the *shubo*, the main fermentation begins. This stage is called "*moromi*".

i.   *San-dan shikomi*

The ready-to-use *shubo* contains approximately one hundred million (10^8) yeasts per gram, a concentration that prevents most contaminations.

Continuing the fermentation on a larger scale (*moromi*, the main fermentation) by adding rice, *kome-koji* and water dilutes yeasts, leading to a risk of contamination. In order to limit this dilution, the ingredients (*shikomi*) are added three times (*san-dan*), thus giving the yeasts time to multiply as the volume of the wort increases.

The first step is to transfer the *shubo* into a large tank, able to contain the *moromi*. A tank with a capacity 20 to 30 times greater than the volume of *shubo* is necessary according to the foaming or non-foaming nature of the yeast.

During the transfer, we try not to "shock" the yeast, so the *shubo* is moved as delicately as possible. Traditionally it is poured into the tank through a bunghole near the bottom, using a funnel.

1st day (after the transfer): *hatsu-zoe* (or simply *zoe*)

Kome-koji, water and rice are added to the tank, doubling the *shubo*'s volume. A temperature of about 12-15 °C / 53-59°F should be reached after addition, thanks to a careful dosage between the temperature of steamed rice (hot) and water (cold). The yeasts awakening following *karashi* is a delicate phase and the temperature must be watched scrupulously. In a large tank, the small volume of *moromi* tends to cool rapidly. Also, an intermediate-sized tank is sometimes used for *hatsu-zoe*.

The addition of water, pumped above the tank breaks any clumps of freshly added rice. Subsequently, the tank must be homogenized regularly, using long wooden rods. The rice has a tendency to sink and it must therefore be brought up to avoid the formation of a compact and dry layer of rice at the bottom of the tank. In addition, some of the rice is brought to the surface by the carbon dioxide bubbles released during fermentation. The tank mixing movement is thus double, both bringing down the surface rice and lifting the bottom rice.

These movements within the tank also have the function of supplying yeasts in oxygen. Indeed, as we have seen above (see "Yeast metabolism", p.120), the respiration allowed by oxygen releases much more energy than fermentation. If it is undesirable in the following stages (since it does not produce alcohol), respiration is however the preferred metabolic pathway for yeast multiplication.

2nd day: *odori*

The *moromi* is left to rest one day so that the concentration of yeasts is reconstituted. The energy released by fermentation usually raises the *moromi* temperature by 1 °C. *Odori* means "dance" in reference to the fact that there is nothing to do that day, except to homogenize the tub, and all the other *kura* works.

3nd day: *naka-zoe*

The second addition doubles the volume of *moromi* again. This time a temperature, after the addition, of about 8-10 °C / 47-50 °F is sought. The progressive decrease of the temperature during the additions has two objectives:

- On the one hand, the fermentation of sake being conducted at low temperature (see "Temperature control", p.166), the transition avoids a thermal shock to the yeasts.

- On the other hand, the microorganisms of contamination being less active at low temperature, it completes the doubly antiseptic action of the *shubo*'s acidity and the yeasts concentration, which begin to dilute.

4th day: *tome-zoe*

The third and last addition doubles the volume of *moromi* again. A temperature after addition of about 6-8 °C / 43-46 °F is sought.

An example of the quantities used during *san-dan shikomi* is given in Table 16 next page.

When considering the final proportions of *moromi*, *koji-buai* (= *kome-koji*/total rice) is generally used. This ratio is usually 20-25%, with a legal minimum of 15% for *tokutei-meisho-shu*. However, the *kome-koji*/*kakemai* ratio is a good mnemonic for retaining the proportions of the *san-dan shikomi* (see Table 16 on the next page).

The *komi-mizu-buai*, or total water volume (*komi-mizu*) on the weight of rice ratio, varies according to the style and quality of the sake. However, we can consider that the final ratio is always in the 125-135% range. In the given example, it is exactly 130% (3900 L of water/3000 kg of rice).

These ratios are a legacy of the old Japanese measurement system (see "Japanese measurements units", p.208) because a rice "*koku*" (150 kg) was used at the time for 1 *koku* of water (180 L) giving a ratio of 120%. This standard ratio was called *to mizu* ("ten water"), but "eleven" or "ten and a half" ratios, respectively 198 L and 189 L of water for 150 kg of rice, were also common.

	Kakemai (kg)	Kome-koji (kg)	Water (L)	Temperature (°F)	Temperature (°C)	kome – koji / kakemai	Komi-mizu-buai
Moto	160	80	260	42	6	50%	110%
Hatsu-zoe	330	130	440	53-59	12-15	40%	85-100%
Naka-zoe	660	190	1000	46-50	8-10	30%	120%
Tome-zoe	1150	300	2200	42-46	6-8	20-25%	130-150%
Total	2300	700	3900	-	-	25-33%	125-135%

Table 16. Standard parameters for the production of *honjozo* sake (low premium sake category, see "Official classification", p.216).

Moromi

Much lower ratios (around 65%) could occasionally be used to produce highly concentrated sakes used in blends or diluted by traders. The sake "Edo Genroku" from the *kura* Konishi is still produced according to this method based on a recipe dating from 1702.

As a result of these additions, the volume of the ferment has been multiplied by 10 and the main fermentation begins. It is conducted at low temperature (<18 °C / 65 °F), lasts from 2 to 4 weeks and produces a raw sake containing 18-22% alcohol.

ii.   Fermentation management

The *kura* activity during fermentation is relatively limited but very technical. It is mainly a daily monitoring of the tanks by analysis, the control of fermentation temperatures and the homogenization of the tanks by mixing. For *kura* using foaming yeast, it is necessary to add to that the control of the volume of foam and the cleaning of the tank's walls when the foam falls.

During the main fermentation, rice dissolves in the wort, releasing mainly starch and proteins that will be broken down respectively into sugars and amino acids by the action of *koji* enzymes. At the same time, yeast uses these nutrients and produce alcohol through alcoholic fermentation.

This simultaneity of the transformation of starch into sugar then alcohol is atypical: for other grains alcohols such as beer or whiskey, these two stages are separated in time and space.

It is thanks to this singularity that sake is the fermented alcoholic drink with the highest potential alcoholic degree. If all the sugar converted into alcohol during sake fermentation (300-340 g/L) was present from the beginning, the fermentation would stop at around 13-15%, as in the case of sweet wines. This is explained by the combined toxicity for yeast of sugar and fermentation products (mainly alcohol). Indeed, sugar is toxic to microorganisms when present in high concentrations because of its impact on osmotic pressure. To simplify we can say that it retains water, thus drying yeasts. The same phenomenon allows honey to almost never expire.

During the fermentation, the *toji* must therefore control these two transformations to proceed at the same rate. If the alcoholic fermentation takes precedence over the hydrolysis of the starch, sugar runs out and the fermentation stops because of a lack of nutrients. In the opposite case, the sugar accumulates and the fermentation stops for the reason described above. In both cases, it is extremely difficult to restart the fermentation and the quality of the product is irretrievably affected.

The activity of *kome-koji* enzymes depends on its mode of production (see "Cultivation methods and enzymatic activity", p.102) and current temperature. The metabolic activity of yeasts depends on nutrients and temperature. For a given raw material, the main adjustment variable is therefore the temperature.

Highly polished rice contains few nutrients, effectively limiting the rate of fermentation. It is therefore necessary to perform the fermentation at low temperature in order to slow down the enzyme activity. The opposite reasoning is equally true for low polished rice.

Of course, this is a simplification. Other parameters must also be taken into consideration: the rice variety, the type of water, *koji*, the yeast strain, etc. For this reason, each *kura* has its own "recipes", adapted to its ingredients and difficult to transpose.

In order to ensure the concomitance of parallel fermentations, *toji* must therefore adapt the different ingredients and control the daily parameters of the wort: alcohol content, density (see "*Nihonshudo* and derivatives", p.157), acidity and amino acids. If necessary, (s)he can control the pace of alcoholic fermentation (easier to control than enzymatic activity) via the techniques described in the next chapter.

iii.   Sake analysis methods

In this chapter, we will study the main analyses and indicators used to follow the fermentation of sake.

1. *Nihonshudo* and derivatives

The *nihonshudo* (literally "sake degree" or "sake level") is a measure inspired by the Baumé degree, an invention of Antoine Baumé, French pharmacist of the 18th century. It indicates the density of sake relative to a reference point: the density of pure water at 4 °C / 39 °F, for which the *nihonshudo* is 0.

The *nihonshudo* (NSD) of a liquid is calculated by the formula:

$$NSD = 1443 \times (\frac{1}{density} - 1)$$

Practically, *nihonshudo* is measured directly by means of a graduated hydrometer (see Figure 14 on the next page) placed in the liquid.

The value of *nihonshudo* mainly varies according to two concentrations: of alcohol and sugar. Alcohol is less dense than water (density of ethanol = 0.789) while sugar is denser (density of glucose syrup at 850 g/L = 1.32). *Nihonshudo* therefore increases with the degree of alcohol but decreases as the sugar concentration increases. In general, it is around 0 and the vast majority of sake are between -10 and +10.

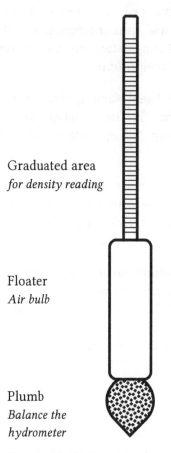

Graduated area
for density reading

Floater
Air bulb

Plumb
Balance the
hydrometer

Figure 14. Hydrometer.

The average value of Japanese sake *nihonshudo* varies with fashion. In the 1980s, consumers preferred lightly sweet sakes and the average value was slightly negative. Today, dryer sakes are in fashion and the average *nihonshudo* value is between +4 and +5.

Almost every *kura* indicate on the bottles and in their brochures the *nihonshudo* of their sake. It is generally accepted that a negative *nihonshudo* indicates sweet sake while a positive *nihonshudo* indicates dry sake.

However, apart from extreme values (greater than +6 or less than -10) one can not really rely on *nihonshudo*. First of all because the degree of alcohol makes its value vary greatly, but also because the sweet perception depends on other elements, in particular the acidity. So the Japanese government has imagined other, more precise, indicators: *amakarado* and *noutando*. These indicators combine *nihonshudo* and *sando* (acidity, see "*Sando*" below) to give a measure of the perception of sweetness.

$$Amakarado = \frac{193593}{1443 + NSD} - 1.16 \times sando - 132,57$$

Amakarado values fluctuate around 0, between -0.3 (very dry) and 0.3 (very soft). Despite its relevance, it is not used by the industry outside of research.

2. *Sando*

The *sando* is the total acidity of sake, due to the presence of several types of organic acids produced by the different microorganisms involved in fermentation.

Acid	Average concentration (mg/L)	Yeast	Koji	Lactic acid Bacteria
Succinic	200-500	+++	+	
Lactic	200-700	++	++	+++
Malic	100-400	++	++	
Acetic	50-100	+++	++	+
Pyruvic	15-100	+	+	+
Citric	80-100	+	+++	
Fumaric	10-20	+	+	

Table 17. The organic acids of sake and their origin.

Sando is expressed in gram equivalent of succinic acid per liter. This means that a sake with a *sando* of 1 has the same acidity as a sake whose only acid is succinic acid at a concentration of 1 g/L (= 1000 mg/L).

This is an arbitrary standard; the total acidity of wine is expressed in sulfuric acid equivalent in France or equivalent tartaric acid in the English-speaking world. To pass from an acidity expressed in succinic acid to an acidity expressed in sulfuric acid or tartaric acid, it is multiplied, respectively, by 0.83 and 1.27 (the ratios of the molar masses of the two acids).

The average *sando* is between 1.2 and 1.5 but we can find sakes with an acidity of 1 to 1.8. The higher the *sando*, the more acidic the sake, but the perception of acidity also depends on other parameters such as sugar, which can hide the acidity.

During the fermentation, the *sando* follows the same type of curve as the *amino-sando*, the *gen-ekisu-bun* and the alcohol content. From 6 to 7 in the *shubo*, it decreases abruptly (0.3-0.6) during the initial additions (dilution) then rises asymptotically until reaching its final level. Monitoring the *sando* makes it possible to uncover a possible contamination of the wort by an undesirable microorganism. Indeed, such contamination is usually manifested by a rapid rise in acidity.

Junmai sakes generally have a higher *sando* due to the dilution effect that affects non-*junmai* sakes (see "Fining Raw Sake", p.175). Traditional *moto* sakes also have a slightly higher *sando* due to their lactic fermentation.

In recent decades, too much acidity has been considered a defect and many types of yeast that are known to be "too acidic" have been abandoned. However, consumers are now returning to slightly more acidic sakes, perhaps because of new taste habits, particularly due to wine.

3. *Amino-sando*

Amino-sando is the total amino acid concentration of sake. It is determined by formalin titration (Sörensen method) and expressed in grams of glycine (an amino acid) per liter. As in the case of *sando* expressed in succinic acid equivalent, the *amino-sando* is therefore expressed considering that the only amino acid present is glycine.

Measuring *amino-sando* during fermentations makes it possible to follow the enzymatic (proteolytic) activity of *koji* and to make sure that the yeasts do not lack nutrients (risks of deficiency for an *amino-sando* lower than 0.75 in the wort).

The average *amino-sando* is 1.3 to 1.5. The only source of amino acids in sake is rice. Also *junmai* sakes generally have a higher *amino-sando*. Similarly, the lower the *seimaibuai*, the lower the *amino-sando* (rice proteins being mainly concentrated in the outer layers of the grain (see "Rice polishing (*seimai*)", p.72). Also, protein content varies from one rice variety to another, modifying the *amino-sando*.

During fermentation, the *amino-sando* follows the same type of curve as the *sando*, the *gen-ekisu-bun* and the alcohol content. From 1 to 3 in the *shubo*, it decreases abruptly (0.1-0.3) during the initial additions (dilution) then rises asymptotically until reaching its final level.

Amino acids are one of the main components of umami. Sakes rich in amino acids (high *amino-sando*) will therefore have a richer and savory character.

4. Glucose

Measurement of the glucose concentration is obtained by the Fehling method, a standard method used in oenology.

It allows monitoring both the yeast fermentation activity and the enzymatic activity (amylase) of *koji* to ensure a sufficient presence of yeast nutrients. During a well-controlled standard fermentation, the glucose concentration gradually decreases from about 5 g/L on the day after the *tome-zoe* (day 3) to 2-3 g/L at the end of fermentation. Except for atypical methods (see "Sweet sake", p.168), if the goal is to obtain a sweet sake, it is preferable to use a sugar addition as high sugar concentrations at the end of fermentation tend to disturb the fermentation's finish.

Thus, the monitoring of the glucose concentration also makes it possible to know the amount of residual sugars of the sake at the end of fermentation and to calculate with precision a possible addition.

This measure also makes it possible to apprehend a given sake's sweetness with more precision than the *nihonshudo*. However, it is never given on bottles.

5. Alcohol content

The alcohol content of sake is expressed, as for all fermented beverages, in percentage of alcohol by volume (distilled spirits alcohol content is often expressed as "proof", 100-proof being 50% alcohol by volume, that is the volume of pure alcohol in milliliters in 100 milliliters of sake). It can be measured simply by the so-called distillation and hydrometry method, recognized as an official oenological method.

To do this, a distillation of a given volume of sake is carried out in order to extract all of the alcohol. Then the distillate (the extracted alcohol) is brought back to the initial volume of sake by addition of water. Finally, a hydrometer is used to directly read the alcoholic degree of the hydroalcoholic solution (water + alcohol) obtained.

A second method based on the same principle exists: density measurements are taken of the sake before boiling and of the residue diluted to the same volume (the residue is the water and the remaining sugar as opposed to the distillate, which is the extracted alcohol). The difference in density is due to the amount of alcohol evaporated that can thus be calculated.

These methods work because the two main elements influencing the density of sake (sugar and alcohol) react differently to heat: the alcohol evaporates at 78 °C / 172 °F while the sugar remains in the solution.

The average alcohol level of sake is 15% to 16%, but a wide range exists from 9% to 20%. Measuring the alcohol content makes it possible to monitor the fermentation progress. If it rises too quickly, the yeast may poison itself and it is necessary to slow down the fermentation, if it stagnates, it is necessary to revive or restart the fermentation.

6. Ekisu-bun

Ekisu-bun is the dry extract of sake, that is to say the measurement of non-volatile compounds: sugars, amino acids, organic acids, mineral salts, etc.

It is measured by weighing the residue after total boiling (dry extract) of 100 milliliters of sake and is therefore expressed in grams per 100 milliliters.

This measure can be replaced by an empirical calculation involving *nihonshudo* and the alcohol content:

$$E = \left(\frac{1443}{1443 + NSD} - A_d \right) \times 260 + 0.21$$

Where A_d is the density of a hydroalcoholic solution with the same alcohol content as the analyzed sake.

In this formula, the term $\frac{1443}{1443+NSD} - A_d$ corresponds to the part of the density due to the elements other than water and alcohol (density of sake - density of the equivalent hydroalcoholic solution), corrected by [×260 + 0.21] to obtain a residue weight in grams per 100 milliliters.

The average *ekisu-bun* is 4.3 to 4.5. It is higher for sakes rich in sugars, acids and amino acids. The measurement of *ekisu-bun* is never specified on sake bottles.

7. *Gen-ekisu-bun*

The *gen-ekisu-bun* or "original dry extract" is a calculation of the dry extract of sake, to which is added the glucose that has been converted into alcohol by fermentation. It is therefore a measure of all the elements of rice that have dissolved in the wort.

$$gE = E + 0.7947 \times A_\% \times 2$$

Where E is the *ekisu bun*, $A_\%$ the degree of alcohol expressed as a percentage alcohol by volume, and 0.7947 the density of ethanol at 15 °C in g/mL. Thus $[0.7947 \times A_\%]$ is the weight of alcohol in grams in 100 mL of sake. A factor of 2 is applied to represent the weight of sugar used to produce 1 g of alcohol ($M_{glucose} = 180$ and $M_{ethanol} = 46$). Of course this factor is a simplification because the yeast consumes more sugar than could be suggested by a simple balanced equation. Oenology uses the figure of 16.83 g/L of sugar per 1% of alcohol (here the figure used would be 15.89 g/L).

Gen-ekisu-bun is used in fermentation monitoring as an indicator of rice solubilization.

8. BMD

BMD, short for "Baumé Multiple Day", is a simple calculation of the sake density expressed in Baumé degree (see "*Nihonshudo* and derivatives", p.157) multiplied by *moromi-nissu* (the number of days of fermentation, taking *tome-zoe* as day 1).

The BMD makes it possible to analyze the fermentation dynamics and to estimate an approximate date of pressing as early as mid-fermentation. By drawing the BMD bell curve on a graph with the number of days after *naka-zoe* as the abscissa. The descending part of the curve generally forms a straight line and it is therefore possible, by continuing the curve, to predict a day of pressing where the line crosses the abscissa (see the example given on Graphs 18 and 19 below).

Depending on the curve's appearance, it is also possible to classify the fermentation kinetics in a family of classic kinetics: there are about ten types, named according to the fermentation pace during the two phases of fermentation materialized by the

BMD bell curve: fast/slow, fast/fast, slow/slow, slow/medium, etc. We can simplify these kinetics into four major standard profiles.

Standard fermentation kinetics

Profile	Duration	Maximum temperature		Final sake
Fast	14 days	63 °F	17 °C	*Futsushu*
Classic	20 days	59 °F	15 °C	*Honjozo*
Long	25 days	55 °F	13 °C	*Junmai*
Ginjo	40 days	50 °F	10 °C	*Ginjo*

Table 18. Standard fermentation kinetics.

Fast fermentations are conducted at high temperature, thereby stimulating both microbial and enzymatic activity, and maximizing rice yield (minimizing *kasu-buai*). However, the heat generated creates a risk of runaway fermentation, which can lead to fermentation stoppages and the production of acidic and aromatic deviations. A strict temperature control must therefore be ensured, requiring adapted equipment. This type of modern fermentation is suitable for entry-level sake production.

Classic fermentations are used for the majority of sakes according to the methods and proportions described in this book. They are adapted to entry-level sakes and more widely used than fast fermentations.

Lowering fermentation temperature lengthens its duration and promotes the appearance of fruity and floral aromas while limiting the production of acids. It allows the production of delicate sakes of which *ginjo* style is the paragon. This type of fermentation requires an adaptation of methods but also ingredients.

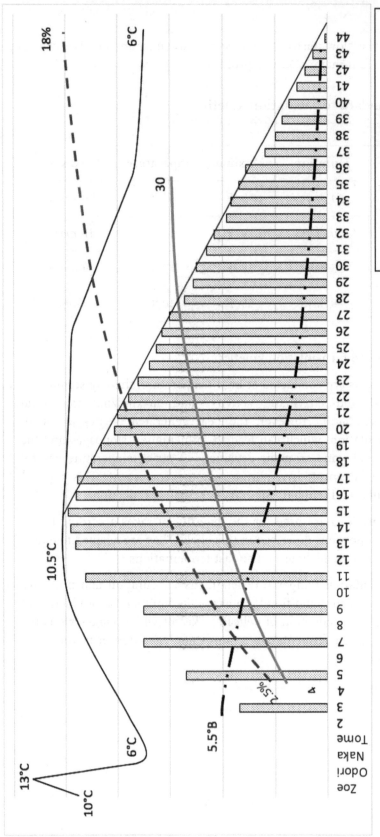

Graph 18. Monitoring of a typical fermentation, *ginjo* style.

Final *sando* = 1.8; final *amino-sando* = 1.7

Legend:
- – – – Alcohol (%)
- ——— Temperature (°C)
- ——— *Gen-ekisu-bun*
- – · – Density (Baumé degree)
- ▨ BMD

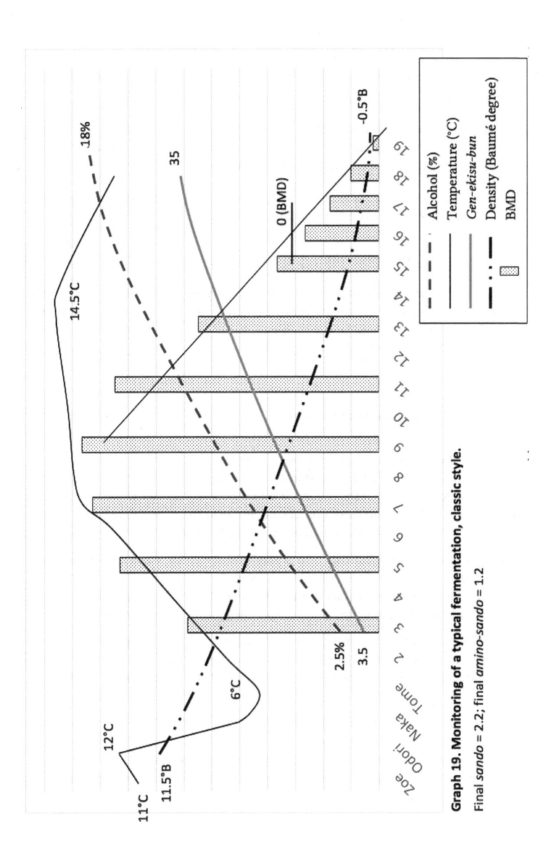

Graph 19. Monitoring of a typical fermentation, classic style.

Final *sando* = 2.2; final *amino-sando* = 1.2

Legend:
- Alcohol (%)
- Temperature (°C)
- *Gen-ekisu-bun*
- Density (Baumé degree)
- BMD

Axis labels: Zoe, Odori, Naka, Tome

Values shown: 18%, 35, 14.5°C, 12°C, 11°C, 11.5°B, 6°C, 2.5%, 3.5, 0 (BMD), -0.5°B

9. Aroma

It is possible to track the concentration of certain flavors through advanced technologies such as HPLC (high performance liquid chromatography).

The desired flavor compounds that usually characterize *ginjo* sake are isoamyl acetate and ethyl caproate. The average concentrations for *ginjo* sake are, respectively, 1.5 mg/L and 2.1 mg/L (see "Fermentation aromas", p.172).

However, the equipment for performing such analyses is extremely expensive and they are therefore used only exceptionally, in research departments for example.

10. Yeast count

During *shubo,* just as during fermentation, it may be desirable to analyze the quantity and quality of the yeasts present. Microscopic observation, counting and several staining methods make it possible to identify the yeast strains present, the yeast concentration and the ratio of living cells.

iv.   Temperature control

As seen in the "Fermentation Management" chapter (p.158), temperature is the main means of action to coordinate the transformation kinetics of starch into sugar and sugar into alcohol. Since fermentation is an exogenous reaction (releasing energy), the wort tends to warm up naturally. Temperature control is therefore a key point of sake fermentation and various means are available to the *toji.*

Traditionally, *kura* were built in such a way that the cellar was exposed to winter winds and protected from the sun. Thus the atmosphere of the cellar is always cold (6-10 °C / 43-50 °F), either thanks to natural cold air in small *kura* producing sake in winter or to air conditioning in large *kura* producing sake all year round.

The tanks are usually thermo-regulated by "jackets" (outside) or "plungers" (inside) in which the *toji* can circulate a cold liquid (water or brine). When this is not the case, artisanal methods such as bags or steel tubes filled with ice cubes play the same role.

As a last resort, *toji* can add cold water (*oimizu*) directly to the tank. The latter method has the double advantage of cooling the tank and diluting the wort, thus slowing the fermentation (and therefore the warming). For this reason, the quantity of water in the *tome-zoe* is generally reduced in order to keep the possibility of adding water during fermentation without changing the ingredients balance.

The temperature of the wort follows a bell curve during fermentation. It rises initially under the effect of fermentation, then it reaches a plateau fixed by the cooling methods mentioned above, and finally decreases when the fermentative activity slows down.

In case of a fermentation "accident", if it slows down or if the amount of sugar increases dangerously, it is possible to quickly heat the tank, using *daki* or small electric or gas heaters.

v. End of fermentation

The end of fermentation is a delicate aspect of sake production that must be managed with care.

While the alcoholic strength of the ferment rises to levels that should wipe out most yeasts (>16%), fermentation continues. This exceptional resistance of yeasts in sake is explained both by the low fermentation temperatures, which slow down their metabolism, and by the parallel fermentation, which steadily supply the yeast with nutrients.

However, this medium remains particularly hostile and yeasts tend to produce undesirable aromas toward the end of fermentation such as ethanal (a.k.a. acetaldehyde, oxidized apple note).

The *toji* must therefore choose the right moment to end the fermentation taking into account both the amount of unfermented rice (*kasu*) present in the tank and the possible appearance of negative aromas. If the amount of *kasu* is too significant to stop the fermentation, (s)he can try to prolong it by adding water to the tank to reduce the alcoholic degree and thus preserve the yeast. *Kasu-buai* (*kasu* ratio) is an important tool for monitoring the end of fermentation.

$$Kasu\text{-}buai = \frac{Kasu \text{ (kg)}}{Total \text{ rice (kg)}} \times 100$$

Thus one could say that *kasu-buai* is the "unused" rice ratio. This is, however, a gross simplification. Indeed, *kasu* is not made of whole grains of rice but partially dissolved rice, which is the unused fraction of rice whose elements useful for fermentation have been extracted.

Thus, the desire to "optimize" rice by obtaining close-to-zero *kasu-buai* for some entry-level sake via, for example, rice liquefaction methods described above, results in a marked deterioration in quality.

Kasu-buai increases when rice solubilizes with difficulty, that is to say when the amount of *koji* or its enzymatic activity is low, when the rice used is poorly soluble (variety or low polishing), when the *komi-mizu-buai* is low (low amount of water) or when fermentation temperatures are low.

Kasu-buai is also strongly dependent on the pressing method: one can not compare the weight of a very wet *kasu* obtained by *fukurozuri* and that of a dry sake obtained by *assaku-ki* (see "Pressing (*assaku* or *joso*)", p.185), since the weight of water present in *kasu* will distort the calculation. Nevertheless, by integrating these variations due to pressing, *kasu-buai* varies to the extreme between 20% for a *futsushu* and 60% for a high-end *daiginjo*. A *kasu-buai* of 25% is standard.

It is also possible to adopt the opposite approach, using the *niku-tare-buai*, which gives a "yield" of rice in sake:

$$Niku\text{-}tare\text{-}buai = \frac{\text{Final sake (L)} - \text{Added water (L)} - \text{Added alcohol (L)}}{\text{Total rice (kg)}} \times 100$$

As such, both *kasu-buai* and *niku-tare-buai* can not be measured before pressing but can be estimated by other indicators such as *gen-ekisu-bun*, described above.

When the *toji* considers that the fermentation must be stopped, he makes the last fining operations (see "Fining Raw Sake refining", p.175) before pressing the sake. Remember that yeasts cultivated in traditional *shubo* are more resistant at the end of fermentation than yeasts cultivated with modern methods (see "Shubo use and impact on quality", p.138). They thus allow the prolonging of the end of fermentation to obtain dryer sakes.

vi.   Atypical fermentations

Moromi is a fundamental step in the production of sake and by playing on different parameters it is possible to radically change the result. There exists both old and new methods to produce atypical sakes.

1. Sweet sake

Although it is possible to produce sweet sake by simply adding sugar (see "Sugar", p.183), there are two traditional methods that give more interesting results.

a. *Zenkoji*

Literally "all-*koji*": all the rice used for the production of these sakes is *kome-koji*. The amount of enzymes and therefore the rate of saccharification is multiplied by 5 (versus a classic sake with a *koji-buai* of 20%).

Yeasts can not sustain such a pace of sugar intake and the fermentation ends quickly, with a larger amount of residual sugars. For the same reasons, *zenkoji* sakes are also richer in amino acids, acids and *koji* (mushroom/chestnut) aromas.

b. Kijoshu

Kijoshu is obtained by a "mutage" with sake of a fermenting vat. Mutage consists in stopping a fermentation by adding a substance, here sake. The abrupt rise in alcohol levels, which is toxic for yeasts, stops fermentation. Enzymes, on the other hand, continue their action and the levels of sugar and amino acids increase. Depending on the desired sugar level, sake can be added at different stages. The most common method is to substitute the *tome-zoe* water (about half of the total water) with sake.

This sake is inspired by a method made famous by the Susanoo kami legend of how he defeated the eight-headed dragon Yama no Orochi. He allegedly made the dragon drunk with sake fermented eight times (understood as a large number of rice and *koji* additions to continue the fermentation thus obtaining a high alcohol sake). The "*goshu*" sake described in the Engishiki (see "A short history of sake", p.16) used this same method, which was brought up to date and formalized for modern production in 1973 by Makoto Sato at the fermentations research laboratory of the Ministry of Finance.

The two types of sake described here are generally aged prior to commercialization. Because of their higher sugar and amino acid levels, they have a deep yellow to dark brown color (see "Aging", p.198) and caramel, nutty/chestnut flavors. In addition, these sakes are generally produced using high-acid yeasts in order to balance the sweet sensation in the mouth and to maintain a certain freshness.

2. Low-alcohol sake

To attract an audience of female drinkers, several *kura* developed low-alcohol sakes (5-13%) in the 2000s. It is of course easy to reduce the degree of a sake by diluting it with water, however this deteriorates the taste and quality, which is not the goal.

A low-alcohol sake with aromatic characteristics close to a classic sake is obtained by decreasing the amount of alcohol produced while maintaining the fermentation time. To do this, the fermentation takes place at low temperature, in a sugar-depleted wort, obtained thanks to a low *koji-buai*.

With 5 to 10% of *kome-koji* (versus about 20%) the enzymatic activity is greatly reduced, decreasing the production of sugar and therefore alcohol. In contrast, yeasts continue to produce aromatic compounds, and rice and *kome-koji* "infuse" their aromas in sake.

The sakes produced are aromatically subdued. To give them a little more relief, and to please their target audience, it is possible to aromatize and/or give them a sparkling appearance.

3. Sparkling sake

Since the mid-2000s, a sparkling sake fashion has appeared in Japan. In the '90s only a handful of *kura* produced these atypical sakes but today, driven by demand, more and more *kura* are trying this new approach.

Sparkling sake comes in many forms to meet the different categories of consumers: cloudy or clear, only slightly fizzy or straight sparkling, natural or flavored. Since most production methods are inspired by the world of wine, we will name them accordingly.

a. Forced carbonation

As demonstrated by commercially available carbonation machines (soda), there now exists the technical means of obtaining a carbonated beverage by simply adding carbon dioxide to the beverage. However, this simple and economical method has little qualitative interest. It is mainly used for products sold at low prices.

b. Direct bottling (*kasseishu* or *nigorizake*)

This was probably the original method for obtaining slightly sparkling sakes. It consists of preserving the fermentation gas by bottling sake as quickly as possible, without filtration. The sakes thus produced are generally not pasteurized and just slightly fizzy. If so, they are called "*kasseishu*" and still contain active yeasts. As such, they are still fermenting and must be consumed very quickly. They are the equivalent of the "bourru" wine consumed around harvest time.

For more stability, it is possible to pasteurize *kasseishu*, which then becomes a sparkling *nigorizake*. For more details, history and production methods, see "A special case: pressing *nigorizake* ", p.191.

c. Closed-tank (Charmat method)

Just as in the case of beer or some sparkling wine, here sake is fermented in a closed (and reinforced, to resist pressure) tank, to keep the fermentation gas in. It is perfectly possible to filter and/or pasteurize in-line this kind of sake during bottling.

This relatively simple and economic method however requires a certain technical mastery and rather large equipment. It can produce quality sake but does not fundamentally alter the characteristics of the product.

d. Bottle fermentation (ancestral method)

Bottle fermentation involves bottling the *moromi* to allow the fermentation to finish in the bottle. It is not necessary that all the fermentation takes place in the bottle to obtain a high level of gas: less than 10% of the total fermentation of sake is enough to obtain the same sparkle as a Champagne. In addition, the beginning of the fermentation in vats allows a better control and ensures a greater homogeneity between bottles.

At the end of fermentation, *kasu* is present in the bottle. It is therefore necessary to disgorge (as in Champagne) if one wishes to market a clear sake. Disgorging consists of "riddling" (slow, spiral movement) the bottles in order to accumulate the *kasu* in the neck of the bottle and then expel it by opening it ("disgorging"). A small amount of sake is then added to replenish the bottle. The process can be facilitated by freezing the *kasu* accumulated in the neck of the bottle by immersing it in a brine at -18 °C / 0 °F. It is however impossible to pasteurize such sake as the temperature elevation combined with the gas would provoke a dramatic rise in pressure inside the bottle (CO_2 solubility in water at 65 °C is a third of that at 20 °C)

e. Secondary fermentation (traditional method)

Unlike the previous method, the sake is pressed then bottled with a liquor consisting of *kasu* and/or rice, *kome-koji*, water and yeasts. A second fermentation then occurs in the bottle. Sake can then, just as in the previous method, be disgorged or not.

This method is equivalent to that used in Champagne and in most regions producing sparkling wines. However, the degree achieved by sake at the end of fermentation is higher than that of wine and it is impossible to restart a fermentation from a basic sake at 18% vol. So it is necessary to dilute this sake with water or to stop the fermentation to a lower degree, between 10 and 14% vol. In addition, unlike wine, there is no or little ageing in sake, especially sparkling, and the second fermentation is usually triggered directly after the first. The distinction between first and second fermentation is therefore not as clear in the case of sake as in the case of wine. In this respect, it can be said that this method is in fact a compromise between traditional and ancestral methods, more adapted to the constraints of sake.

The methods using bottled fermentation are the most complex to master and require several years of research at each *kura* to find the right recipe. The first sake thus produced presented strong deviations. However, these methods open up new possibilities for the sake world through the production of truly unique sake.

e. Fermentation aromas

We can distinguish four origins of sake aromas, in order of importance: fermentation, *koji*, rice and finally aging, the importance of which varies according to its duration (see "Aging", p.198). If fermentation has such an important place in the aromatic profile of sake, it is because rice and *kome-koji* are relatively poor in aromatic compounds and these can be transformed during fermentation. In addition, most sakes do not undergo aging (or very little).

The richness in aromatic precursors may, however, vary depending on the types of rice and *koji*, influencing the final aroma composition of sake. For more details on the impact of rice and *koji* varieties on sake flavors, see "Influence of rice on the final product", p.42, and "*Koji* aroma", p.110.

Sake contains more than 300 aromatic compounds from fermentation that can be classified into five broad categories:

1. Fruity aromas

These are the most present and most sought after flavors of sake, and are usually caused by esters. The star of the fruit flavors is the famous *capron-san* (ethyl caproate or ethyl hexanoate). This ester has a strong aroma of fresh fruit, green apple or pineapple. It is the marker of "*ginjo-ka*", the aromas of *ginjo*.

In contrast to these fresh fruit aromas, isoamyl acetate is responsible for notes of ripe fruit and banana. Two other esters play an important role in fruity aromas: ethyl acetate, fresh and vegetal (grass, grapes, strawberry), and the heavier ethyl octanoate (apricot, wax, creamy). At high concentration, ethyl acetate confers acescence to sake.

At lower concentrations, a long list of esters contributes to the fruity aroma of sake: these include propyl acetate (raspberry, pear), butyl acetate and iso-butyl (banana), ethyl isovalerate (apple, pineapple), ethyl isocaproate (lychee), and ethyl keto-isovalerate (melon, pineapple, rhubarb).

2. Spicy aromas

Fusel alcohols, furfural and terpenes that give spicy character to other alcoholic beverages are little produced during fermentations at low temperatures. We find them rather in entry-level sakes.

The higher alcohols with the most important fusel notes are isoamyl alcohol and isobutanol.

3. Floral and vegetal aromas

The compounds mainly responsible for the floral flavors of sake are 2-phenylethanol (floral or rose) and propanol (floral/woody). The production of these higher alcohols is minimal for low temperature fermentations.

Greener notes can also be seen, especially at the end of fermentation, or in unpasteurized sakes: these are caused by propyl acetate (celery), ethyl pyruvate (vegetable), phenylpyruvic acid (honey, almond, green), hexanal (green, fatty), etc.

4. Lactic aromas

These aromas are especially represented in the lactic-fermented sakes, that is to say the sake produced by the *kimoto* and *yamahai* methods. Lactic acid bacteria produce diacetyl with notes of cheese and butane-2,3-diol with a butter/cream smell.

Other aromatic molecules may also participate in the lactic profile of sake, sometimes in a negative way: these include isobutyric acid (cheese, rancid), isovaleric acid (foot, sweat), isohexanoic acid (fatty, sweat), isocaprylic acid (fat, wax, rancid), and oleic acid (fat, wax, lard).

5. Earthy/moldy aromas

There is generally little interest in this fifth category because of its negative nature. However, it is necessary to pay attention to identify these potential deviations caused by propionaldehyde and methional/methanal.

6. Concentration and aroma perception

Some molecules are mentioned here several times for different categories of flavors because these molecules are perceived differently according to their concentration and the aromatic environment (the other aromatic components of sake).

It is necessary to distinguish for a given molecule its detection threshold and its recognition threshold. Indeed, at a concentration higher than the detection threshold, the taster is able to feel the presence of the molecule but not to identify it whereas at a concentration above the recognition threshold, the trained taster can recognize and name the molecule.

Between these two levels, the molecule brings complexity to the sake by creating an aromatic background and influencing the perception of other aromatic molecules. The perception thresholds depend on the aromatic molecules, from a few tenths of grams per liter to a few hundred micrograms per liter. Here are some examples of thresholds:

Category	Molecule	Detection (mg/L)	Recognition (mg/L)
Fruity	Ethyl caproate	0.12	0.27
Fruity	Isoamyl acetate	0.27	0.52
Floral	2-phenylethanol	29	56
Spicy	Isoamyl alcohol	68	140
Lactic	Isovaleric acid	0.41	0.81

Table 19. Detection and recognition thresholds of some aromatic molecules in sake.

Chapter III

Fining Raw Sake

Chapter III: Fining raw sake

At the end of fermentation, the *toji* obtains a "raw" sake. Cloudy, sparkling and unstable, it must be refined before commercialization. We will now look at the different fining methods used.

a. Additions

As the name suggests, additions consist of adding various ingredients to sake, thus changing its taste. The main additives used are water, alcohol, sugar, acids and amino acids.

In the current context, the use of additives has a bad press, and some claim that *junmai* (sake without additives) are the only real sake. This is explained by the conjunction of a global trend towards so-called "natural" products and by the excesses of the past (see the "*Sanbaizoshu*: original sin" insert opposite). However, we must recognize that:

1- The use of additives is a historical practice.

2- The vast majority of sake sold today use these techniques.

3- Excellent sake can be produced using these techniques.

So let's try to be discerning and not to reject a technique that can be interesting.

i.   Water

Water occupies a special place in sake additives as it is one of the only additives allowed in *junmai* sakes (see another exception, "*Yon-dan*", p.183), and the only one to be used almost systematically.

The alcoholic strength reached at the end of the fermentation, although depending on the *toji*'s choices, is generally of the order of 18% (see "End of fermentation", p.167). Since most sakes are bottled at 15-16%, it is necessary to add water in the vast majority of sake. Note that even sakes called "*genshu*" (without added water) generally are closer to 17%, and therefore require a water addition; more details of this are given later.

There are two methods for adding water, each with advantages and disadvantages, and often used together.

Sanbaizoshu: the original sin

During the Second World War, the shortage of rice jeopardized sake production. In order to survive and continue to produce, the *kura* resorted to palliatives, especially to dilution. Thus was "invented" the *sanbaizoshu* (sanbai = three times and zo = increase).

As is implied, it consists in diluting three times the sake produced (a liter of sake giving 3 liters of *sanbaizoshu*), by adding water, alcohol, sugar, acids, amino acids, etc. This results in very low quality sake at very low cost.

If this method could be justified in times of war, it is much more questionable in times of peace. In fact, the share of these sakes in total production has become very low. However, these methods lasted long after the war because of the large margins generated. Even today less extreme techniques but originating from a similar state of mind remain.

These products can unfortunately be called "*seishu*" (since the different additions represent less than 50% of the total weight of rice used) and producers are careful enough not to communicate about these practices when they use them. Thus, these products create in the minds of neophytes confronted with them, a confusion extremely harmful to sake's reputation.

For these same reasons, many connoisseurs demonize the use of additives without taking the time to separate the wheat from the chaff.

It should be noted that since the Second World War *goseiseishu* or synthetic sake have also been produced, solely by blending alcohol, flavorings, sugar, acids and other additives, sometimes with a small proportion of rice flour.

1. Adding water before pressing

The proportion of rice and water used for fermentation varies from one *toji* to another. A small amount of water increases the nutrient concentration of the wort and prompts a rapid fermentation. It is thus possible to deliberately reduce the amount of water used for *san-dan shikomi*, in order to ensure an efficient fermentation.

As we saw in the "Managing temperatures" section (p.169), it is possible to add water during fermentation to slow it down. It is also possible to add this water at the end of fermentation. The added water allows for the extraction of certain elements (such as aromas and alcohol) sequestered in the *kasu*, thus limiting the dilution effect. The operation of this phenomenon is explained in the following chapter, "Alcohol" (see Figure 15, p.181).

Because of these elements released by *kasu*, it is difficult to predict the exact consequences of a water addition, especially in terms of final alcoholic degree. It is possible to make several additions in order to get as close as possible to the desired result. One can also choose to correct the degree by a second water addition after pressing.

Sakes to which no water have been added after pressing (or a water addition lowering the alcoholic strength by less than 1%) may be called "*genshu*". A *genshu* sake can very well have undergone a significant water addition before pressing and thus have a low degree of alcohol. However, commercialized *genshu* usually have a high degree, of the order of 18%, which corresponds to the expectations of consumers for this category of sake.

2. Adding after pressing

The addition of water after pressing is a simple dilution; in that regard it is less desirable than an addition before pressing. However, with this method, the *toji* can be certain of the result (s)he will get. (S)he just need to take a sample of sake to be diluted and to perform tests with several proportions of added water. (S)he will then taste the samples, usually with the owner of the *kura* and/or his team to choose the exact amount to add to get the desired sake.

3. Benefits of water additions

First of all, let's underline that there is nothing shameful about adding water to sake. Without water, sake would only be dry rice.

If there is an obvious economic interest in diluting sake (if we can then sell it at the same price, it is even the oenological equivalent of the philosopher's stone), this is not what motivates producers to use this technique. As stated, at the end of fermentation the sake is usually 18% ABV or more. At this level, alcohol might give you a burning sensation and mask certain aromas. Adding a small amount of water can reveal those aromas by decreasing the alcoholic sensation. It's the same process that drives most spirit producers to reduce their ABV to around 40%.

This phenomenon can be perfectly illustrated by tasting "*genshu*" sakes: having a higher alcoholic degree (usually 17-18% TAV), they are generally identified as being a "manly" drink with rich and powerful aromas, but sometimes a little "rustic". They are sometimes served with an ice cube to smooth them out. However, ice might freeze the sake aromas and it is better to add a few drops of cold water, as for a whiskey.

ii.   Alcohol (*jozo arukoru*)

Contrary to what one might imagine, the objective of an alcohol addition is never (today) to increase the ABV of a sake, but to maintain it during water addition.

The addition of industrial alcohol in some sake is a tradition that is more than 400 years old. This method was largely developed during the Genroku era (1688-1704). *Shochu* made from *kasu* called "*Hashira shochu*" was used. At the time, the addition of distilled alcohol ensured better preservation by sterilizing the sake thanks to an increased ABV.

Thanks to better control of fermentations and pasteurization, this is no longer necessary, but the addition of alcohol has other advantages.

During the Second World War, when rice shortage jeopardized sake production (see "*Sanbaizoshu*: Original Sin", p.177), the goal of this practice was simply to make up for the lack of rice. It is unfortunately still possible today to use the addition of alcohol to inflate artificially and inexpensively the volumes produced.

Of course, this only makes sense for entry-level products, but we're going to see why even today a very important part of the most recognized sakes, and especially "competition" sakes, contain added alcohol.

1. Type of alcohol

The base alcohol used for additions is a 96% neutral industrial alcohol (*jozo arukoru*). It has no other aroma than that of alcohol and thus has no adverse impact on the product.

Some producers choose to use other alcohols, such as *shochu* (distilled alcohol mainly from rice, barley, brown sugar, *kasu* or sweet potato, between 25% and 50%). However, this practice strongly modifies the character of sake and it remains extremely marginal despite the unmistakable quality of certain products made this way.

Note that only the use of neutral alcohol or *shochu* is allowed under the name "*seishu*" (their use should not exceed 50% of the total weight of rice).

2. Addition method: 25-35%

Although the alcohol is bought and delivered to the *kura* in the form of a 96% neutral alcohol, it is generally not stored or used in this form.

Indeed, 96% alcohol is a highly flammable product that requires very specific storage conditions, rarely available to small *kura* (large producers are, by their significant use of industrial alcohol, generally much better equipped). In addition, the use of highly concentrated products is a source of error and inaccuracies: it is easier to mistake a few centiliters than a liter.

Since the alcohol content of the sake should not increase during the addition, it is possible to reduce the distilled alcohol by adding water before storage and use. A final degree of 25% to 35% ABV makes it possible to obtain a stable solution (microbiologically and in terms of safety).

3. Method and quantity

The addition of alcohol is carried out before pressing in proportions determined by the *toji*. The amount of added alcohol is usually determined by the *kura's* "recipe" but it can be adjusted according to the characteristics of the treated batch. The weight of alcohol added (based on a 95% ABV spirit) may not, however, exceed 10% of the weight of rice in the case of *honjozo* and *ginjo* sake. This amount corresponds to an increase in the final volume of about 25-33% (depending on the final degree), which is already considerable.

There is also a restriction on the use of alcohol by *kura*: a *kura* can not use more than 280 L of pure alcohol per ton of rice processed in the year. This "restriction" is however far too high to constitute any real obstacle to the use of distilled alcohol in large quantities. During the addition, special attention is paid to the homogenization of the tank, which can be provided by mechanical mixing. Once the addition is complete, the tank is left standing for 12 to 48 hours before pressing.

4. Benefits and impact of alcohol addition

Once fermentation is complete, two phases can be distinguished in the tank: a liquid phase and a solid phase that after pressing will respectively become sake and *kasu*.

The solid phase, consisting mainly of yeasts and rice residues, retains some fermentation aromas adsorbed on the solid particles. Among others, those flavors give *kasu* its unique taste and make it a popular ingredient in Japanese cuisine. These flavors are soluble in alcohol but do not migrate to the liquid phase before pressing because it is already saturated.

However, if the liquid phase is diluted by water and/or alcohol addition, its concentration decreases and the aromas of the solid phase can join the liquid phase. A new equilibrium is established between the aromas of the two phases (see Figure 15, next page). The mixture of *kasu* and water called *amazake* perfectly illustrates the ability of water and alcohol to extract the aromas of *kasu*.

Additions

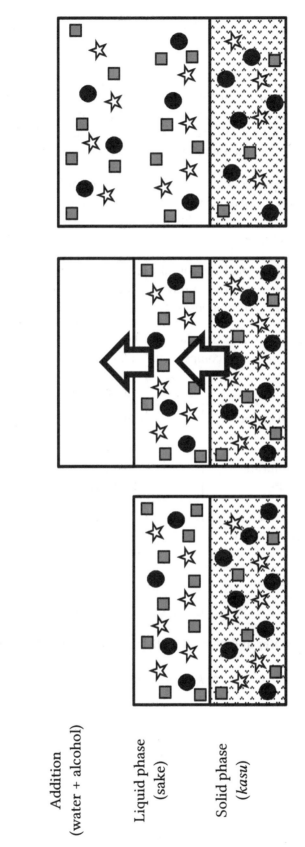

Figure 15. Simplified model for dilution of sake components during addition of water and alcohol.

Considering an addition that doubles the volume of the liquid phase, it is found that the different components shown react differently to the dilution, depending on their concentration in *kasu* and the balance of concentrations between the two phases. The concentrations found in sake after addition compared to initial concentrations are as follows ■ : -50% ☆ : -33% ● : -25%

Sakes produced with the addition of alcohol are called *aruten*, as opposed to *junmai* sakes.

Thus, the addition of alcohol and water before pressing does not result in a pure and simple dilution of the aromas: all the flavors do not react in the same way to the dilution. The most concentrated aromas are sufficiently present in the *kasu* to compensate for the dilution effects, while the secondary aromas are directly impacted by the dilution and their concentration in the mixture decreases.

What are the sensory consequences of these mechanisms? Since the secondary aromas are diluted, some of them pass under the recognition or detection thresholds: respectively the concentration thresholds from which a man is able to recognize a flavor or to detect its presence.

The aromatic "background" consisting of all the molecules analyzed by the taster is reduced. The main aromas are thus promoted, giving an impression of elegance, finesse and sharpness that can compensate for the loss of aromatic complexity.

These qualities being particularly popular with Japanese consumers, producers seek this effect, especially in so-called "competition" sakes.

Addition effect	Components
Slight dilution <10%	Isoamyl alcohol Amino acids Lactic acid Potassium
Average dilution ≈20%	Isoamyl acetate Succinic acid
Major dilution ≤50%	Iron Copper

Table 20. Effects of a water and alcohol addition on the concentration of different components of a sake.
Addition of 10 kg of pure alcohol per 100 kg of total rice (10%), legal maximum for the honjozo and ginjo categories. Source: NRIB.

iii. Sugar

The vast majority of sakes contain "residual" sugars. These are sugars not converted into alcohol during fermentation. The amount of sugar present at the end of fermentation can be controlled by adjusting the temperature during fermentation (in order to modify the respective speeds of transformation of starch into sugar and sugar into alcohol, see "Fermentation management", p.156). *Toji* may also choose to add sugar to sake after fermentation: either to "sweeten" sake or, more often, to compensate for the dilution caused by adding water (or water and alcohol).

Whatever the purpose, there are two distinct methods:

1. Industrial sugar

The first method is to add commercial sugar (cane or beet for example) into the finished product. This addition may take place at any time between fermentation and bottling; it is reserved for *futsushu* sakes. This technique has little qualitative interest but there is a historical clientele for sweet sake (*amakuchi*).

Note that in the world of wine, this method called "sugaring" is prohibited, except for sparkling wines during the "dosage".

2. *Yon-dan*

The second method is called "*yon-dan*" (of "*yon*" = four(th) and "*dan*" = step) with reference to the *san-dan shikomi* described above (three-step addition method). Here, the added sugar comes from rice.

To do this, a mixture of rice, water and amylases is macerated. These can be pure enzymes purchased from a specialized company, or just *kome-koji*. In this second case, amino acids will also be extracted from the rice and thus added to the sake.

The maceration is carried out at high temperature (around 50 °C / 122 °F) and in a significant amount of water (minimum *komi-mizu-buai* of 150%) in order to optimize the solubilization of the rice. It lasts from 8 to 10 hours, then the mixture is cooled before being added to sake (*yon-dan uchi*) shortly before pressing. If an alcohol addition is to take place, it is done after adding the *yon-dan*.

3. Comparison of the two methods

If the addition of industrial sugar is simple and economical, *yon-dan* has several advantages:

- The use of *yon-dan* is allowed for *tokutei meisho shu* while any sake that has been industrially sweetened is downgraded to *futsushu*.

- It is possible to add elements other than sugar via *yon-dan*. A *toji* wishing to bring only sugar will use a glutinous rice (easily degradable) and commercial enzymes. But if he also wants to provide amino acids, he can replace enzymes with *kome-koji* and rice with *kasu*. He can also choose to use the *sakamai* already used in fermentation to reinforce his aromas in sake by infusion.

Via these complementary elements (amino acids and rice flavors), *yon-dan* makes it possible to better compensate for the dilution due to the addition of water and alcohol than would an industrial sugar addition. It is considered that for each 20 L of pure alcohol added per ton of rice, 10 kg of rice (i.e. 1%) in the form of *yon-dan* is required to compensate for the dilution. We will see however that these elements can also be brought by other techniques used in the context of *futsushu*.

iv.   Acids

The addition of acids is made necessary by the large dilutions made in the lowest-end sakes. The added acids are chemically manufactured and bought from specialized firms. These are the same acids that are naturally present in sake, however *toji* generally use a single commercial acid rather than a cocktail of acids reproducing the natural proportions of sake. For this reason, acidified sakes may have an imbalance in acid perception.

v.   Amino acids

In the same way as for acids, the addition of amino acids is rendered necessary by the large dilutions made in the lowest quality sakes. The added amino acids are chemically manufactured and bought from specialized firms. The focus is generally on glutamate, the most umami-contributing amino acid, marketed as MSG (monosodium glutamate), an additive widely used by Japanese food business companies. Amino acids can also be provided by the *yon-dan* technique (see "Sugar", p.183).

b. Pressing (*assaku* or *joso*)

Sake pressing consists of separating the raw sake, properly speaking, from "*kasu*". *Kasu* consists of the solid residues of fermentation: mainly undissolved rice and yeasts (alive and/or dead).

The difficulty of this operation lies in the fact that *kasu* is a paste too liquid to be retained by a press but that quickly obstructs a conventional filter. There are currently three methods that we will describe.

Kasu

Kasu obtained from pressing sake is marketed in Japan for use in cooking or consumed as a snack, just grilled. It is appreciated for its nutritional qualities (average content: 54.5% water, 15% proteins, 18% sugar, 8% alcohol, 3% fibers and 1.5% lipids) and its aromas of sake.

Among the many recipes using *kasu*, we can name *amazake*, a sweet and slightly alcoholic drink made from *kasu* and water, or *kasu*-macerated *tsukemonos*, small pickled vegetables.

Kasu can also be used more industrially for the production of rice vinegar, *shochu* or *goseiseishu* (synthetic sake, see "Sanbaizoshu: original sin", p.177).

Kasu takes different forms depending on its moisture content and therefore the pressing method used. The most humid and expensive *kasu*, made from mild presses used on high-end sake (see "Cotton bags: *fukurozuri*" on the next page), are marketed in the form of pastes, in plastic boxes or bags.

The driest *kasu*, resulting from press-filter (see "The press-filter: *assaku-ki*", p.188), are marketed in the form of 40x20 cm flexible plates. This aspect is due to the Yabuta machine whose each pressing plate is divided into eight 40x20 cm segments in order to facilitate the cleaning, thus molding the *kasu* according to the same dimensions.

i. Cotton bags: *fukurozuri*

This method, although traditional-looking (and often promoted as such), was formalized in 1965 in order to obtain finer tasting sake for competition. The sake is poured manually into cotton bags (*fukuro*, of variable capacity, about 15 liters), which are then hooked to a bamboo stem and suspended over a tank. The sake then flows drop by drop for about 8 hours.

The "free run" or "drop" sake that flows from the bags, named *shizukuzake*, is usually placed in demijohns called *tobin* (glass bottles, traditionally 18 liters, sometimes between 10 and 25 liters, see "Japanese measurements units", p.208). The sake placed in *tobin* is then called *tobin-gakoi*. The purpose of these small containers is twofold: the first is to allow sedimentation of the sake, as the cotton mesh of the bags allow some small particles to pass. These cloud the sake and must be removed (see "Clarification (*oribiki*)", p.192).

The second purpose of the *tobin* is to separate the different fractions that drip because even within *shizukuzake*, the quality is not constant. As the bags drain themselves, it is the least extractable fractions of sake, more rustic, less elegant, that drip. This will be all the more true for the sake extracted later by pressing (called *fukuro-shibori*, *shibori* = squeeze/wring and no longer *fukurozuri*).

The use of the demijohns allows the producer, *a posteriori*, to taste the different fractions in order to distinguish between the best quality and the remainder. In general, a producer will sell only one *shizukuzake*, the rest of the lot being then mixed with other lots.

When the flow of the bags dries up, the *kasu* is not yet dry and it is still possible to extract sake, so the *toji* uses one of the two pressing methods described below on the remaining fraction.

Fukuro

The cotton bags (*fukuro*) used for *fukuro-shibori* or *fune-shibori* undergo significant stress during pressing and often tear. Traditionally, astringent *kaki* (*kakishibu*) juice was used to strengthen the bags.

The *kakishibu* is obtained by macerating in water for half a day the pulp of astringent persimmons. After filtration, the resulting liquid contains tannins and a resinous gum that make it more effective than many other tanning agents to strengthen fabrics, wood and paper. The repeated soaking (every year before the first pressing) gives the bags a brown hue. Today, some designers look for these patched brown bags to create fashion accessories.

ii.   Vertical press: *fune*

This method can be considered to be the traditional one. Here, the cotton bags, rather than being suspended, are stacked in a wooden box whose size may vary but are of the following sort of magnitude: 2 m long, 50 cm wide and 1 m deep. Its shape evokes that of a boat, hence the name of the method (*fune* = boat). At the base of the box, on one side, an opening allows the sake to flow out.

At first, the simple weight of the bags on each other allows for the collection of a fraction named *arabashiri*. One will note a similarity to the *shizukuzake* method, except the weight of the bags, which adds to the pressure. The second time pressure is applied, the *nakadori* then *seme* fractions are liberated. It might be necessary to restack the bags inside the *fune* to extract the *seme* fraction. These three fractions respectively represent approximately 60%, 35% and 5% of the pressed sake.

Arabashiri and *nakadori* are both good quality, the first is the image of new sake, sparkling and intensely aromatic, the second is more refined and has a denser palate. The third is considered of lower quality.

Pressing before *fune*?

Few changes are noticeable between the 300-year-old *fune* press observable in Sawanotsuru museum (Nada) and a modern *fune* press, except for the old weighted lever being replaced by an hydraulic motor. But one can wonder if some pressing techniques pre-existed *fune*?

Pressing or squeezing bags to extract juice is an age-old technique as attests the 4000-year-old carvings in the Tomb of Mereruka (Egypt). Thus there is no doubt that similar techniques pre-existed the "invention" of sake in Japan. However the standard *fune* was probably not always used. Even if *fukurozuri* was only formalized in 1965, there is a high chance that dripping sake before extracting the remaining juice was a common technique when pressing techniques were less refined and required man force. We can see an example of that in old *ukiyo-e* (woodblock prints) showing two groups of men pressing hanging bags of sake between two large wood panels. However, there is no trace of separating dripping sake from pressed sake in order to obtain two qualities.

We can easily guess that these kind of primitive pressing techniques were good enough as long as sake production remained small-scale and local, but *fune* pressing became a necessity as soon as specialized production appeared.

iii. Press-filter: *assaku-ki*

The press-filter (*assaku-ki*, or Yabuta according to the name of the best known manufacturer) is a technology used in many fields to filter liquids heavily loaded with residues, such as sake. Because of its ease of use and its yield (the amount of sake extracted is larger and the *kasu* obtained is drier) this machine has been adopted by almost all producers, although some continue to produce some sake with the techniques described previously.

The operation of this machine consists of filtering the sake through filtration membranes (which replace the cotton bags) under the pressure of compressed air. The machine is an assembly of vertical metal plates covered with the said filtration membranes.

There are two types of plates, filter plates and pressing plates, placed alternately.

The sake to be filtered is placed between the two plates, then compressed air is injected into the pressing membrane of the pressing plate which inflates and compresses the sake to be filtered against the filtration membrane of the filter plate. The sake passes through the latter and is evacuated through a specific opening at the base of the filter plate. Once the sake is completely filtered, there remains between the two plates the *kasu*: solid residues that could not pass through the membrane. The plates are then loosened and the *kasu* is removed with spatulas (it usually sticks to the membranes).

Compared with the previous methods, *assaku-ki* produces much clearer sake (and thus more stable) and reduces contact with oxygen, limiting the risk of oxidation.

Izakaya, sake houses

In Japan, restaurants often specialize in a unique dish: soba (buckwheat noodles), yakitori (skewers), ramen or udon (noodle soup), tempura (deep fried vegetables, seafood, etc.), okonomiyaki (pancakes stuffed with vegetables meat or seafood), sushi and sashimi, etc. It is the customers who move between restaurants during the evening, depending on their desires.

However, one type of institution includes a wide variety of styles: *izakaya* (居酒屋), which can be translated as "sake house". These are places of sake consumption par excellence, where sake is drunk between colleagues or friends, while eating simple and iconic *o-tsumami*: edamame (soya beans), yakitori (skewers), sashimi, karaage (fried chicken), etc.

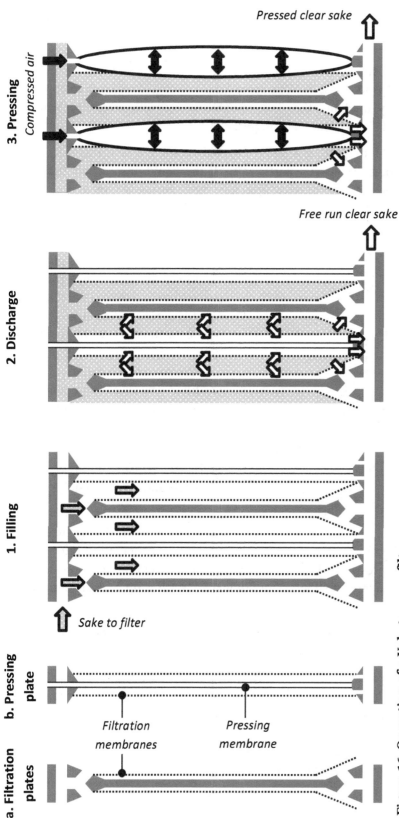

a. Filtration plates

b. Pressing plate

Filtration membranes

Pressing membrane

1. Filling

Sake to filter

2. Discharge

Free run clear sake

3. Pressing

Compressed air

Pressed clear sake

Figure 16. Operation of a Yabuta press-filter.

The filtration (a) and pressing (b) plates are assembled, then the sake to be filtered is pumped into the Yabuta and fills the inter-plate space (1). The most liquid phase of the sake then flows through the filter (2). When this first phase of discharge is complete, compressed air is injected into the pressing membranes (3). These then swell and squeeze the sake to filter contained between the plates. Several pressure build-up and running off cycles are required to completely deplete the *kasu*. When it is dry, the plates are again spread and the *kasu* can be evacuated.

iv.   Centrifugation

Traditional filtration methods have two major disadvantages: they are discontinuous and labor intensive. It is for these reasons some *kura*, conducted research to apply to sake a method widely used in other food industries: centrifugation (try Yamato Shizuku "Yama-tornado" or Dassai "centrifuge").

The principle is simple: by putting a liquid in rapid rotation, a centrifugal force is exerted, thus separating the heavier particles from the liquid. In practice, this is a mechanical acceleration of the gravity principle used during sedimentation (see "Settling (*orisage*)", p.192).

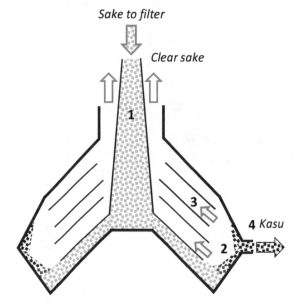

The sake to be filtered is pumped continuously into the rotating centrifuge (1). The heavy particles accumulate at the end of the centrifuge (2), while the clear sake springs upwards (3), pushed by the continuous arrival of sake to filter. The relief valve opens at regular intervals to evacuate the accumulated *kasu* (4).

Figure 17. Operation of a continuous centrifuge.

Continuous centrifuges make it possible to process large volumes of sake and to integrate the operation into an in-line processing logic: pressing, filtration, pasteurization. In addition, they are easy to use and maintain compared to the tedious hours of setting up and cleaning the press-filter plates.

From a qualitative point of view, the centrifuge also has various advantages related to its selectivity:

During filtration, the particles retained by the filter accumulate against it, creating a surface deposit. The filter clogs up little by little, reducing the diameter of the pores to the point of retaining desirable particles (aromas, acids, amino acids, etc.). This is especially true in the context of very heavy fluids such as sake. In the case of centrifugation, this type of phenomenon is almost non-existent. The particles to be eliminated are therefore targeted very precisely.

Moreover, centrifugation can sometimes replace pressing, filtration and pasteurization. Indeed, by using high rotation speeds, it is possible to precipitate very small particles (eliminated during filtration), up to the proteins eliminated during pasteurization (see "Pasteurization (*hiire*)", p.195). However, this technique requires fine management of the centrifugation parameters (rotational speed and feeding), at the risk of stripping out the sake. Well controlled, the centrifugation preserves the qualities of sake and can contribute to the stabilization of unpasteurized sake.

v.   A special case: *nigorizake* pressing

Nigorizake is a cloudy sake, very popular in the United States, that could be described as "unfiltered". However, this term is relatively vague and covers a broad set of technical realities.

In the early days of sake production, it was consumed directly after fermentation, without separating the *kasu*. Then, when production techniques began to be refined by monks, filtration appeared, until it became a norm, then a legal obligation at the end of the 19th century. At the time, only individuals producing sake for their personal consumption still consumed cloudy sakes.

In 1966, the "Tsuki no Katsura" *sakagura*, wishing to reproduce an "old-fashioned" cloudy sake developed a new filtration technique that was approved by the government. It became possible to market *nigorizake* provided that it was obtained after filtration through a sieve with a diameter of less than 2 mm. In practice sake is directly pumped from the tank through a "cage" pierced with 2 mm-wide holes.

This method requires a special treatment of sake and therefore additional labor costs. So, many producers, rather than using the official technique, were content to mix a little *kasu* with their sake, after a conventional filtration, to obtain the desired cloudiness. This method was so widespread that the law was eventually changed to allow this technique. Today only some *nigorizake* are produced by loose filtration.

Doburoku and *nigorizake*

The terms "*doburoku*" and "*nigorizake*" are written in a similar way in Japanese: 濁酒 and 濁り酒. They both contain the character 濁 for "cloudy" and the character 酒 for alcohol or sake and indeed, they both designate a type of cloudy sake. However, *doburoku* refers to homemade sake, generally of low quality, rustic, acidic and low in alcohol, while the term *nigorizake* refers to a cloudy sake, but of marketable quality. Today, doburoku is consumed especially at festivals, and it is rare to see such a product marketed.

c. Clarification (*oribiki*)

The sake that emerges from one of the three pressing systems described is never perfectly clear. It contains particles or sediments (yeast, starch or insoluble proteins, etc.) called "*ori*" that should be removed by an additional clarification step or "*oribiki*".

i.   Settling (*orisage*)

Sedimentation or "*orisage*" consists of separating the heavier sediments by gravity: the sake is left to rest, the heaviest sediments fall to the bottom of the tank (low temperatures favoring the process), then the clear sake is pumped from the top. The sake present at the bottom of the tank, in which is concentrated all the sediments, called "*orizake*", must undergo a new stage of clarification. Depending on its degree of turbidity, it can be assembled with another batch of sake for a new pressing or filtered on suitable equipment (sometimes with an addition of 2 to 3% *kasu*, favoring the aggregation of sediments).

The duration of the sedimentation depends on the level of clarification expected. Sedimentation of 5 to 10 days at 5-10 °C / 41-50 °F is standard, however it can be prolonged if sediments are slow to settle. It may also be desirable to speed up the process so that the following stabilization steps (filtration and pasteurization) can be performed quickly to avoid any deterioration due to overly long storage.

ii.   Fining

Sedimentation can be promoted by the use of fining agents: substances capable of dragging certain undesirable particles while sedimenting. The three most popular fining agents for sake are activated charcoal, persimmon tannins and alginates.

Activated carbon acts on solid particles, pigments and aromas, and is available in the form of a coal powder. It has a very large exchange surface and therefore a high adsorption capacity, allowing to clarify sake and remove any traces of browning and negative aromas. However, as it is not very selective, it must be used with care so as not to strip out the final product. A dose of a few tenths to a few grams per liter is used depending on the needs.

Kaki tannins, on the other hand, specifically eliminate peptides and can therefore be used to stabilize a sake that is too rich in proteins (see "Aging", p.198, about the consequences of a high peptide ratio on sake preservation). Kaki tannins are traditionally used in the form of *kakishibu.*

Alginates, of more recent use, are nevertheless of natural origin as they can be found in algae. Chemically neutral, they promote the coagulation of sediments and can be used in combination with activated carbon. The main obstacle to their use is the need to dilute them in a large volume of water before use to avoid the formation of alginate gels. They are therefore almost exclusively used when a post-pressing water addition is planned. As we have seen above, dilution before pressing is generally preferred, which effectively limits their use.

The fining agent is usually left to act for at least one day. The time required depends on the amount of particles to be removed and the amount of agent used. After incorporation, the agent acts by agglomerating the particles to be removed, thus dragging them down.

iii.   Filtration

Sedimentation, with or without fining, does not result in perfectly clear sake. However, the presence of sediment can, apart from aesthetic considerations, pose difficulties during pasteurization: the sediments may react to heat and obstruct the exchanger's pipes. For this reason, unfiltered sakes (not to be confused with *nigorizake* obtained by adding *kasu*) are rarely pasteurized or, when they are, pasteurized in bottles.

Sedimentation is usually followed by a filtration that can take place on different types of media (cotton, cellulose, synthetic fibers, earth, etc.). Depending on the type of support, the porosity varies, retaining larger or smaller molecules. We can distinguish coarse filtrations, whose purpose is to give clarity and shine to sake by separating the elements at the origin of the turbidity, from fine filtrations. These can change the taste of the product by eliminating some large macromolecules. They can be used sometimes to refine and round a sake but overly fine or excessive filtration may strip out the product.

Filtrations under 0.5 micrometers, such as tangential filtration, are called "sterile" as they can eliminate microorganisms, yeasts or bacteria that could cause contamination once in the bottle.

Filtrations under 0.01 micrometers, such as ultrafiltration, additionally eliminate enzymes that could modify sake once bottled. In that regard, they can replace pasteurization (see "Pasteurization (*hiire*)", next page) and allow for production of more stable unpasteurized sakes. These same filtration methods can be used to purify water used during the production process.

Another form of filtration is commonly used: activated carbon filtration. It produces the same effects as the fining agent active carbon, and usually replaces it. In both cases, it is sometimes criticized for stripping out sake. Thus, many *kura* now produce *muroka* sakes (literally "without filtration", an inappropriate term), without the use of activated charcoal.

However, activated carbon filtration is not the only filtration that can alter a sake. There is a whole battery of Japanese terms describing the deviations caused by different filter media: these include *kami-shu* or paper smell, *momen-shu* or cotton smell, *fukuro-ka* or bag smell, and *tansho-shu* or coal smell.

For this reason, particular attention must be paid to the quality and cleanliness of the filter media. For example, cotton bales used for filtration are cleaned multiple times in running water before use. Activated carbon must be recent, used in moderate quantities and quickly removed.

Historical sake stabilization techniques

Sake was historically stable in winter thanks to low temperature; however, it was not the case in summer when *Hiochi-kin* (spoilage bacteria) could easily develop in tepid sake (keeping sake cool was not an option; underground cellar are not available in Japan due to earthquakes).

Thus, since the 16th century, sake was pasteurized to an estimated 50-55°C (120-130°F) as a mean to control the *Hiochi-kin* population and mitigate the risks of spoilage. However, after pasteurization, sake returned to its initial wooden vessel, which contained enough bacteria to contaminate the pasteurized sake again. After a few weeks, the population of *Hiochi-kin* would develop again, necessitating another pasteurization. Despite all this care, the repeated cycles of *Hiochi-kin* development and pasteurization would end up deteriorating the sake and late summer sake couldn't compare with freshly brewed sake.

In 1876 Mr. Korschelt wrote a pamphlet advocating the use of salicylic acid, which was proven efficient at 0,2g/L. Considering this a makeshift solution (he estimated the stability of salicylic acid in sake to around a year) Mr. Atkinson proposed new and optimized pasteurization parameters in his 1881 book (higher temperature at 60°C/140°F, pasteurization of the destination vessel and tighter closure as well as storage in smaller vessel/cask to limit the consequences of a punctual spoilage).

Despite the proven efficiency of Mr. Atkinson solution, salicylic acid became widely used as sake preservative until it's negative health impact forced the Brewing Society of Japan to stop distributing it in 1969.

d. Pasteurization (*hiire*)

i.   The purpose of pasteurization

Due to the double nature of its fermentation, sake contains (even after fermentation) nutrients and, unless it has undergone sterile filtration, a high load of microorganisms. These conditions generate a high risk of contamination.

The most suitable microorganisms for this medium rich in alcohol are lactic acid bacteria of the *Lactobacillus* (*L.*) and *Leuconostoc* groups, grouped under the term *Hiochi-kin* (*L. homohiochi, L. fructivorans, L. plantarum, L. acidophilus, L. fermentum, L. hilgardii, L. casei, L. paracasei, L. rhamnosus* and *Leuconostoc mesenteroides*). While developing, they produce lactic acid and in some cases diacetyl, giving a cloudy and acidic sake, with buttery and fermentary aromas, unfit for consumption.

In order to avoid these contaminations, three methods are available. Sterile filtration suppresses the inoculum, but is rarely used because of its negative impact on sake aromas. The addition of salicylic acid, which inhibits the growth of lactic acid bacteria, was abandoned in the 1970s when it was shown that the third method, pasteurization, is 100% effective. Pasteurization destroys microorganisms by a rise in temperature, but it also has another function: the inactivation of *koji* enzymes.

These enzymes necessary for fermentation remain active after pressing and can modify the product once in the bottle. The amylases and peptidases in particular continue to transform the residual polysaccharides and polypeptides of sake respectively into sugars and amino acids. These reactions alter the taste balance of sake and create nutrients that could promote bacterial contamination. Pasteurization denatures enzymes by modifying their structure, rendering them inactive.

Thus, pasteurization both destroys microorganisms and inactivates enzymes. However, this process is not without consequences on the organoleptic quality of the product. The rise in temperature denatures proteins but also favors Maillard reactions, lipid oxidation, etc. For this reason, some *kura* choose to market unpasteurized sakes called "*namazake*" that boast fresh and crisp aromas. However, these sakes are more sensitive to aging and should be stored at low temperatures and consumed quickly.

ii. Sake pasteurization methods

Sake pasteurization takes place at relatively low temperature (65 °C / 149 °F for 10 minutes) to destroy microorganisms and denature enzymes while limiting its organoleptic impact. It can be carried out on bulk or bottled sake (*bin-ire*).

In the first case, sake is circulated through a series of heat exchangers:

Sake to pasteurize

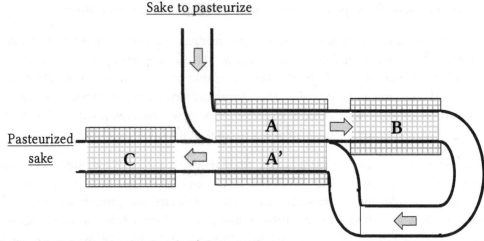

Figure 18. Sake pasteurization with heat exchangers.
Exchanger A: warming on contact with the outgoing sake (countercurrent).
Exchanger B: actual pasteurization (60-65 °C / 140-149 °F).
Exchanger A': cooling on contact with incoming sake (countercurrent).
Exchanger C: cooling.

This type of system, widely used in the food industry, represents a clear improvement over the traditional equipment called "*jakan*" (= snake), a long spiral metal pipe (a snake-evoking shape). The latter acts as a heat exchanger between the hot liquid in which it is immersed and the sake circulating inside. This method of rudimentary pasteurization has almost disappeared today even if we still find some *jakan*, improved by the addition of a double wall to establish a countercurrent. Heat exchangers allow for better control of the process.

In the second case, sake bottles can be immersed in a hot water bath and then quickly cooled in a cold water or ice bath. In order to control the temperature, fake bottles containing a thermometer are placed at several points in the bath. There are also automatic systems, transporting the bottles on rails in hot (autoclave, steam or hot water jets), then cold (jets of cold water) compartments.

In either case, controlling the duration and speed of the rise and fall in temperature is fundamental to ensure an efficient and harmless pasteurization. Most sakes are pasteurized twice: once after the fermentation ends (in vats), then a second time before shipping (bottled). This ensures that no microorganisms that could have been introduced during tank aging (see "Aging", next chapter) survive in the bottle.

Some producers simply pasteurize before shipping. This is sufficient to ensure the quality of the sake in the bottle and allows the sake to undergo a period of non-pasteurized aging that, well controlled, can bring complexity to the product. These sakes are called *nama-chozo*. Conversely, some producers consider that their storage conditions are sufficiently healthy to overcome a second pasteurization and market once-pasteurized *nama-zume* sake, unpasteurized before shipment.

There are also totally unpasteurized sakes called *namazake*. These must be stored at low temperature and consumed quickly in order to avoid risks of degradation in the bottle due to contamination or the activity of *koji* enzymes. Note however that modern methods of pressing (such as *assaku-ki* or centrifugation) and clarification can produce relatively stable *namazake*.

New sake stabilization techniques

Over the course of the 20th century, sake-making conditions evolved drastically toward better sanitation: enamelled tank, *sokujyo-moto*, selected yeasts, higher average alcohol content (11-13% ABV sake was common at the end of the 19th century), higher temperature pasteurisation, etc. At the same time, sake-pressing techniques evolved toward tighter filtrations, progressively reducing the amount of potentially harmful micro-organisms contained in sake; first with the invention of the Yabuta filter-press in 1963 then with the introduction of centrifugation followed by cross-flow filtration, sterile filtration, ultra-filtration, etc.

Theses technology advances offer new opportunities to produce stable non-pasteurized or low-pasteurized sake with the obvious advantage of preserving a maximum of the new sake aroma and freshness. New ideas and technologies appear regularly and we can safely beat that the standard 60-65°C/10min pasteurization will soon be replaced.

One recent discovery imported to sake industry from water treatment technologies is called microbubbles. It consists in generating air bubbles under 50 μm in diameter in sake during pasteurization. It has been shown that those bubbles effectively allow to lower the pasteurization temperature to around 50°C/120°F while retaining the benefit of pasteurization. The consequences in terms of energy savings and sake quality are not to be minimized and some kura already created sake using this technique (one commercially available product is Dassai 23 Hayata). Amusingly, this new technology allow to lower the pasteurization temperature back to what it was for almost four centuries (see the insert included p. 192).

e. Aging

Since the 17th century, when the first sake of the year (*hatsu-shibori* in November) is pressed, a ball of *sugi* (Japanese cedar) called *sugidama* is suspended at the entrance of the *kura*. It is said that when the *sugidama* goes from green to brown, all its branches being faded, the sake is ready to be consumed. The process takes 3 to 4 months, and the first *hatsu-shibori* sakes are usually marketed between February and spring.

Outside the picturesqueness of this tradition, it covers a technical reality. Released from the press, sake is still very active and although it can be consumed, it is necessary to let it rest for several months, before obtaining a stable product that meets the criteria of modern distribution. During these few months it will lose, in particular, the residual fermentation gas that makes it slightly sparkling out of the press.

Beyond this "minimal" aging, a *kura* can choose to age all or part of its sake over long periods (up to more than 30 years) to change its character. These sakes are then marketed under the name of *koshu* or *jukuseishu*. This second term that specifically means "aged sake" avoids any ambiguity as to whether this sake has been intentionally aged by the *kura* (a *koshu* could be a sake forgotten on a shelf).

Due to the rarity and price of these sakes, a variety of more poetic names exist to describe them: *hizoshu* (treasure), *kokoshu* (very old sake), *daikoshu* (big old sake), etc. We will study here the influence of aging.

i.   General principles

The aging of alcoholic beverages is due to slow physicochemical reactions that transform some of their compounds. Of course, only the compounds having an impact on the organoleptic perception of the product interest us here, specifically the aromatic compounds.

During aging, aromas disappear, appear or are transformed according to the following three types of schematic reactions:

Aroma loss:

Aromatic molecule + X ➜ Non aromatic molecule + Y

Aroma transformation:

Aromatic molecule 1 + X ➜ Aromatic molecule 2 + Y

Aroma formation:

$$\text{Non aromatic molecule} + X \rightarrow \text{Aromatic molecule} + Y$$

The same principles apply to all molecules having an impact on the other organoleptic qualities of sake (such as texture, sweetness, umami, etc.). The main protagonists of these reactions are: aroma, sugars and their precursors (polysaccharides), amino acids and their precursors (polypeptides), enzymes and oxygen.

The latter is involved in a large part of these transformations, because of its reactivity and its constant presence, ensured by the exchanges of gases that take place with the outside air.

Moreover, because of the concomitant activity of enzymes and yeasts during fermentation, sake is naturally rich in sugars and amino acids (yeasts consume these two elements, but the environment is constantly enriched by the enzyme activity).

This allows "Maillard reactions", a family of reactions between sugars and amino acids that occur in the process of cooking meat and roasting coffee or cocoa beans, to take place. In sake, sugars and amino acids react to form empyreumatic aromas and brown pigments.

ii. Organoleptic changes

1. Color changes

While aging, sake gradually takes a more and more pronounced yellow then brown hue. This coloration is mainly due to melanoidins resulting from Maillard reactions and to ferrichrysin (see "Purpose of polishing", p.79). Color is a good indicator of the oxidative nature and thus the "aromatic" age of a sake.

We speak here of "aromatic" age because the "real" age alone does not make it possible to presume the oxidative character of a sake, which strongly depends on the conditions of conservation (see "Aging management", p.201).

2. Aroma changes

During aging, the aromatic profile of sake evolves. The fresh fruit (pineapple, green apple, melon, etc.), floral (lily, lily of the valley, etc.) and green (celery, fresh grass, etc.) aromas tend to disappear to give way to a more complex profile, mixing spicy (vanilla, curry), dried fruits (almond), empyreumatic (burnt, caramel) and balsamic (honey, wax) aromas.

Negative aromas (sulphide/garlic) can also appear during aging, in extreme cases it is called "*hineka*" (aged smell), or for non-pasteurized sake, *nama-hineka* or *mureka* (musty). Sake rich in amino acids (low polished rice) and fermented at high temperatures are more likely to develop *hineka*.

The main molecules responsible for evolution aromas are as follows:

Spicy	**Vanillin**: vanilla
	Vanillic acid: lactic, vanilla bean
	Sotolon: fenugreek, curry, hazelnut
Dried fruits	**Furfural**: almond
	Benzaldehyde: bitter almond
Empyreumatic	**Ethyl vanillate**: phenolic, burnt
	Maltol: cooked sugar
Floral	**Phenylacetaldehyde**: sweet floral, hyacinth
	Phenylacetate ethyl: honey, rose
	Phenylacetic acid: honey, floral, wax
Negative	**Dimethyltrisulphide (DMTS)**: garlic, onion, simmered meat, mainly responsible for *hineka*
	Dimethyldisulphide: garlic, onion, cabbage
	Dimethylsulfide (DMS): truffle, cabbage, supports fruity aromas
	Methional: moldy, earthy, potato
	3-Methylbutanal: acrid, aldehyde, main responsible for *mureka*

3. Taste changes

During aging, the amount of amino acids present in sake decreases due to the various chemical reactions in which they are involved. Some of these reactions produce bitter and astringent compounds.

These compounds also tend to emphasize the umami character of sake. In small quantities, the result may be positive, but a sake with a high concentration of amino acids (low polishing) has a high risk of developing an umami/bitter negative character during aging.

In unpasteurized sake, the evolution of sugar and amino acid concentrations is modified by the residual action of *koji* enzymes on, respectively, polysaccharides and polypeptides. The sugar concentration of unpasteurized sakes increases during aging and their concentration in amino acids is relatively constant (at least in the first years). Unpasteurized sakes thus provide a greater sensation of sweetness or roundness as they get older, but they are at high risk of developing negative bitter characteristics (it is not recommended to age unpasteurized sake).

iii. Aging management

The organoleptic evolutions described above depend on several parameters that the *toji* handles in order to obtain the desired evolution profile.

1. Temperature

Most chemical reactions are temperature dependent. *Kura* therefore choose to keep their sake at different temperatures depending on the speed and type of aging desired.

The higher the storage temperature, the faster and stronger the aging will be, promoting rapid browning and nut/caramel aromas to the detriment of the more delicate aromas of pear/white flower.

The most common aging temperatures are:

-4 °C or 0 °C / 25-32 °F: Very slow to slow changes. Ideal for long aging of high-end sake (3 to 10 years).

4 °C / 39 °F: Classic low aging temperature, most sakes can benefit from such aging over a few months, and gain depth and umami.

10 °C / 50 °F: Classic high aging temperature, aromas and color evolve relatively quickly, some sake can degrade beyond 2 years.

Ambient temperature: Very fast reactions, an obvious browning and nuts/curry/caramel/coffee aromas appear in just a few months. Atypical sakes can be produced this way but most sakes degrade under such conditions.

Theoretically, time and temperature can compensate each other, but a long aging at low temperature will give a finer, less obvious, and globally more qualitative result than a short room-temperature aging, which must be reserved for specific styles of sake.

2. Containers

Sake can be aged in a wide variety of containers: glass bottles, stainless steel or enamel tanks, ceramic jars, cedar barrels (*taru*), etc.

The type of container has consequences on two aging parameters: the supply of oxygen and aromatic contribution.

With the exception of wood, whether traditional *sugi* or imported oak barrels, whose main purpose is flavoring, the materials used to preserve sake are aromatically neutral. The supply of oxygen is therefore the central issue in choosing an aging container.

Oxygen is involved in many chemical reactions typical of aging: oxidations, Maillard reactions, etc. It comes from gas exchange with the outside air via openings (e.g. stopper or bung) or with the air included in the walls of porous containers (ceramic or wood).

In both cases, it is the type of container (porosity, size, openings) and therefore the relationship between the exchange surfaces and the volume of sake contained that determines the importance of the oxygen supply during aging. We can consider as a general rule that the larger the container, the slower the aging.

a. Type of container

As mentioned above, *toji* have at their disposal a wide range of containers for sake aging. We will study the main ones:

-Tanks (stainless or enamel steel)

Tanks are the most commonly used aging container today. *Toji* use their brewing tanks or dedicated tanks to store sake before bottling and commercialization. They are generally used to minimize the impact of aging thanks to their low surface/volume ratio. In this perspective, the tank must be closed in order to limit the exchange of oxygen with the outside air.

It should be noted that tanks generally have a thermal regulation system that makes it possible to maintain the sake at low temperature and thus to further limit the effects of aging. Open fermentation tanks (U-shaped) can be closed for aging by either a traditional double-leafed wooden lid or a stainless steel lid, which is more airtight, allowing longer storage.

-Glass bottles

It is possible to age a bottled sake either in its final commercial form or as a stage in the production process. In the first case, the sake is stored in 72 cl or 1.8 L bottles (see "Japanese measurements units", p.208) for aging and then pasteurized (or not for a *nama-zume*) in the bottle, labeled and put on sale.

In the second case, the sake undergoes another manipulation before marketing, which requires opening each bottle for blending before a new bottling. It is therefore rarer to keep sake in 72 cl bottles, as 1.8 L bottles or 1 to 4 *to* demijohns (see " Japanese measurements units", p.208) are generally preferred for ease of handling. These bottles, which are larger, also offer less oxidative aging conditions thanks to a lower exchange surface/volume ratio.

The Sohomare *kura* for example ages sakes in *isshobin* before blending, a method that is reminiscent of the Bollinger house of Champagne.

- Ceramic jars

Ceramic pots were traditionally used in the 13th century to store sake. This type of container has disappeared, replaced by cedar and glass. However, we can see the impact of jar aging via "cousin" drinks of sake: *awamorishu* in Okinawa or huangjiu in China.

The permeability of certain low temperature terracotta allows a controlled oxidation of the product by a slow but constant supply of oxygen. This makes it an excellent potential container for producing an atypical sake. The renewed interest in the world of wine for aging and fermentations in jars (or "amphorae") could inspire some *toji*.

-*Taru*

Taru as a container for aging, storage and transport was widely used until the appearance of glass bottles in the twentieth century. It is now limited to *taruzake* only, because of its very strong flavor (it is said that it takes 10 years before the cedar aromas of a new *koji-muro sugi* cladding are no longer detected in sake; imagine the impact of direct contact with *sugi* in a *taru*).

Today, sake can be stored in *taru* for 1 to 3 weeks for flavoring, it is then marketed under the *taruzake* name. Over such short periods, the reactions described above can not take place and the sake retains its original freshness.

If one appreciates its heady notes and when the aging is well mastered, cedar aromas marry well with sake to give very beautiful products, rich and complex, in a rather "autumnal" style. The Choryo *kura* excels in this respect and produces one of the finest examples of *taruzake*, complex and elegant.

Note that it would be possible to use one *taru* for several years, thus exhausting its powerful cedar aromas by the successive passage of sake. These *taru* would then allow carrying out long periods of aging without masking the aromatic profile of the sake with strong notes of cedar. Thus, the permeability of wood (as well as that of terracotta) can produce atypical sakes of high quality.

- Cedar vats

Used as a replacement for jars since the 15th century, cedar vats have since been replaced by enameled steel and then stainless steel, which are simpler to maintain and easier to thermoregulate.

Some *kura* choose today to reintegrate some *sugi* tanks to return to traditional methods (sometimes also for the purpose of image and communication). However, these tanks are more often used for fermentation than for sake storage because of their open shape, less suitable for conservation.

However, like U-shaped stainless steel tanks, cedar vats can be closed with a traditional two-leaved wooden lid for sake storage and aging. If the tank is properly sealed, it can make an excellent aging container, thanks to its thermal inertia (superior to that of a stainless or enameled steel tank) and the very fine micro-oxygenation it allows. A vat that is too young will be very likely to mark the sake with a cedar note, but the lifetime of a vat is over a century.

- Oak barrels

The fashion of wine in Japan has pushed some *kuramoto* to age sake in oak casks. French oak that has contained famous white wines is generally favored for obvious marketing reasons, but also technical reasons. A new oak barrel would bring too many wood aromas and tannins, which could deteriorate the sake, and a barrel that contained red wine would color the sake. The cask aging allows, as for terracotta jars or *taru*, a mild oxidation of sake, but also brings some elements of the wine previously contained in the cask (mainly acids and flavors).

b. *Taru* making

Taru have been used in Japan for centuries for the manufacture, preservation and transport of food products. The manufacturing method used today in Japan is considered to have been introduced from China around the 13th century.

Initially made of willow wood appreciated for its strong volumetric shrinkage (ability to swell when moistened, thus preventing leaks), it was quickly abandoned for Japanese cedar for its strength and its rot-proofness.

The same method makes it possible to produce containers of all sizes, from wooden buckets and *daki*, to *taru*, to fermentation tanks.

Forestry

Wood resource management is a historical concern in Japan (see insert *"Sugi"*, p.22) and cedar forest management methods are aimed at obtaining high quality timber: the methods used can be defined as "regular even-aged high forest" management.

First of all, the future plot is deforested. It is usually a plot of mature cedars that have just been cut. Branches and woods of no commercial value are piled up and burned on site to fertilize the soil.

Young seedlings of cedar are then planted, about 1100 per hectare. These were previously grown in nurseries to about 40 cm. Between 2 and 5 years old, the area should be regularly weeded to prevent fast-growing trees or weeds from overwhelming the cedars. Between 10 and 20 years old, cedars should be pruned to remove the lower branches. The growth of the tree is thus directed in height and the log (the usable part of the tree) will be free of nodes (departures of branches that create zones of weakness in the wood).

From the age of 30, every 10 years, regular thinnings should be done. These consist of cutting the less promising trees (poorly placed, twisted, diseased, etc.) to encourage the growth of the best cedars. Depending on their size, these trees can be used for firewood or timber. The goal is to obtain 200 to 300 quality cedars per hectare at the end of the process.

The trees are harvested between 50 and 100 years according to the desired diameter, and the cycle is then resumed.

Manufacturing

Once the cedars are cut down, the logs undergo a first natural drying outdoors. Cedar is quick to deform during drying, so this first drying step is necessary.

After several months of drying, the logs are cut into smaller logs of the desired length, that is to say equal to the height of the future *taru*. The logs are then axially slit (see Figure 19, below) on their long axis, forming smaller logs that are then split again into staves following the annual rings of the wood, using a curved axe and a mallet.

The first stave to be extracted is the one that straddles the sapwood and the heartwood. The sapwood consists of the youngest rings of the tree, corresponding to the last 15 years of growth. The heartwood consists of older, hardened rings, whose obstructed vessels are no longer functional.

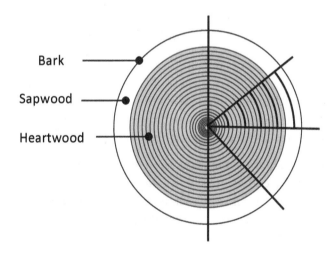

Figure 19. Cross-section of a *sugi* log.

The sapwood of the *sugi* is a very attractive white wood but it does not have the solidity, the tightness, or the aromas of the heartwood. Also the first stave is positioned between the heartwood and the sapwood to make a *taru* whose external appearance is that of the sapwood but whose resistance, waterproofness and aroma are that of the heartwood. For the same format, such *taru*, named *koutsuki-taru* are 15% more expensive than classic *taru*, named *akami-taru*.

The following staves consist only of heartwood. Depending on the diameter of the tree, it is possible to obtain 3 to 4 staves per slit log. Once the staves are formed, they can be dried a second time, in open air or in an oven. Traditionally, the staves were stacked in circles to form chimneys several meters high.

When the stave is dry enough to use, it is planed, tapered, beveled, hollowed and backed to give it its final shape: a smooth, slightly curved and trapezoidal stave of constant thickness. The staves are then assembled to form a frustoconical barrel and then held together by bamboo circles.

The circles are braided using freshly cut bamboo slats, 3 cm wide and 8 m long. For a standard *taru*, a single slat is enough to braid a circle, but for a tank, a large number of slats are needed. Once the staves have been held by the circle, a groove (the "croze") to accommodate the barrel bottom is milled in the staves. The barrel bottom, made of cedar planks assembled with a pin and holes, is then put into place. The bamboo circles are then hammered to the wide part of the barrel to tighten the staves and seal the *taru*.

Seven circles, arranged from top to bottom in a "2+2+2+1" pattern enclose a standard *taru*. The lid, pierced by a bung, is placed in the barrel and can be removed (or broken for *kagami-biraki*, see below) to access the beverage.

Kagami-biraki

The *kagami-biraki* (literally "mirror opening") is a Japanese New Year celebration involving breaking *mochi* (rice cakes) by hand or with a mallet. This ceremony, originally held for the lunar new year, was moved in 1652 so as not to coincide with the (monthly) death anniversary of the shogun Tokugawa Iemitsu. It was later decided to set the date to January 11th.

In this ceremony, as per the Shinto symbolism, the *mochi* represent a mirror (*kagami*) to "open" (*biraki*). By extension, we call *kagami-biraki* the opening of a sake barrel using a mallet because the same symbol is present in this gesture. It is said that the practice of *kagami-biraki* was popularized by shogun Tokugawa Ietsuna who opened a sake barrel to bring good luck to his troops before a battle from which he emerged victorious. Today *kagami-biraki* is practiced during weddings, inaugurations or sports competitions.

Commercialization

It is possible to buy a *taru* of sake directly from a *kura*. In this case, the *taru* is covered with a mat of rice straw (or "*komo*", today replaced by an interlacing of synthetic fibers) painted in the colors of the *kura*.

The casks thus covered are named "*honnidaru*" or "*komodaru*", as opposed to bare "*hadaka-taru*" casks. Apart from the aesthetic aspect, the *komo* and rope which cover the *honnidaru* maintain the *taru*'s lid and ensure a tight closing. It is in this form that *taru* were traditionally transported for sake trade.

This type of *taru* is part of traditional Japanese imagery and can be seen empty in front of sake stalls or Shinto temples. These are called "*kazaridaru*" (literally "decorative casks").

Taruzake can be either bought in a bottle (it is then a *taruzake binzume* (bottled)) or in a barrel (it is then a *taruzume*). In this second case, the aging duration depends on the buyer. If the sake is not drunk on one occasion, it continues to gain cedar aromas. To represent this phenomenon, the sake that remains in the barrel is named "*tarunaka*" then "*taruzoko*", respectively the "middle" and the "bottom" of the *taru*.

Kagami-biraki ritual today

Generally, the *komodaru* is prepared before the ceremony: its lid must be cleared of the straw mat that covers it, without cutting because of the negative symbolism it could bring. Then, the two strings surrounding the *taru* around the lid are lowered by a few centimeters to loosen their embrace. The lid is then removed with a mallet and a crowbar (or equivalent) and replaced by the "mirror": an uncovered lid that will easily dislocate under the blows of a gavel (*kizuchi*). It is quite possible to use as the "mirror" the original lid of the *taru* whose staves have been previously unriveted.

If originally the lid was probably broken with mallets, this practice is no longer really suitable for current ceremonies: imagine a bride splashed with sake when her husband finally breaks the solid cedar lid. Instead, "fake" reusable *komodaru*, whose interior consist of a small stainless steel basin, exist.

Once the *komodaru* is ready, a speech is usually given and then the "mirror" is "broken" using a small wooden mallet (*kizuchi*) to which are attached two ribbons, one white and the other red. Depending on the type of ceremony, several participants may hit the mirror at the same time (for example, the bride and groom). Once the sake is uncovered, it is served to the participants using a *hishaku* (traditional wooden ladle).

---

c. Japanese measurements units

The formats and measures used in the sake world are the traditional Japanese standards. These measurement units have their origin in the Chinese system, modified and unified during the Edo period, which saw the development of Japanese commerce and the merchant class. It would then be replaced by the metric system during the Meiji era.

The reference unit can be considered the "*koku*", defined as the quantity of rice needed to feed a man for one year, i.e. 150 kg. This unit served among other things to define the wealth of a *han* (region), the salary of a samurai, or the capacity of a boat.

Koku is derived from the "*go*" or 1/1000 of *koku*. At the time the quantities of rice were measured using "*masu*" (Japanese cedar boxes) of standard size. The 1 *go masu* being a very common object at the time, it is probably its (proven) use as a sake cup that has resulted in the use of this format as a reference.

$$1 \ go = 1/1000 \ koku = 150 \ \text{g of rice} \approx 180 \ \text{mL}$$

From the "*go*" being taken as the basic unit of measurement, follows:

- The **tokkuri**, a 1 or 2 *go* pitcher (180 or 360 mL),
- The **yongobin**, literally "4 *go* bottle" (720 mL),
- The **isshobin**, literally "1 *sho* bottle" (1 *sho* = 10 *go*, or 1.8 L),
- The **taru** of 1, 2 or 4 *to* (1 *to* = 100 *go* or 18 L).

Unit	Go	Sho	To	Koku
Character	合	升	斗	石
Value	180 mL	1.8 L	18 L	180 L

Table 21. Traditional Japanese measuring units (volume).

The *koku* is again at the top of the scale, this time as a unit of volume (1 *koku* = 1.000 *go* = 180 L). *Koku* is still used today to measure *kura*'s production capacity.

The most used aging containers are the 4 *go* bottle, the 1 *sho* isshobin, the 4 *to* taru and the 10 *koku* tank. The containers used on the market are the 4 *go* bottle, the 1 *sho* isshobin and the famous "sake cup" or glass of sake. Invented in 1964 by the Ozeki *kura* on the occasion of the Olympic Games, it consists of a sake glass closed by an aluminum operculum. Its capacity of 100 mL makes it one of the few containers deviating from the traditional canons.

f. Blending

Sake tanks produced in a given year are rarely bottled individually, but rather blended. Several blending methods with various objectives exist:

Blending sakes produced with identical methods

The goal here is to produce a larger volume of the same cuvee with homogeneous characteristics. If tanks were bottled and then marketed one after the other without prior blending, despite identical production methods, small differences could exist between batches.

Blending sakes produced with different yeasts or rice

Sake produced with different yeasts or rice are often blended to obtain a more complete and complex product. As a perfumer builds its scent with head and heart notes, a *toji* may decide to blend an aromatic sake and a richer sake.

Blending sakes produced in different years

The aim may be the homogeneity of the product from one year to another and/or greater complexity. As they age, some sakes get better (see Chapter IV "Sake Tasting", on the next page) and blending a fraction of aged sake in a younger sake can help give it some body and complexity. Few *kura* carry out this type of blending and it is generally reserved for high-end products, as only high quality sake improves over time. Sohomare and Kenbishi *kura* are the most famous *kura* for this type of blend.

Chapter IV

Sake Tasting

Chapter IV: Sake tasting

a. The different types of sake

A sake label, even a translated one, can be difficult to decipher if you do not know the main categories of sake. Here is a compendium:

i.   Official classification

The Japanese government recognizes three main quality terms for sake: *honjozo, junmai* and *ginjo*. These three types of sake are grouped under the term "*tokutei-meisho-shu*". It should be noted that for Japanese legislation, "*daiginjo*" is a subcategory of "*ginjo*".

The criteria for awarding these mentions (see Table 22, on the next page) concern the rice polishing rate, the addition of distilled alcohol and the color and taste of the product. This last obligation (flawless aroma and aspect) is reminiscent of the international "sound and fair merchantable quality". Any sake not belonging to one of these three categories is called *futsushu*.

Another sign of quality, "*tokubetsu*", can sometimes sneak in among these: *tokubetsu junmai* or *tokubetsu honjozo*. "*Tokubetsu*" means "special" and indicates that this sake was produced according to a specific and qualitative process. The process in question must be specified on the label but the scope is largely left to producers. The use of a *shuzo-koteki-mai* or a *seimaibuai* of 60% can, for example, constitute a criterion. In the latter case, the producer chooses to "downgrade" a sake that he could market as a *ginjo*. Motivations can be multiple; often it is to avoid having two *ginjo* in the range, which could confuse consumers.

Here's how to recognize these terms on a bottle:

Futsushu 普通酒

Honjozo 本醸造

Tokubetsu 特別

Junmai 純米

Ginjo 吟醸

Daiginjo 大吟醸

		Seimaibuai	Distilled alcohol	Quality
	Honjozo	≤ 70%	≤ 10% of rice weight	Good aroma, flawless aspect
Junmai	Junmai	-	0	Good aroma, flawless aspect
Junmai	Junmai Ginjo	≤ 60%	0	Good aroma, flawless aspect
Junmai	Junmai Daiginjo	≤ 50%	0	Distinctive flavor, very good aroma, flawless aspect
Ginjo	Ginjo	≤ 60%	≤ 10% of rice weight	Good aroma, flawless aspect
Ginjo	Daiginjo	≤ 50%	≤ 10% of rice weight	Distinctive flavor, very good aroma, flawless aspect

Table 22. Official classification of *tokutei-meisho-shu* sakes.
Source: National Tax Agency of Japan.

- The "qualities" as defined in the table refer to fair and merchantable quality, and the absence of defects.
- The above designations may not be assigned to sake produced with "non-graded" rice or equivalent quality (see "Rice quality assessment systems", p.67) or whose *koji-buai* is under 15%.
(Note that the old *seimaibuai* limitation of maximum 70% for *junmai* sake has been repealed.)

To be designated as "*futsushu*" is any product not meeting the criteria listed above but:
- under 22% ABV,
- resulting from the fermentation of rice, *kome-koji*, water and the following products (which cannot exceed 50% of the mass of rice used): *sakekasu*, acids, sugar, amino acids, sake (in addition as for *kijoshu*), alcohol and *shochu*.

Futsushu and *tokutei-meisho-shu* constitute the "*seishu*" category under the Japanese National Tax Agency regulations and can claim the "*Nihonshu*" Geographical Indication if they are produced in Japan, using Japanese ingredients.

ii. Other signs of quality

Other mentions, relating to the mode of production and thus to the quality of the sake, can be affixed on the labels. All these terms have already been mentioned throughout the book, and the various chapters related to the mode of production can be referred to for more details.

Amakuchi 甘口: sweet sake, a generic term also used for entry-level sake.

Arabashiri あらばしり: free-run sake obtained before an *assaku-ki* or *fune* pressing. This noble fraction of sake is highly regarded.

Genmaishu 玄米酒: sake produced with unpolished rice, rare and atypical.

Genshu 原酒: sake produced without water addition after pressing (or an addition modifying the degree of less than 1%), usually around 17-18% ABV.

Goseiseishu 合成清酒: synthetic sake produce without or almost without rice.

Hiyaoroshi ひやおろし: seasonal *nama-zume*, marketed in autumn.

Kasseishu 活性酒: sparkling *nama-nigorizake* marketed while still fermenting, should be drunk immediately.

Karakuchi 辛口 or *cho-karakuchi* 超辛口: dry to very dry sake whose *nihonshudo* is above +6. Those generic terms can be used for entry-level sake.

Kijoshu 貴醸酒: sake produced by replacing some of the *san-dan shikomi* water with sake. It is usually very sweet and aged for several years before sales.

Koshu 古酒, *jukuseishu* 熟成酒, *hizoshu* 秘蔵酒, *kokoshu* 古古酒 or 古々酒, *daikoshu* 大古酒: sakes aged before sales, the last three usually imply long aging, more than 5 years old.

Muroka 無濾過: sake produced without using activated charcoal.

Namazake 生酒, *nama-chozo* 生貯蔵, *nama-zume* 生詰: sake respectively produced without any pasteurization (*namazake*), without pasteurization before aging (*nama-chozo*) or without pasteurization before bottling (*nama-zume*). These sakes are fresh, juicy and aromatic but must be stored at low temperature and consumed quickly.

Nigorizake 濁り酒: cloudy sake, "unfiltered", often sweet, sometimes sparkling.

Shiboritate 搾立て: freshly pressed sake, often *nama* and lightly sparkling.

Shizukuzake 雫酒: sake obtained through *fukurozuri*, without pressing. This slow and costly process is only used for the most high-end sakes.

Taruzake 樽酒: sake aged in *sugi* barrels, with strong cedar aroma.

Zenkoji 全麹: sake produced with only *kome-koji*, sweet and usually aged before sales.

The former sake classification

In 1943 the Japanese Ministry of Finance introduced a classification of sake into three categories: Special, 1st Category and 2nd Category. By default, a sake was considered to belong to the 2nd category, unless the producer presented his sake to the Ministry for tasting and was certified as Special or 1st Category. Higher taxes levied on higher categories discouraged a significant portion of the producers who did not necessarily need the label to sell their products. For this reason, but also because of the logistical and political difficulties posed by such a system, it was abandoned in 1989.

Tokkyu 特級: Special   *Ikkyu* 一級: 1st Category   *Nikyu* 二級: 2nd Category

---

b. Sake and terroir

Since December 25, 2015, the term "*nihonshu*" has been recognized and protected as a "Geographical Indication" (GI) in Japan. Only sake produced in Japan from rice produced in Japan can therefore use the term "*nihonshu*".

The pressure of international trade rules, trade agreements and WTO should lead to a rapid and worldwide recognition of these GI. However, this is not Japan's first step towards recognizing the territoriality of sake. Since 2006, the term "Hakusan" (referring to the city of Hakusan in Ishikawa Prefecture) is also protected under the GI regime in Japan. Only five *sakagura* from the region (Tengumai, Kikuhime, Tedorigawa, Manzairaku and Kanaya Shuzo) can use this label. The existence of an American *sakagura* named "Hakusan sake garden" (closed in 2004) was probably not unrelated to the creation of this GI. Previously, four other attempts at geographical protection had emerged (Niigata, Hokkaido, Saga, and Nagano), inspired by the initiative of Niigata Prefecture in 1997: NIIGATA.O.C. These acronyms, inspired by the French AOC model, are not recognized by the Japanese government as GI but are locally controlled and protected by trademark law.

In 2016, after 2 years of administrative procedures, Yamagata became the first Japanese prefecture to benefit from an official GI for its sake, in recognition of its excellent water, cold winter and the local professionals' efforts for producing quality sake, especially *ginjoshu*, resulting in "silky and clear" sakes.

214   Classification

The terms and conditions may vary from region to region, but the criteria are the same: local rice and/or water, production in the region, evaluated by a pre-market tasting committee. Qualitative conditions such as maximum *seimaibuai* (60% for Niigata) can also complement these criteria.

All of these projects highlight the geography of sake and the existence of regional particularities. For all that, can we talk about terroir? The concept of terroir has four main dimensions: climate, soil, man, and plant. Let's study each of these elements in relation to sake.

1. Climate

The climate impacts both rice cultivation and sake production. As seen above, a cold climate was historically necessary for sake production to control fermentation temperatures. The use of air conditioning has lifted many constraints, but so far the geography of sake has seldom changed and rare are the *kura* in southern Japan.

In addition, the climate of a region strongly influences the possibility of cultivating a given variety of rice and the quality of the grain. The climate of a given year or "vintage" strongly influences sake through the quality of the rice produced (e.g. homogeneity, tendency to solubilization, see "Irrigated rice farming", p.35).

2. Soil

Rice is a cereal and one can doubt the impact of soil quality on grain quality. Nevertheless, the type of soil plays a fundamental role in the availability of nutrients for the plant and therefore in its development. For example, deep soils, rich in swelling clays (smectite and vermiculite), and the presence of silica-rich fossil woods, make Yokawa the most recognized region for the quality of its Yamadanishiki.

The soil (more precisely the subsoil) also plays a large role in the quality of the spring water (and therefore brewing water) available. In fact, spring waters load themselves with various mineral salts along their underground route according to the type of rock encountered (see "Water minerals ...", p.113).

3. Man

As seen above (see "*Toji* guilds", p.20), knowledge about sake production has long been passed on in regional guilds. This system favored the appearance of regional styles related to the production methods used by each guild. Although most guilds have now disappeared and knowledge has been democratized, the style of the main guilds remains.

The Nanbu Guild, originally from Iwate region, largely dominates the world of *toji* with one-third of affiliated *toji* and regular diploma courses. Also, its style can now be considered "classic": fine and aromatic sake, characteristic of the *ginjo* style and sake of the North of the archipelago. The Echigo Guild (from Niigata) is known for its "*tanrei-karakuchi*" style: dry and light, almost crystalline, with a clean finish. The Tanba Guild, originally from Hyogo Prefecture, tends to promote a "masculine" style: aromatic, powerful and rich in umami. The Noto Guild, originally from Ishikawa Prefecture, is known to produce juicy and aromatic sakes with a short finish, and so on. Small differences in *koji* production or fermentation temperature are at the root of these styles.

Although a guild-affiliated *toji* may practice in another region, few are those who emigrate because the guilds that survive today and form *toji* are all based near the major labor pools (the main producing regions) of sake. In addition, if all the competent *toji* are able to produce sake by disregarding the traditional style of their guild, one generally finds some common traits in all of their production.

Thus, although their influence has greatly diminished, guilds still impose their mark today in the regional style of sake, playing a role in the definition of sake terroirs.

4. Plant

Rice varieties are at the crossroads of the three factors mentioned above: selected by humans to adapt to a given soil and climate, they can be at the foundation of a regional style: Gohyakumangoku has become part of Niigata *tanrei-karakuchi* style thanks to its light, fruity and elegant style, the same goes for Miyamanishiki in Nagano.

All these elements plead for the existence of real sake terroirs. The presence and even dominance of "standardized" products obtained from modern methods (standard rice variety imported from other regions, corrected water, air conditioning, etc.) does not in any way call this truth into question. Sakes produced locally using local ingredients are called "*jizake*". If this name was obsolete and a bit negative when fashion in the 20th century was for the so-called "modern" methods, it is regaining its credentials in the 21st.

The geographical analysis of the technical data highlights the relevance of this regional analysis. Figure 20, below, shows that major trends in style can be seen along the North-South and East-West axes.

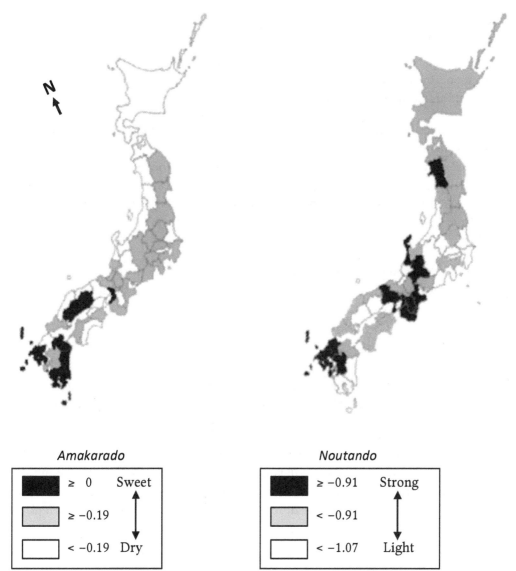

Figure 20. Regional variations of *amakarado* and *noutando*.
Source: National Tax Agency of Japan.

Hirezake: an atypical sake

An atypical method of serving sake that illustrates the excellent relationship between sake and fish is the famous "*hirezake*". This sake is served hot, containing a dried and grilled dorsal fin of a "*fugu*" fish, the famous Japanese deadly fish. Fortunately for the sake enthusiast, the *fugu* fins are never toxic. The grilled fin brings to sake both pleasant roasted notes and an interesting visual aspect.

c. When to drink sake?

In Japan, sake is consumed on all occasions, usually accompanied by *sakana*, literally "sake food", the equivalent of our appetizers. The first and simplest *sakana* is the salt that could traditionally be offered as a side dish for sake.

There is no real culture of "marrying" food and sake in Japan, but rather the idea that sake should not interfere with food and rather support it. Since the style of sake has developed for centuries in contact with local cuisine, the question was not really to know which sake to choose, as local sake or *jizake* was a perfect match with local food. As a result, coastal sake tends to be fresh and elegant to match seafood, while sake from central Japan is quite rich, and go well with meat and dried or salted products.

Sake is an ideal companion for an aperitif, but also throughout the meal. A general rule for marrying dishes and sake is to choose a sake whose richness and power equal that of the dish.

1. Seafood

Of course, the first association that comes to mind with sake is the sake/sushi or sake/sashimi combination. Although working perfectly with elegant *ginjo* sakes, it is a somewhat reductive vision of the place of sake at the table.

On all types of seafood, sake is a good substitute for white wine, avoiding the formation of certain negative fishy flavors. This is mainly due to the absence in sake of iron and sulphites (present in wine), which can produce certain aromatic aldehydes in contact with fish. The difference is substantial for the saltiest or iodized seafood: sea urchins, oysters, fish roe, dried fish, etc.

2. Meat

With meat, better serve a sake with a little body and strength. The umami-rich sakes (*junmai*, and traditional *moto*) are particularly suited to red meats and game birds. Avoid overly sweet sakes that might make for a heavy combination.

Sake and charcuterie is an amazing combination to discover. The sake umami emphasizes that of charcuterie while the saltiness blends in. Choose a sake whose power is equal to that of the chosen ham or sausage: *kimoto junmai* for a Spanish ham, a wild boar or donkey sausage, *daiginjo* for a "San Daniele" ham or rosette.

3. Cheese

Just like charcuterie, and for the same reasons, cheese goes perfectly with sake: goat cheese with an aromatic *ginjo*, aged cheeses with a traditional *shubo* or *koshu*, washed rinds and blue cheeses with a sweet sake such as *zenkoji* or *kijoshu*. Soft cheeses are often an exception to the rule.

d. How to choose your sake?

Now knowing all types of sake and their method of production, the technical terms of labeling and the style of sake you want to serve your guests; but you do not feel much more confident when the fateful moment of choice is in front of you. Looking for a lightly earthy *yamahai* to accompany your ribeye with mushroom, but where to buy it? How to choose a brand? How much to spend?

Outside Japan, availability may be limited. However, more and more specialty shops and wine shops are offering a selection of sakes. Online stores have blossomed in recent years and if you make preparations in advance, it is perfectly possible to get a bottle of sake that corresponds to your needs.

The notion of price is decisive for sake. Excellent sake can be found in Japan for a price ranging from 1500 yen to 6000 yen (10 to 60 $/€/£), transport costs and importers margin tend to double or triple the price to 30-150 $/€/£. The good news is that the great crisis crippling Japanese sake since the 1970s, combined with technical progress and an industry renewal have eliminated most bad products.

With rare exceptions, including some cooking sakes produced outside Japan (check the labels, some are good such as "Les larmes du Levant" in France or SakeOne in the USA (OR)), all the sake offered on the market are good. In addition, apart from some "good plans" and some fashionable sake, their price is an honest reflection of their quality.

The question of the style remains; each *kura* has its own methods that make its signature style. Here, no other solution exists than to taste and form your own opinion. Don't rely too much on guides, taste is personal and you are the only person to know what you really like. But if you like a sake, explore the other cuvee of the same *kura*, it's a safe bet that you will find something else you enjoy in the range. Similarly, observe if your tastes are rather about certain categories of sake, certain regions or some rice, you will undoubtedly find sakes that you will appreciate by analogy. In that regard, do trust your regular dealer if they understand what you like.

e. Serving sake

i.   Etiquette

The rules of Japanese good manners are quite specific and sake is not exempt from these. If everyone is free to drink his own way in Western countries, and if the Japanese are always indulgent towards foreigners, it is still always good to know how to behave.

The consumption of sake in Japan has always been considered as a social act. From the Heian period (794-1185) appeared formal banquets during which sake was consumed in a single cup that circulated from hand to hand in an order established by the protocol. This type of banquet was slowly formalized until the 14th century with the appearance of *honzen-ryori* or "meal on tray". Three formal passages of the cup constitute the prelude to the actual meal, served on trays placed in front of each guest. The cup continues to circulate during the meal, and well after for libations usually accompanied by shows (of music, dancing, poems).

Today, the social aspect of sake and drinking in general remains imprinted in Japanese culture and drinking alone or even serving oneself is frowned upon. Thus, at a banquet, each guest serves his neighbors and waits to be served by them in return. This mutual service, called "*o-shaku*", is the best-known sake "ritual".

In practice, a sort of ballet is played then, each taking care of the cup of his neighbor, competing politely to "snatch" the carafe from the hands of the "server" to serve him back, heavy drinkers desperately seeking a cup to fill to indicate their thirst and small drinkers gently raising their cup while being served to stop the flow while taking care to leave some space in their cup so that a friend can signify his thirst by pouring them a few drops. This practice explains the smallness of sake cups, allowing diners to take turns pouring each other numerous times over the course of an evening.

During service, carafe and glasses are always raised with both hands, one holding the object and the other placed underneath as if to support it lightly. Serve or receiving sake with one hand may seem too casual.

The more or less formal application of the rules of *o-shaku* depends on the context, the age, the intimacy and the degree of intoxication of the guests. Paradoxically to serve oneself can be a great mark of relaxation and thus of friendship.

During the same evening, several sakes can be presented. The order of service may surprise Western consumers who tend to present products from the entry-level to the most prestigious. However high-end sakes are often the finest and guests may not appreciate all their subtlety at the end of service. It is therefore classic to serve sakes from the most prestigious to the most standard. This allows the drinkers both to fully appreciate the quality of the best sake and to finish the evening with a simple and comforting, sometimes hot, sake.

ii. Serving temperature

One of the unique characteristics of sake is its ability to reveal new facets at different temperatures. There are at least 11 designations covering service temperatures between 0 °C and more than 55 °C (see table opposite).

Of these, the most commonly used are *atsu-kan* for hot sake and *suzu-hie* for cold sake.

Temperature		Japanese name	Meaning
°C	°F		
55+	130+	*Tobikiri-kan*	Extreme
50-55	120-130	*Atsu-kan*	Hot
45-50	113-120	*Jyoh-kan*	Warm
40-45	105-113	*Nuru-kan*	Lukewarm
35-40	95-105	*Hitohada-kan*	Body temp.
30-35	85-95	*Hinata-kan*	Sun warmed
15-30	60-85	*Jo-on*	Room temp.
10-15	50-60	*Suzu-hie*	Cool
5-10	40-50	*Hana-hie*	Flower
0-5	30-40	*Yuki-hie*	Snow
-5	20	*Mizore-zake*	Sleet (slush)

Table 23. Sake serving temperatures.

1. How does temperature impact perception?

Temperature has an impact on both the perception of taste and the perception of aromas. Heat favors the perception of sweetness and umami, while cold favors saltiness and bitterness. It seems that acid perception is not very temperature-dependent. Aromas are volatile molecules that are released into the ambient air at a certain temperature. Whereas lighter molecules can be released at low temperatures, larger molecules need more energy and therefore more heat.

By heating the sake, we therefore favor the evaporation of these heavier aromas that we would not have been able to perceive otherwise. Heating also promotes the perception of the most present aromas, including alcohol.

2. How to choose a serving temperature for a given sake?

Traditionally, sake was always drunk hot, and there are still some diehards who say that this is the only acceptable way to drink sake. However, with the refinement of production methods, the need to erase the aromatic defects of sake by warming disappeared. Indeed, it was at the Emperor's Court that sake was served cold for the first time.

As a general rule, it should be remembered that the most aromatic sakes are ideally served *suzu-hie* (beware, too low a temperature will freeze the aromas) while richer sakes are served at room temperature or hot. In this field, nothing replaces experience and personal taste, and I can not invite you enough to try serving the same sake at different temperatures. Still, on the following page is a base of advised sake serving temperatures, according to category. These recommendations are, of course, valid for a standard sake of a given category because, as you know now, not all of them are.

3. How to warm sake?

Traditionally, quality establishments had an *o-kan-ban* or hot sake specialist. The job of this employee was to serve each sake at the right temperature, according to the client's requests or habits. This function was highly recognized, just as the sommelier role can be in Western countries.

The drop in sake consumption and the development of sake being served cold have relegated this function to obsolete folklore but it carries the myth of a complex and risky technical act. Fortunately for all sake lovers, this is not the case if you follow a few simple rules: sake must be warmed slowly, homogeneously and under 65 °C / 149 °F. Here is the accepted best method:

1. Pour the sake to heat in a pitcher made of metal or ceramic (see "Glassware" on the next page). Ideally the sake should be at room temperature.

2. Place the pitcher in a boiling water bath. The water level must reach at least half the height of the pitcher. There is no point in continuing to heat the water while the sake is in the water bath.

3. If you have a thermometer available, wait until the sake reaches the desired temperature. Otherwise, 2 to 5 minutes are sufficient depending on the desired temperature, the volume to be heated and the type of pitcher (a metal pitcher leads to better heat and warms the sake faster). You can taste the sake as you go to check its temperature.

4. Serve, if possible, in previously warmed glasses (in the oven or in the microwave, for example).

Temperature			Futsushu Honjozo	Junmai	Ginjo Daiginjo	Nama Nigori	Genshu	Taru	Koshu
Atsu-kan	50 °C	125 °F	●	●				○	
Hitohada-kan	35 °C	95 °F	○	○	○			○	●
Jo-on	20 °C	70 °F	○	○	○		○	●	○
Suzu-hie	10 °C	50 °F	●	●	●	●	●	●	●
Yuki-hie	0 °C	30 °F				○	●		

Table 24. Serving temperature of the different sake categories.

● : ideal   ○ : good   empty: not recommended

This simple system has the merit of being very adaptable. For example, it is perfectly possible to heat a bottle of sake in a simple hotel room electric kettle.

However, you may wish to heat your sake by other methods: it is possible to use an oven (conventional or microwave), a direct flame, or any other method involving a heat source. Just keep in mind that the warming should be gradual and the sake should not boil. If sake vapors escape the pitcher, it's pretty hot already.

iii.   Glassware

1. Decanters

When sake was still transported and stored in jars or barrels, it was presented and served in carafes, the four main types of which are: *tokkuri* (ceramic bottle), *chirori* (metal pitcher), *katakuchi* (ceramic cup) and *chioshi* (lacquered wooden teapot).

The shape and material of these containers may change but the four described here are the most typical. The *tokkuri*, quite common, could be used to buy and carry sake from a dealer. *Chirori* is generally used to heat sake because the metal easily conducts heat and its shape is adapted. *Katakuchi* and *chioshi* are utensils of service exclusively, the latter being traditionally reserved for ceremonies.

Today, sake is almost exclusively marketed in bottles, so it can be served directly and the use of a carafe has become superfluous. Thus, the choice to use a carafe arise more out of aesthetic considerations than practical ones.

2. Glasses and cups

The choice of glass for a tasting depends on the context, the sake and its temperature of service. To help you in this choice, here are some of the main containers at your disposal:

Ceramic *choko* or *guinomi*

Ceramic is the most used material for sake cups. This container can be criticized for the thickness of its rim and its shape, which are not suited to the expression of aromas, but the pleasure of using a beautiful piece of ceramic will always enhance the pleasure of the taster.

There are many traditional forms, among which are the *tsutsu-gata* with vertical edges, the *soba-choko* with slightly flared edges, the open *wan-gata* and the very open *hira-gata*, the stemmed *bajohai*, the hexagonal *rokaku* or the *tenmoku* with its typical glaze. Choose from this variety of shapes, materials and colors, the style that suits you.

There is a specific type of *choko*, the "*kikichoko*", made of white porcelain, whose bottom is decorated with two concentric blue circles. These *choko* are frequently used in *kura* and professional tastings as the alternation of blue and white allow the drinker to easily observe the color and turbidity of the sake.

"Amber" glass

"Amber" glass is a type of brown-orange glass with straight edges, used in professional tastings instead of *kikichoko*, when tasters want to disguise the sake's visual features. This type of glass is not interesting outside these special tastings.

Metal or glass *choko* and *guinomi*

Metal and glass conducts heat and allows the taster to feel the temperature of the sake served through the cup. These are not classic materials for *choko*, however many Western liquor glasses can be converted to beautiful sake glasses.

Wooden *masu*

The *masu* is a utility object related to rice measurement (see "Japanese measurements units", p.208), sometimes used in sake service. It exists in raw or lacquered wood. Some raw cedar *masu* flavor the sake they contain. Neither its shape nor its material are ideal for tasting sake and it is not recommended in this context. We can however appreciate the traditional features of the object and try the experiment.

Lacquered wood *sakazuki*

This is a ceremonial cup of a very delicate form. Some magnificent examples exist. Its large surface emphasizes the main aromas of the sake and disperses the others while the smoothness of the rim refines mouthfeel. It is perfectly adapted to aromatic sakes such as *daiginjo*.

"Tulip" glasses

"Tulip" glasses have appeared very recently in the world of sake, driven by the desire for modernization and the influence of wine. The tulip shaped glasses concentrate the aromas and therefore focus on the nose as opposed to the traditional approach of sake tasting that focus especially on the mouth. For this reason they are especially suited to aromatic sakes or professional tastings.

> **Forms and perception**
>
> The shape of a glass changes the perception of aroma and taste of sake:
>
> - A wide open rim ("v"-shaped) disperses the aromas and encourages large sips, enhancing the sake body on the palate. It is therefore suitable for full-bodied and lightly aromatic sakes (or *junshu*, see Figure 21, p.237).
>
> - A tightened rim concentrates the aromas but only delivers a fine trickle of sake. It is therefore suitable for aromatic and light sake (or *kunshu*).
>
> In addition, a fine rim (glass, metal or wood versus ceramic) is perceived by the lips and influences the taster, emphasizing the elegance of the sake. Also, different materials conduct heat at different speeds, from the most conducting to the least: metal, glass, ceramic, wood. Provided that you touch the part of the cup that contain sake, this will highly influence your perception of a warm or cold sake.

f. Storing your sake

Sakes are systematically marketed when ready to drink. However, one may wish to store them, either for short periods waiting for the right drinking opportunity, or for aging purposes. In both cases, here are the main rules for storing sake:

i. Storage conditions

1. Light

Like wine, sake is sensitive to light rays, so it is necessary to keep it away from light, especially daylight that contains ultraviolet (see "Manganese", p.113).

This explains why most sake bottles are tinged with a deep green or brown color that blocks some of the light rays.

2. Temperature

Kura choose to keep their sake at different temperatures depending on the speed and type of aging desired (see "Aging", p.198). However, in a basic approach and for the consumer who only seeks to keep his sake as close to its initial qualities, it is advisable to keep sake at around 4 °C / 39 °F. In most cases, a simple refrigerator is sufficient but as the number of stored bottles increases, the purchase of a dedicated refrigerator or refrigerated cellar is required.

As with wine, the consistency of the storage temperature is fundamental: sudden variations can be particularly damaging, but seasonal variations of a few degrees do not cause harm.

3. Humidity

The caps used for sake are not as sensitive to moisture as cork. Also, moist storage conditions for sake are not as important as in wine. However, for long storage, it is best to avoid too dry places that could cause some harmful evaporation.

4. Position

Two types of stoppers are mainly used for sake bottles: screw caps and a mixed plastic/aluminum "T" plug. The latter, more rare, is used on almost all *isshobin*.

In both cases, it is best to keep the bottle upright, especially for long periods. Unlike wine cork stoppers, these do not need to be in contact with the liquid to keep them watertight.

In addition, and despite the food quality of the materials used, the seals are made of plastic whose contact with sake is not desirable. Moreover, unlike wine, everything is done in the sake production line to keep sake bottles vertical: crates, shelves, refrigerators, etc. despite the resulting loss of space.

ii.   Drink or age?

1. Sake with aging potential

Sakes with the best cellaring potential are the richest sakes with deep aromas but deep rice polishing (*seimaibuai* <60%). The following characteristics are positive for aging: traditional *moto* (*kimoto* and *yamahai*), *junmai, muroka, genshu,* certain varieties of rice (such as Yamadanishiki and Omachi), etc.

The following characteristics are not good for aging: *sokujyo, nama, nigori,* sparkling, *aruten,* etc.

The *ginjo* and *daiginjo* tend to better sustain aging because of their polishing and careful attention to their production, but the *ginjo-ka* disappear quickly during aging. The less aromatic *ginjo* are therefore more appropriate for bottle aging.

Koshu sakes have been specially aged in the *kura*. It is therefore not necessary to age them longer. This is also often the case with *kijoshu* sakes. If they have not been aged previously, they are however excellent candidates.

2. Containers

The size of the opening of a sake bottle varies little depending on the size of the bottle. Also, exchanges, including oxygen, which may take place with the external environment are more or less constant while the amount of sake inside the bottle changes.

For this reason, a sake will age more slowly in an *isshobin* than in a smaller bottle. So it is best to buy the sake you want to age in *isshobin*.

3. Aging time

At present, the vast majority of sake is produced for consumption in the year following bottling, all bottles bearing this indication (see the insert "Age indications on sake bottles", next page). *Kura* usually age themselves the sakes they consider to be age-worthy. Thus, *kijoshu* for example, are marketed after an aging ranging from a few years to a few decades.

However, aging sakes within the *kura* requires a large capital immobilization and therefore represents a cost. In addition, drinking sake young or old is also a matter of personal preference. Also aging sake outside the *kura* can be interesting.

However, the subject is complex, highly dependent on consumer taste, product and storage conditions, and there is no better advice than personal experience in this area. As part of a first attempt at aging, it is best to choose a low aromatic *yamahai* or *kimoto*, *junmai* sake, for aging 2 to 3 years at 4 °C /39 °F or in a conventional refrigerator, away from any light.

iii.   A special case: keeping open bottles

Once opened, a bottle of sake can keep its qualities from a few days to several months depending on the type of sake. As with aging, it is the most delicate flavors (*ginjo-ka*) that disappear first. Thus, more rustic sakes with deep aromas or having already undergone a first aging will keep longer. As a general rule, it may be considered that a duration of 2 weeks after opening is reasonable. Beyond that, the risks of deterioration are important.

Ideally, the bottle should be kept upright, cool and protected from light; a fridge door is perfectly suited. Using a neutral gas or a vacuum cap can somewhat extend the life of the bottle.

Age indications on sake bottles

Two types of dates are found on a sake bottle: the official date and the "BY" date.

The first is a legal obligation and takes the form of a year and month according to the Japanese or Western calendar. For June 2016 it reads for example: "28年6月", "28.6", "2016.6" or "16.6". This date is the date on which the sake was bottled "for sales purposes". Thus, in the case of sakes aged in bottles within the *kura*, this date corresponds to the date of first marketing (labeling). We can therefore consider that, according to the *kura*, this sake is ready to be consumed from this date on. It is therefore a starting point for any consumer wishing to age his sake in the bottle.

The second date is, again for 2016, in the form "28BY" or "H28BY", the 28th year of the Heisei era (current Japanese era since 1989 = H1). The acronym "BY" is the abbreviation for "brewing year". This date indicates the year of production and can be compared with a "vintage".

Historically, the production year began on October 1st (Nihonshu no Hi), after the new rice harvest and extended throughout the winter before the production crews returned to the fields in the spring. Modern air conditioning and permanent employees are now able to produce sake throughout the year, and the production year officially begins on July 1st.

Thus, a sake produced in spring 2016 will be considered as produced during the 2015 "season" (27BY). This gap can be justified by the rice harvest from which sake is produced (autumn 2015). On the other hand, a sake produced during the summer of 2016 with this same rice will be considered as produced during the 2016 season (28BY), so the year of rice production is not a rule.

A third indication may appear on the label, this is the duration of aging for sake aged more than one year in the *kura*. The age of sake is expressed in years of aging, rounded down. Age indication for blended sake must corespond to the youngest sake of the blend.

g. Sake tasting

As with other alcoholic drinks, sake tasting (or *kikizake*) takes place in four stages: eye, nose, mouth and finish. On the other hand, quality evaluation criteria are specific to sake. For the sake-taster wannabe, it is important not to copy a reading grid or criteria from other alcoholic drinks.

i.   Appearance

1. Color

The color of a sake can go from a very light yellow, almost transparent, to brown. When it has just been squeezed, sake has a slight green glow that disappears quickly during aging.

The main pigments in sake are: flavins from rice or produced by sake microorganisms, ferrichrysin formed in the presence of iron in water, and compounds derived from Maillard reactions involving sugars and amino acids.

The sake's color is therefore an indicator of its richness (sugar and umami) and its possible aging. A very lightly colored sake is rather a sign of a light sake (*honjozo* or *ginjo*), a slightly deeper color indicates a deeper sake (*junmai*) and a brown hue is the sign of a rich and aged sake (*koshu, kijoshu* or *zenkoji*).

The color has little impact on the overall quality assessment, however it is generally expected that sake will reflect its aromatic characteristics. If the color of the sake is darker than expected, this may be a sign of bad storage conditions that can be confirmed in the nose or mouth.

Some sakes have a pink hue due to the use of a specific yeast. This is an extremely rare case.

2. Turbidity

Apart from *nigorizake*, a sake has to be perfectly clear.

In the case of *nigori*, the sediments present in the glass can range from a thin white *haze* to a creamy or granular texture. This does not bode well for the quality of the sake but can identify the type of *nigori*. For a fine turbidity one can speak of "*usunigori*".

3. Effervescence

Apart from the particular case of sparkling sakes, some sakes have a fine effervescence. These are usually young sake, sometimes unpasteurized.

In the case of sparkling sakes, it may be interesting to evaluate the amount and fineness of the bubbles and the persistence of the foam. These impressions will be related to the sensation in the mouth. However, effervescence is highly dependent on the container. In addition, sparkling sakes are so unusual and their production methods so diverse that it is difficult to compare them.

4. Legs and tears

The tears or legs of the sake are the drops coming down the walls of a glass after swirling it. Their aspect depends in particular on the viscosity of the sake (degree of alcohol, sugar, etc.). If the observation of tears had its hour of glory in the world of wine, it is actually very uninformative and impractical in a sake cup.

ii. Aroma

The fashion of *ginjo* has put aromatic sake front of stage. However, outside this category, the aromatic profile is not regarded as a fundamental aspect. This explains the shape of sake cups such as *sakazuki* that do not emphasize the aromas. Apart from *ginjo*, a discreet aromatic is not necessarily a defect as long as it is pleasant.

A good sake must have a clear, distinct and clean aroma. The fruity and floral aromas are the most classic. Some aromas are markers and special attention should be paid to them:

Lactic notes: They are the marker of a traditional *shubo* (*yamahai*, *kimoto*, etc,). The buttery or yeasty notes are desirable but they should not dominate or lean towards cheese or perspiration.

Rice notes: They are rather rare, even for *junmai* sakes. They usually indicate the use of a powerful rice, such as Omachi.

Koji **(Mushroom/Chestnut) notes**: Apart from *zenkoji* sakes, they are quite rare. These relatively heavy aromas are more desirable in rich sake (*junmai*, *yamahai*, etc.). They can, however, bring a welcomed complexity if they are unobtrusive.

Cedar notes: Apart from *taruzake* for which they are sought, they may be the sign of new cedar equipment within the *kura* and are then considered a defect. The aroma of cedar is complex and consists of a set of molecules of the terpenes family including sesquiterpenoids and diterpenes.

Sulphured notes: They are negative and often the sign of overaged or poorly stored sake (*hineka*).

Spicy notes: They are rather rare and the sign of a "high" temperature fermentation (as opposed to *ginjo*). They are not negative, as long as they remain discreet and pleasant.

Aging notes: Apart from deliberately aged sakes, they are negative.

In the case of *ginjo* sakes, the aromatic must be explosive. The main markers of *ginjo* are green apple, exotic fruits (pineapple), ripe banana and rose. For more details on the constituent molecules of these flavors, see "Fermentation aromas ", p.172, "*Koji* aromas", p.110, and "Organoleptic changes", p.199.

iii.   Taste

The palate is the most important part of the tasting. Several dimensions are studied but it is the balance between them that makes a quality sake. A sake, even if it can be rich, should not be heavy in order to be easily drunk and rinse the palate.

1. Flavors

The complexity and the aromatic power are not prerequisites of quality. A very delicate, almost watery sake can be appreciated for its crystalline fluidity while an overly complex flavor can be considered as a mess.

We generally find in the mouth an aromatic profile close to that of the nose and the different aromatic notes described for the nose are valid for the taste. A sake will be judged negatively if the two sensations are dissociated and, just like on the nose, it is fundamental to present a clear and flawless aromatic.

2. Acidity

As can be seen from Table 17, below, the acidity of sake is highly variable and has multiple origins.

	Average concentration (mg/L)	Yeasts	*Koji*	Lactic acid bacteria
Succinic acid	200-500	+++	+	
Lactic acid	200-700	++	++	+++
Malic acid	100-400	++	++	
Acetic acid	50-100	+++	++	+
Pyruvic acid	15-100	+	+	+
Citric acid	80-100	+	+++	
Fumaric acid	10-20	+	+	

Table 17. The organic acids of sake.

A strong acidity is usually the mark of a traditional *shubo* (lactic), an old type of yeast (malic) or an atypical *koji* (citric). With experience, it is possible to partially recognize these acid profiles and to deduce some clues about the production methods.

Lactic acid has a relatively mild acidity, malic acid is more persistent and citric acid emphasizes lemony notes. Acetic acid, for its part, is recognizable by its vinegary aroma, which can bring complexity to a sake but quickly becomes negative at high concentrations (especially if it exceeds one third of the lactic acid concentration).

The acidity must balance the sweetness of the sake to maintain a certain freshness. For this reason, highly acidifying yeasts are generally used for the production of very sweet sakes such as *kijoshu*. The acidity of a sake, however, should not be overly marked: it is on average 10 times lower than that of a wine (pH 3-4 for a wine, 4-5 for a sake), so do not expect the same freshness/tension.

3. Sweetness

Depending on the *nihonshudo*, a different level of sweetness is expected. A very dry sake (*karakuchi* or *cho-karakuchi*) must be sharp and clear. For a sweet sake (*amakuchi, kijoshu, zenkoji*, etc.) the sugar impression must be integrated into the rest of the body and should not be cloying.

Apart from these extreme cases, sake should appear neither sweet nor dry, and the sweetness should only contribute to a round, full bodied palate.

4. Alcohol

Alcohol should not be overly present, which can be the case with *genshu* over 18% ABV or when the addition of alcohol has been poorly controlled: a significant dilution can emaciate the sake and bring out the burning of the alcohol.

This is one of the reasons why *yon-dan* is commonly used to "compensate" for alcohol additions.

5. Umami

Umami is the fifth taste. It indicates the presence of amino acids and is perceived as "savory" (think of dry Parmesan cheese, tomato, biscuits or grilled meats). Umami is an important concept in sake, especially for *junmai* and low polished rice.

Sakes with *amino-sando* under 1 are low in umami and called *tanrei* or "light". Conversely, sakes having an *amino-sando* greater than 2 are called *noujun* or "rich". Sakes too rich in amino acids or poorly stored are unbalanced and present a note called *zatsumi*, mixture of bitterness and umami.

6. Texture

The texture impression is often linked to other characteristics mentioned above: acidity, umami, alcohol. We are talking more specifically about trigeminal sensations that are related to astringency, sediments and effervescence.

Astringency or *shibumi* can give a chewy texture and a welcome thickness to some *junmai* sakes. However, it is a relatively rare and undesirable feature when it is overly present. Bitterness or *nigami* is always negative.

The sediments of *nigori* sakes can be very variable, both in quantity and quality, depending on the desired style. However they must always bring a textural element (e.g. milky or creamy) and integrate into the sake without dominating.

Effervescence is present in sparkling sakes, some *nama nigori* and young sake. Depending on the style of sake a greater or lesser presence of bubbles is expected but in any case, the bubbles must bring freshness to the sake and not provide a pungent sensation but rather a thin evanescent foam.

7. Finish

The finish is one of the reasons for the misunderstanding between wine and sake tasters: for sake, a long finish (persistence) is not essential. A clean finish without aftertaste, called "*kire*", is particularly appreciated because it will not disturb the aromas of the dish that follows.

In another style, more powerful, a persistent and pleasant finish called "*shirinpin*", or "*pin*", can also be sought.

iv.   A global approach to sake tasting

Through evolution, the development of taste has allowed humans to distinguish the foods that are beneficial to them: bitterness and acidity are indicators of toxicity or low nutritional value (green fruits for example) while sweetness and umami indicate the presence of nutrients (respectively, sugars and amino acids). The first two are therefore instinctive repulsors while the last two attract us naturally (the appetence of children and even newborns for sugar is universal).

On these four dimensions, sake is placed as the most "physiological" alcoholic drink: 10 times less acidic than wine, without beer-like bitterness, and rich in sugars and amino acids. This is what makes it an "easy to drink" alcohol and fully justifies a certain traditional approach to its consumption: <u>sake is meant to be drunk</u>.

The set of analytical tasting elements described in this chapter reveal a desire to describe and analyze from a professional or Western approach. The traditional vocabulary of sake tasting contains more negative terms than positive terms, highlighting the search for a certain ataraxia or perfection by the absence of defects, which would define a perfect balance between all the elements of the sake.

The spirit of sake can thus be summed up by a term, which is added to those analyzed in this chapter, the "*nodogoshi*" that could be translated as the way sake "goes down". This is the feeling given by sake when it is swallowed. Ideally, it should be soft, as easy to swallow as water. The set of descriptors given above thus become almost secondary.

Sake can then be categorized according to two dimensions: aromatic power and taste power.

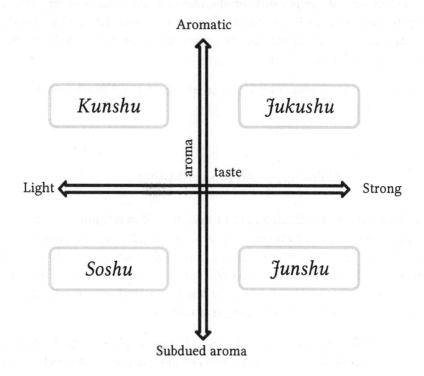

Figure 21. A simple categorization of sakes by their taste profile.

We can easily distribute the known categories of sake in these four styles. *Futsushu* and *honjozo*, simple and easy to drink are *soshu*. *Ginjo*, aromatic and light, are *kunshu*. *Junmai*, rich and powerful are *junshu*. Old sakes *koshu*, *kijoshu*, etc. are *jukushu*.

However, it is interesting to note that while the traditional categories (*futsushu*, *honjozo*, *junmai*, *ginjo*) imply a qualitative judgment, this is not the case here. These four terms give us a tasting lesson: each style is respectable and beautiful sakes can be found in all categories. Do not confine yourself to prestigious sakes and appreciate elegance, finesse, evanescence as well as power, savoriness and length.

Good tasting,

Kanpai !

Gautier Roussille

Glossary

This glossary describes briefly the main technical terms of this book. For a more detailed explanation of each term, go to the referenced page.

Aerobic: which involves oxygen **p.120**

Aikoji: *kurabito* assistant to the *taichi* **p.94**

Akami-taru: classic red *taru* as opposed to *koutsuki-taru* **p.206**

Alkaline: syn. of basic, chemical opp. of acidic

Amakarado: taste indicator combining *nihonshudo* and *sando* **p.158**

Amakuchi: sweet sake **p.183**

Amazake: sweet beverage, blend of water with rice and *kome-koji* or *sakekasu*, low or non-alcoholic **p.185**

Amino acids: molecules that constitute proteins **p.93**

Amino-sando: measurement of amino acids in sake **p.160**

Amylopectin: large and branched type of starch molecule **p.30**

Amylose: small and straight type of starch molecule **p.30**

Anaerobic: which involves an absence of oxygen **p.120**

Anka: use of heaters for *shubo* warming **p.128**

Arabashiri: free-run sake from *assaku-ki* or *fune* presses **p.187**

Aruten: sake with added alcohol, opp. of *junmai* **p.182**

Aspergillus oryzae: scientific name of *koji* mold **p.95**

Atsu-kan: hot sake **p.222**

Awa: lit. "foam", formed during fermentation **p.147**

Awamorishu: traditional Japanese distilled spirit (Okinawa) **p.105**

Baijiu: Chinese distilled spirit, improperly named sake **p.10**

Bara-koji: modern *kome-koji* as opposed to *mochi-koji* **p.96**

Bin-ire: bottle pasteurization **p.196**

BY: acronym for «Brewing Year », vintage **p.229**

Capron-san: ethyl hexanoate, fresh fruit aroma, base of *ginjo-ka* **p.172**

Chioshi: wooden lacquered teapot used for (ceremoniously) serving sake **p.225**

Chirori: metal pitcher used to warm and serve sake **p.225**

Cho: length unit ($\approx$110 m) also a surface (1 $cho^2 \approx$ 1 ha) **p.34**

Cho-karakuchi: very dry sake **p.213**

Choko: type of sake cup **p.225**

Conidia: asexual reproduction spore for mold/mushrooms **p.97**

Conidiophore: asexual reproductive organs carrying conidia **p.97**

Croze: groove holding the barrel head or bottom **p.206**

Daiginjo: sake with a *seimaibuai* under 50% **p.213**

Daimyo: Japanese local lord, governing a *han* **p.21**

Daki-daru: *shubo* warming method using *daki* **p.128**

Dango: balls of sweet *mochi* (delicacy) **p.110**

Deijo-kobo: type of marketed selected yeasts **p.151**

Dekoji: *koji* production step **p.101**

Doburoku: "homemade" sake, unfiltered, acidic and low in alcohol **p.191**

Dougumawashi: *kurabito* in charge of cleaning **p.94**

Doyo-no-Ushi-no-i: day of the ox during summer **p.119**

Ekijo-kobo: type of marketed selected yeasts **p.151**

Enzyme: category of protein that favors biochemical reactions **p.93**

Ferrichrysin: negative red/brown pigment formed in presence of iron **p.80**

Flavins: category of natural yellow pigments **p.230**

Fugu: highly prized fish, mortal if improperly prepared **p.218**

Fukure: first CO_2 release during *shubo* **p.130**

Fukuro: cotton bag used in traditional pressing **p.186**

Fukuro-ka: "bag smell", filtration flaw **p.194**

Fukuro-shibori: sake pressing in cotton bags (*fukuro*) **p.186**

Fukurozuri: sake dripping in cotton bags (*fukuro*) **p.186**

Fune: lit. "boat", traditional press, shape reminiscent of a boat **p.187**

Futa-*koji*: *koji* cultivation in *kojibuta* **p.99**

Futsushu: entry-level sake not classified as *tokutei-meisho-shu* **p.213**

Genmai: unpolished rice (syn. cargo or brown rice) **p.74**

Genmaishu: sake made with *genmai* rice **p.74**

Genshu: sake without a water addition after pressing **p.178**

Ginjo: sake with *seimaibuai* under 60% **p.213**

Ginjo-ka: typical *ginjo* aroma **p.172**

Glycerolipids: category of esterified lipids (reserve) **p.81**

Go: volume unit equal to 180 mL **p.209**

Goseiseishu: synthetic sake **p.177**

Goshu: historical type of sake **p.16** and **p.169**

Guinomi: type of sake cup **p.225**

Hadaka-taru: uncovered *taru* as opposed to *komodaru* **p.212**

Hako-koji: *koji* cultivation in *kojibako* **p.100**

Hakumai: polished rice as opposed to *genmai* **p.74**

Han: ancient Japanese territorial division **p.209**

Hana-hie: a sake serving temperature **p.222**

Hanami: contemplation of cherry blossom (*sakura*) **p.110**

Hanamizake: sake drunk during *hanami*, can contain *sakura* blossoms **p.110**

Hangiri: large bucket made of stainless steel or wood **p.125**

Haplodiploidy: genetic engineering method, producing pure-line individuals in a single generation **p.41**

Hashira shochu: *shochu* made with *kasu* formerly used to produce fortified sake **p.179**

Hatsu-shibori: first pressed sake of the season **p.198**

Hatsu-zoe: first addition during *san-dan shikomi* **p.155**

Haze: white and powdery dots seen on *kome-koji* **p.99**

Heartwood: internal part of the wood, as opposite to sapwood **p.205**

Heterozygote: individual possessing two different alleles for a given gene, example: AB **p.40**

Hiire: low temperature pasteurization of sake (60-65 °C) **p.199**

Hikikomi: *koji* cultivation step **p.98**

Hinata-kan: a sake serving temperature **p.222**

Hineka: overaged sake smell cause by high DMTS concentration **p.200**

Hineri-mochi: pasted rice, kneaded to test its cooking **p.87**

Hiochi-kin: spoilage lactic acid bacteria **p.195**

Hirezake: hot sake containing a grilled *fugu* fin **p.218**

Hishaku: traditional bamboo ladle **p.208**

Hitohada-kan: a sake serving temperature **p.222**

Hiyaoroshi: seasonal *nama-zume* sold during autumn **p.213**

Homozygote: individual with two similar alleles for a given gene, example: AA **p.40**

Honjozo: sake with *seimaibuai* under 70% and maximum alcohol addition of 120 L/t of rice **p.213**

Honnidaru: *taru* covered with *komo*, traditional commercialization form **p.212**

Honzen-ryori: lit. "platter meal", type of banquet formalized during the 14th century **p.221**

Horei: rice cooling after steaming **p.91**

Hydrophilic: adj. having an affinity with water **p.148**

Hydrophobic: adj. having a tendency to repel water **p.148**

Ikkyu: "1st Category" of the former sake classification system **p.215**

Isshobin: 1.8 L sake bottle **p.209**

Iwa-awa: an aspect/stage of fermentation foam **p.147**

Izakaya: type of Japanese bar/restaurant **p.198**

Jacket: cooling system enveloping the fermentation tanks **p.169**

Jakan: lit. "snake", traditional pasteurizing device **p.200**

Ji: an aspect/stage of fermentation foam **p.147**

Jizake: "local" sake, generally produced by a small *kura* **p.222**

Jo-on: a sake serving temperature **p.222**

Joso: pressing **p.185**

Jozo arukoru: distilled alcohol used to produce *aruten* sake **p.179**

Jukuseishu: willingly aged sake **p.198**

Jukushu: style of sake, aromatic and powerful **p.237**

Junmai: sake produced with only *kome-koji*, rice and water **p.213**

Junshu: style of sake, powerful palate and light nose **p.237**

Kabura-gai or **kai-bo**: type of pole-handled wooden masher **p.126**

Kagami-biraki: traditional ceremony, opening of a sake cask **p.207**

Kakemai: steamed rice added in the wort as opposed to *kojimai* **p.14**

Kake-nagashi: continuous water renewal during rice steeping **p.86**

Kakioke: measuring scoop used in *koji* culture **p.100**

Kakishibu: astringent kaki juice used for its tannins **p.186**

Kamaya: *kurabito* responsible for rice steaming helped by an *aikama* or *oimawashi* **p.94**

Kami-dana: small Shinto altar found in Japanese houses **p.33**

Kami-shu: lit. "paper smell", a negative aroma caused by filtration **p.194**

Kani-awa: an aspect/stage of fermentation foam **p.147**

Kanpai: "cheers!" **p.237**

Kanso-kobo: type of marketed selected yeasts **p.151**

Kanzukuri: wintertime sake-making **p.20**

Karakuchi: dry sake with positive *nihonshudo* **p.213**

Karashi: resting/maturation period for polished rice **p.83**, *kome-koji* **p.101** or *shubo* **p.134**

Karashi-ba: a cool room dedicated to *kome-koji karashi* **p.101**

Kashira: lit. "the head", assistant to the *toji* **p.94**

Kasseishu: sparkling *nama-nigorizake* sold while still fermenting **p.170**

Kasu or **Sakekasu**: sake pressing residues made of undissolved rice and yeasts **p.185**

Kasu-buai: lit. *kasu* ratio, used to indicate yield at the end of fermentation **p.167**

Katahaku: sake produced from an unpolished *kojimai* and a polished *kakemai* **p.74**

Katakuchi: type of sake pitcher **p.225**

Kazaridaru: lit. "decorative cask", empty *komodaru* **p.212**

Ki-ippon: *junmai* sake produced and bottled in the same *kura* **p.24**

Kijoshu: sweet sake produced by replacing some water with sake **p.169**

Kikichoko: white and blue *choko* used for professional tastings **p.225**

Kikizake: (serious) sake tasting **p.230**

Kikuzake: Choyo-no-sekku (Sept. 9th) sake with chrysanthemum blossoms **p.110**

Kimoto: traditionnal *shubo* method, with lactic fermentation. Also, sake produced with this method **p.125**

Kire: clean and clear finish in a sake (a positive attribute) **p.241**

Kirikaeshi: *koji* cultivation step **p.99**

Kizuchi: small wooden mallet used for *kagami-biraki* **p.208**

Kobo: fermentation yeast **p.151**

Koji: mold (*Aspergillus*) used in food production **p.93**

Kojibako: middle size *toko* used in *kome-koji* production **p.100**

Koji-buai: *kome-koji*/total rice ratio **p.154**

Kojibuta: small size *toko* used in *kome-koji* production **p.100**

Koji-kin: *koji* "seeds" used to inoculate rice when making *koji* **p.97**

Kojimai: rice dedicated to *kome-koji* production, as opposed to *kakemai* **p.15**

Koji-muro: room dedicated to *koji* cultivation **p.97**

Kokei-kobo: type of marketed selected yeasts **p.151**

Koku: measuring unit equivalent to 180 L **p.209**

Komai: lit. "old rice", rice stored for over a year after harvest **p.74**

Komaishu: defective sake produced with *komai* **p.83**

Komi-mizu-buai: total water volume/total rice weight ratio **p.154**

Komo: rice straw mat **p.207**

Komodaru: *komo* covered *taru*, traditional form of commercialization **p.207**

Konpeito: spiked ball shaped Japanese confectionary, also *kome-koji* produced with *koshiki-hada* **p.89**

Koshiki: traditional rice steamer **p.87**

Koshiki-hada: soggy rice grains steamed at the outskirt of the *koshiki* **p.89**

Koshu: aged sake, willingly or not **p.198**

Koutsuki-taru: white *taru*, more prestigious than the classic *akami-taru* p.206

Kumikake: *sokujyo moto* homogenization using a chimney **p.135**

Kunshu: sake style, aromatic but light-bodied **p.237**

Kurabito: *kura* employee, working in sake production **p.94**

Kuramoto: owner of a *sakagura* **p.94**

Lysophosphoglycerides: a category of cell membrane phospholipids **p.80**

Maedaki: first *shubo* warming period (5th-15th day) **p.127**

Maillard reactions: family of chemical reactions between sugars and amino acids that produce aromatic, flavorsome and brown-colored molecules **p.199**

Masu: traditional wooden square cup **p.209**

Meikueilu: Chinese spirit improperly referred to as sake **p.10**

Meshitaki: *kura* cook **p.94**

Miko: young woman, diviner and guardian of a Shinto sanctuary **p.16**

Milled (rice): "white" rice whose bran has been removed (80-84% *seimaibuai*) **p.79**

Mirin: sweet cooking sake **p.95**

Miso: fermented paste of soy beans and rice or barley **p.95**

Mitosis: cellular division, allowing asexual reproduction **p.146**

Miyamizu: lit. "Miya water", famous sake-making water **p.111**

Mizu-awa: an aspect/stage of fermentation foam **p.147**

Mizu-koji: lit. "water-*koji*" water and *kome-koji* mixed to extract *kome-koji* enzymes **p.134**

Mizu-moto: another name of *bodai-moto* **p.123**

Mochi: rice paste, traditional Japanese food **p.87**

Mochi-koji: historical type of *kome-koji* forming a paste **p.96**

Momen-shu: "cotton smell", negative filtration aroma **p.194**

Mori: *koji* cultivation step **p.99**

Morohaku: sake produced from polished rice as opposed to *genmaishu* **p.74**

Moromi: main fermentation **p.153**

Moto or **shubo**: yeast starter **p.122**

Motomawashi: one of the three *sannyaku*, responsible for *moto* **p.94**

Motosuri or **Yamaoroshi**: rice grinding in *kimoto* method **p.125**

Mureka: stale aroma of 3-methylbutanal (aldehyde) **p.200**

Muroka: sake produced without activated charcoal **p.194**

Mushimai: rice steaming **p.87**

Mycelium: vegetative part of mold and mushroom made of filaments **p.97**

Nakashigoto: *koji* cultivation step **p.100**

Naka-zoe: second addition of *san-dan-shikomi* **p.154**

Nama-chozo: once-pasteurized sake, before commercialization **p.213**

Nama-hineka: overaged sake aroma (*hineka*) of *namazake* **p.200**

Nama-kobo: type of marketed selected yeasts **p.151**

Namazake: unpasteurized sake **p.196**

Nama-zume or **Hiyaoroshi**: once-pasteurized sake, before aging **p.213**

Namizake: old terminology, today "*genmaishu*" **p.74**

Natto: fermented soy beans, a traditional Japanese food **p.101**

Nigami: "bitterness", tasting vocabulary **p.234**

Nigorizake: lightly- or un-filtered cloudy sake **p.191**

Nihonshu: lit. "Japanese alcohol", sake in Japanese **p.12** and Japanese GI **p.215**

Nihonshu no Hi: 1st of October, sake day or sake "new year" (BY) **p.229**

Nihonshudo or **SMV**: sake density measure, used as an imprecise sweetness indicator **p.157**

Niku-tare-buai: rice "yield", indicator used with *kasu-buai* **p.168**

Nikyu: "2nd Category" of the former sake classification system **p.215**

Noujun: tasting term signifying full-bodied, as opposed to *tanrei* **p.234**

Noutando: sake body indicator combining *nihonshudo* and *sando* **p.157**

Nuka: rice flour, leftover from polishing **p.75**

Nukegake: filling the *koshiki* by layers of rice **p.90**

Nukumitori-daki: last *daki* during *shubo*, contains scalding water **p.130**

Nuri-haze: low quality *kome-koji* obtained when the *koji* develops on the grain surface **p.107**

Nuru-kan: a sake serving temperature **p.222**

Ochi-awa: an aspect/stage of fermentation foam **p.147**

O-choko or **choko**: a category of sake cup **p.225**

Oimizu: cold water added into the wort to control fermentation speed **p.166**

O-kan-ban: bar employee specialized in serving hot sake **p.223**

Ori: sake sediments after pressing **p.192**

Oribiki: clarification (removing *ori*) **p.192**

Orikomi: transferring the *shubo* from *hangiri* to *tsubodai* **p.126**

Orisage: settling the *ori* to remove them **p.192**

Orizake: cloudy portion of the sake obtained after *orisage*, some *nigorizake* are sold under this name **p.192**

O-shaku: traditional mutual service of sake **p.221**

Pin: sake tasting term, "finish" **p.235**

Plunger: cooling system placed in the fermentation tanks **p.166**

Polypeptides: small amino acid chains (<100 units) **p.199**

Polysaccharides: complex chains of sugar molecules **p.199**

ppm: parts per million, 10^{-6} **p.80**

Protein: organic macromolecule formed by amino acids chains **p.93**

Reishu: historical type of sake, also sake served cold **p.17**

Romaji: system used to represent Japanese terms in Roman characters **p.12**

Sakagura or **kura**: sake producer (*kura* = cellar/store/shop) **p.14**

Sakamai: rice used in sake production **p.41**

Sakana: lit. "sake food", nibbles served with sake **p.219**

Sakazuki: a category of sake cup **p.226**

Sake no kami: minister of the *sake no tsukasa* **p.17**

Sake no tsukasa: sake production department at the Imperial Court **p.17**

Sake zukuri uta: traditional songs sung during *kura* works **p.126**

Sake: generic term designing alcoholic beverages, habitually *nihonshu* **p.11**

Sakura: Japanese cherry tree and blossoms contemplated during *hanami* **p.110**

Saltpeter: ancient name of potassium nitrate **p.127**

San-dan shikomi: building up the *moromi* in three steps **p.155**

Sando: acidity measurement in sake **p.158**

Sankin-kotai: *daimyos* alternated residency **p.21**

Sannyaku: three qualified *kurabito* responsible for a production step **p.94**

Sanshuro: a historical type of sake **p.18**

Sapwood: young wood, just under the bark, as opposed to heartwood **p.205**

Seikiku: *kome-koji* production **p.97**

Seimai: rice polishing **p.73**

Seimaibuai: rice polishing ratio = final weight/initial weight **p.73**

Seishu: lit. "clear alcohol", "filtered" sake as opposed to *nigorizake* **p.11**

Senmai: rice rinsing **p.84**

Shibori: pressing **p.186**

Shiboritate: freshly pressed sake, often slightly sparkling and *nama* **p.213**

Shibumi: tasting term, astringency **p.234**

Shiki-jozo: year-round sake production, as opposed to *kanzukuri* **p.19**

Shikomi: addition **p.13**

Shimaishigoto: a *koji* production step **p.100**

Shinpaku: white core of certain rice grain **p.29**

Shinseki: rice steeping **p.84**

Shinshu: lit. "new sake", sake sold after minimal aging or right after pressing, historically at the beginning of the year **p.19**

Shinto: traditional Japanese religion **p.33**

Shirinpin: "finish", sake tasting term **p.235**

Shizukuzake: sake obtained by *fukurozuri* **p.186**

Sho: volume measurement unit equal to 10 *go* or 1.8 L **p.209**

Shobuzake: Tango-no-sekku (May 5th) Iris root sake **p.110**

Shochu: traditional Japanese spirit, deserving a dedicated book of its own **p.182**

Shu or *Zake*: alternative readings of the "sake" character **p.11**

Shubo or **moto**: yeast starter **p.122**

Shuzo: often in *kura* name, means "sake producer"

Shuzo-koteki-mai: rice specifically dedicated to sake-making **p.41**

Smectite: a type of swelling clay favorable to wet rice culture **p.216**

So-haze koji: intermediary *kome-koji* between *tsuki-haze* and *nuri-haze* **p.108**

Sokujyo: modern *shubo*, also sake produced with this method **p.134**

Soshu: a style of sake, with light body and aroma **p.237**

Soyashimizu: acidic liquid used in *bodai-moto* **p.123**

Sphingolipids: a category of complex cell membrane lipid **p.80**

Starch: energy reserve molecule in plants, made up of glucose chains **p.30**

Stave: planks of wood constituting a barrel **p.205**

Sterols: a category of lipid (steroid) with a hydroxyl group on one of its rings **p.80**

Sugi: Japanese cedar, *Cryptomeria japonica* **p.22**

Suji-awa: an aspect/stage of fermentation foam **p.147**

Suzu-hie: a sake serving temperature **p.222**

Taishi: one of the three *sannyaku*, responsible for *koji*, helped by the *aikoji* **p.94**

Taka-awa: an aspect/stage of fermentation foam **p.147**

Tama-awa: an aspect/stage of fermentation foam **p.147**

Tane-koji: *koji* "seeds" used to inoculate rice when making *koji* **p.97**

Tanrei: "light", tasting term, as opposed to *noujun* **p.234**

Tanrei-karakuchi: light and dry, sake style typical of Niigata **p.217**

Tansho-shu: "charcoal smell", negative aroma caused by filtration **p.194**

Taru kaizen: boat specialized in *taru* transportation toward Edo **p.20**

Taru: lit. "cask" **p.203**

Tarunaka: sake from the "middle" of a *taru* with strong cedar aroma **p.207**

Taruzake: *taru* aged sake **p.203**

Taruzake binzume: *taruzake* sold in bottles **p.207**

Taruzoko: sake from the "bottom" of a *taru* with very strong cedar aroma **p.207**

Taruzume: *taruzake* sold in a *taru* **p.207**

Te-ire: rice mixing during *seikiku* **p.198**

To mizu: lit. "ten water", traditional *komi-mizu-buai* of 120% **p.154**

To: volume unit equal 10 *sho,* or 18 L **p.209**

Tobin: 18 L demijohns (big bottle) **p.186**

Tobiri-kan: a sake serving temperature **p.222**

Toji: sake production manager, cellar master **p.20**

Tokashu: Momo-no-sekku (March 3rd) peach sake **p.110**

Tokkuri: a type of sake pitcher **p.209**

Tokkyu: "special category" of the former sake classification system **p.215**

Toko: wooden box used in *koji* cultivation **p.98**

Toko-koji: *koji* cultivation in large *toko* **p.100**

Toko-momi: inoculation, *kome-koji* production step **p.98**

Tokubetsu: lit. "special", a quality designation for *honjozo* and *junmai* **p.213**

Tokutei-meisho-shu: superior sakes: *honjozo, junmai, ginjo* and *daiginjo* **p.213**

Tome-zoe: third addition of *san-dan-shikomi* **p.154**

Toshizake: new year herbs and spices sake **p.110**

Tsubodai: small tank used for *shubo* **p.126**

Tsuke-kaye: sequential renewal of water during rice steeping **p.86**

Tsukemono: small pickled vegetables **p.185**

Tsuki-haze koji: type of *kome-koji* with *koji* developed deep in the grain **p.107**

Tsukimizake: sake drunk while contemplating the autumn full moon **p.110**

Tsumikae: *koji* cultivation step (in *futa-koji* method) **p.100**

Umami: fifth basic taste, "savory" **p.234**

Unagizake: sake poured on *unagi* during summertime Doyo-no-Ushi-no-hi **p.119**

Usunigori: *nigorizake* with very fine sediments **p.230**

Utase: rest phase at the beginning of the *shubo* **p.126**

Vermiculite: a type of swelling clay favorable to wet rice culture **p.216**

Wakitsuki: step during which the *shubo* covers with foam **p.130**

Yabuta: famous press-filter brand **p.188**

Yamahai: traditional *shubo*, also sake produced with this method **p.133**

Yamaoroshi or **Motosuri**: rice grinding during *kimoto* **p.125**

Yokozuna: highest rank for a sumo wrestler **p.94**

Yon-dan: lit. "fourth addition" of rice and enzyme or *kome-koji* before pressing **p.183**

Yongobin: standard sake bottle containing 4 *go*, or 720 mL **p.209**

Yuki-hie: a sake serving temperature **p.222**

Yukimizake: snowflake sake drunk in winter **p.110**

Zenkoji: sake produced with only *kome-koji* rice **p.168**

Index of tables, figures and graphs

Tables

Charts and Graphs

Figures

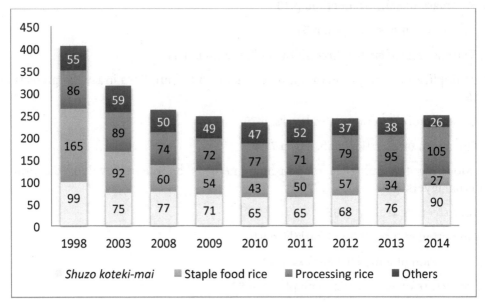

Annex 1. Sources of starch used to produce *Nihonshu* (thousands of tons).

Sources: NTA and Japan Sake and Shochu Makers Association.

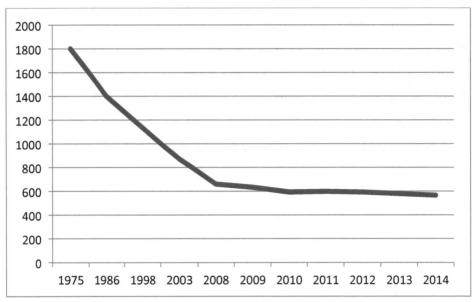

Annex 2. Production volume of *Nihonshu* (Millions of liters).

Source: Japan Sake and Shochu Makers Association.

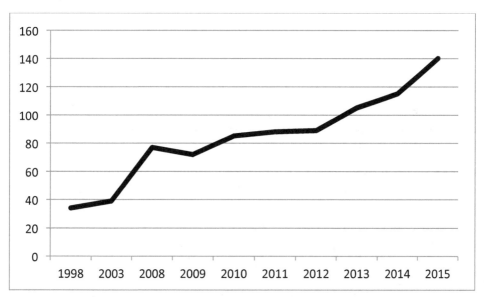

Annex 3. *Nihonshu* export value (Billions yen).
Source: Trade statistics, Japan Ministry of Finance

2016	Volume (L)	Value (1000 JPY)	volume %
TOTAL	19736818	15581063	100%
USA	4648576	4720828	23,6%
S Korea	3694760	1562006	18,7%
Taiwan	2096002	931098	10,6%
China	1910184	1449281	9,7%
Hong Kong	1877112	263011	9,5%
Canada	576473	381127	2,9%
Singapore	508721	600709	2,6%
Thailand	460545	239881	2,3%
Australia	409030	361912	2,1%
Germany	387886	179078	2,0%
Italy	321594	113595	1,6%
Vietnam	389510	287137	2,0%
UK	316574	322572	1,6%
Malaysia	222884	200988	1,1%
Netherlands	182852	108172	0,9%
Brazil	183507	92874	0,9%
UK	168781	196059	0,9%
Philippines	126549	57216	0,6%
New Zeal.	94848	52776	0,5%

Annex 4. Main *Nihonshu* export countries.
Source: Japanese customs

Bibliography

AKIYAMA, H. (2010). Sake, the essence of 2000 years of Japanese wisdom gained from brewing alcoholic beverages from rice. Brewing Society of Japan. 204 p.

ANGLADETTE, A. (1959). Notes sur la riziculture japonaise. Riz et riziculture & cultures vivrières tropicales. 5. 161-187.

ARAMAKI, I. et al. (2004). Correlation between Structural Properties of Amylopectins and the Sake Brewing or Physicochemical Properties of Rice. J. Brew. Soc. Japan. 99. 457-466.

ARAMAKI, I. et al. (2011). Distribution of minerals in rice grains used for sake brewing. J. Brew. Soc. Japan. 106. 837-847.

ASK Co. Ltd. (2015). Cultivation textbook of the proper brewer's rice.

ATKINSON, R.W. (1881). The Chemistry of Sake Brewing. Tokio Daigaku. 108 p.

AULD, W. G. (2012). Brewing Sake: Release the Toji Within. Create Space. 230 p.

BAUMERT, N. (2011). Le saké, une exception japonaise. PUR. 300 p.

BUTTERY, R. G. et al. (1988). Contribution of volatiles to rice aroma. J. Agric. Food Chem. 36 (5). 1006-1009.

CHANG, T. T. (1976). The origin, evolution, cultivation, dissemination, and diversification of the Asian and African rices. Euphytica. 25. 425-441.

FUJINO, Y. (1978). Rice lipids. Cereal Chem. 55(5). 559-571.

FUJITA, A. et al. (2010). Effects of sulfur dioxide on formation of fishy off-odor and undesirable taste in wine consumed with seafood. J. Agric. Food Chem. 58(7). 4414-4420.

GAUNTNER, J. (2002). The Sake Handbook: All the information you need to become a Sake Expert! Tuttle Publishing. 248 p.

GAUNTNER, J. (2014). Sake Confidential: A beyond-the-basics guide to Understanding, Tasting, Selection, & Enjoyment. Stone Bridge Press. 184 p.

HARPER, P. (2006). The Book of Sake: A Connoisseur's Guide. Kodansha. 96 p.

HASHIZUME, K. (2006). Rice Protein Digestion by Sake Koji Enzymes: Comparison between Steamed Rice Grains and Isolated Protein Bodies from Rice Endosperm. J. Biosci. Bioeng. 102. 340-345.

HASHIZUME, K. et al. (2007). Bitter-Tasting Sake Peptides Derived from the N-Terminus of the Rice Glutelin Acidic Subunit. Food Sci. Technol. Res. 13(3). 270-274.

HORIGANE, A. K. et al. (2014). Moisture distribution in rice grains used for sake brewing analyzed by magnetic resonance imaging. J. Cereal Science. 60(1).

HOUSTON, D. F. et al. (1969). Amino Acid Composition of Rice and Rice By-Products. Cereal Chem. 46. 527-536.

IEMURA, Y. et al. (1999). Properties of the peptides liberated from rice protein in Sokujo-moto. J. Biosci. Bioeng. 88(3). 276-280.

IEMURA, Y. et al. (1999). Properties of TCA-insoluble peptides in kimoto (traditional seed mash for sake brewing) and conditions for liberation of the peptides from rice protein. J. Biosci. Bioeng. 88(5). 531-535.

INOUE, T. (trad.). (2016). Textbook of sake brewing. Brewing Society of Japan. 232 p.

ISHIGE, N. (2001). The History and Culture of Japanese Food. Routledge. 284 p.

ISOGAI, A., et al. (2005). Changes in the Aroma Compounds of Sake during Aging. J. Agric. Food Chem. 53 (10). 4118–4123.

ISOGAI, A., et al. (2010). Contribution of 1,2-dihydroxy-5-(methylsulfinyl)pentan-3-one (DMTS-P1) to the formation of dimethyl trisulfide (DMTS) during the storage of Japanese sake. J. Agric. Food Chem. 58. 7756-7761.

KANAUCHI, M. (2013). SAKE Alcoholic Beverage Production in Japanese Food Industry. Dr. Innocenzo Muzzalupo. 26 p.

KATO, H. (1987). Nihon no sake gosennen. Tokyo: Gihodobooks. 261 p.

KITAGAKI, H., KITAMOTO, K. (2013). Breeding research on sake yeasts in Japan: history, recent technological advances, and future perspectives. Annual Review of Food Science and Technology 4. 215-35.

KITAGAKI, H., SHIMOI, H. (2007). Mitochondrial Dynamics of Yeast during Sake Brewing. J. Biosci. Bioeng. 104(3). 227-230.

KOHNO, H., TAKAHASHI, K. (2016). Different Polar Metabolites and Protein Profiles between High- and Low-quality Japanese Ginjo Sake. PLOS ONE. 11(3).

KONDO, H. (1992). Sake, a Drinker's Guide. Kodansha. 128 p.

KOYANAGI, T. et al. (2016). Tracing microbiota changes in yamahai-moto, the traditional Japanese sake starter. Biosci. Biotechnol. Biochem. 80(2). 399-406.

KURIBAYASHI, T. et al. (2012). Analysis of Free Fatty Acids in Sake by an Enzymatic Method and Its Application for Estimating Ethyl Caproate and Selecting Yeast with High Productivity of the Ester. Biosci. Biotech. Biochem. 76(2). 391-394.

LIN, Y. et al. (2014). Optimization of conditions for glucoamylase, α-amylase and acidic protease production by A. oryzae koji. J. Chem. Pharm. Res. 6(9). 360-364.

MACHIDA, M., et al. (2005). Genome sequencing and analysis of Aspergillus oryzae. Nature. 438. 1157-61.

MARSHALL, W., WADSWORTH, J. (1993). Rice Science and Technology. CRC Press. 486 p.

MATSUZAWA, K. et al. (2002). Changes in compositions and microorganisms in Dakusyu-sake brewing using the Bodaimoto method. J. Brew. Soc. Japan. 97(10). 734-740.

257

MIMURA, N. et al. (2014). Gas chromatography/mass spectrometry based component profiling and quality prediction for Japanese sake. J. Biosci. Bioeng. 118 (4). 406-414.

MIZUMA, T. (2007). Water-Absorption Rate Equation of Rice for Brewing Sake. J. Biosci. Bioeng. 103(1), 60–65.

MIZUMA, T. Effects of the rice polishing ratio on water absorption of rice. 7 p.

MORI, K. et al. (2011). Genome Sequence of the White koji Mold A. kawachii Used for Brewing the Japanese Distilled Spirit Shochu. Eukaryotic Cell. 10(11). 1586-1587.

MUTTERS, R., THOMPSON, J. (2009). Rice Quality Handbook. UCANR. 141 p.

NAKAJIMA, A., SAKAGUCHI, T. (2000). Uptake and removal of iron by immobilised persimmon tannin. J. Chem. Tech. Biotech. 75(11). 977-982.

NUNOKAWA, Y. et al. Studies on the Ripeness of koji. NRIB.

OHBA, T., SATO, M. (1986). Chapter 16: Sake. Handbook of Food and Beverage Stability. 773-799.

OKUDA, M. et al. (2009). Influence of Sulfur and Nitrogen Content of Rice Grains on Flavor in Stored Sake. Cereal Chem. 86(5). 534-541.

OKUDA, M. et al. (2009). Relationship between sake making properties of rice grains and meteorological data. J. Brew. Soc. Japan. 104. 9. 699-711.

OKUDA, M. et al. (2009). Influence of starch characteristics on digestibility of steamed rice grains under sake-making conditions, and rapid estimation methods of digestibility by physical analysis. J. Appl. Glycosci. 56. 185-192.

OKUDA, M. et al. (2010). Changes in mean air temperature after heading and starch characteristics of rice grains for sake making among harvest years and areas. J. Brew. Soc. Japan. 105 (2). 97-105.

OKUDA, M. et al. (2014). Changes during polishing in mineral concentrations of rice grains used for sake making. J. Brew. Soc. Japan. 109. 887-900.

OMORI, T. et al. (1997). A novel method for screening high glycerol- and ester-producing brewing yeasts (Saccharomyces cerevisiae) by heat shock treatment. J. Fermentation and Bioeng. 83(1). 64–69.

RICKMAN, J. F. (2015). Operational Manual for Mechanical Transplanting of Rice. csisa.org.

SAITO, T. (1993). Shape of Polished Rice for Sake Brewing and Its Evaluation. J. Brew. Soc. Japan. 88(3). 170-177.

SAITO, T. (1998). Evaluation of Rice Equally Polished from Outerlayer. J. Brew. Soc. Japan. 93(10). 778-783.

SALTER, P. F. et al. (1999). Geostatistical analysis of groundwater chemistry in Japan. Japan Nuclear Cycle Development Inst. 231 p.

SASAKI, K. et al. (2014). Statistical analysis of sake-preparation conditions and dimethyl trisulfide formation. J. Biosci. Bioeng. 118(2). 166-171.

SHURTLEFF, W., AOYAGI, A. (2012). History of koji – Grains and/or Soybeans Enrobed with a mold Culture (300 BCE to 2012). Soyinfo Center. 660 p.

SPITAELS, F. et al. (2014). The Microbial Diversity of Traditional Spontaneously Fermented Lambic Beer. PLOS ONE. 9(4).

STEINKRAUS, K. (2004). Industrialization of Indigenous Fermented Foods, Revised and Expanded. CRC Press. 600 p.

SUGIMOTO, M. et al. (2012). Changes in the Charged Metabolite and Sugar Profiles of Pasteurized and Unpasteurized Japanese Sake with Storage. J. Agric. Food Chem. 60 (10). 2586–2593.

SUMIHARA, N. (2007). Reconstruction of Bodaimoto; the Origin of Modern Sake. Tenri University. 35 p.

TAKAHASHI, H. et al. (2008). Influence of strains of Aspergillus oryzae and kinds of koji rice on production of the proteolytic enzyme in sake koji. J. Brew. Soc. Japan. 103(11). 894-900.

TAKAHASHI, M. et al. (2006). GC-Olfactometry analysis of the aroma components in sake koji. J. Brew. Soc. Japan. 101(12). 957-963.

TAKAHASHI, M. et al. (2007). Change in the aroma of sake koji during koji-making. J. Brew. Soc. Japan. 102(5). 957-963.

TAKEKOSHI, Y. The Economic Aspects of the History of the Civilization of Japan. Routledge. 1632 p.

TALAVERA, K. et al. (2007). Influence of temperature on taste perception. Cell. Mol. Life Sci. 64(4). 377-81.

TAMAKI, M. et al. (2007). Hardness distribution and Endosperm Structure on Polishing Characteristics of Brewer's Rice kernels. Plant Prod. Sci. 10(4). 481-487.

TAMAKI, M. et al. (2008). Varietal Differences in Endosperm Structure Related to High-degree Polishing Properties of "Hattan Varieties" of Rice Suitable for Brewing Original Hiroshima Sake. Plant Prod. Sci. 11(4). 446-471.

TAMAKI, M. et al. (2009). Relationship between the starch properties of white-core tissue and polishing characteristics in brewer's rice kernels. Plant Prod. Sci. 12(2). 233-236.

TAMURA, T. et al. (2009). Iron is an essential cause of fishy aftertaste formation in wine and seafood pairing. J. Agric Food Chem. 57(18). 8550-8556.

TERAMOTO, Y. et al. (1993). Rice wine brewing with sprouting rice, sprouting rice infected with aspergillus oryzae and rice koji. J. Hist. Brew. 99. 467-471.

The Kojiki: Records of Ancient Matters. 2005. Periplus Editions. 592 p.

TOTMAN, C. (1989). The green archipelago: forestry in preindustrial Japan. University of California Press. 297 p.

TOTMAN, C. (1995). The Lumber industry in early modern Japan. University of Hawaii Press. 165 p.

UMEMOTO, S.-I. et al. (1970). The Effects of Trace Iron on Amino-carbonyl Reaction. Nippon Nōgeikagaku Kaishi. 4(2). 64-76.

UTSUNOMIYA, H. et al. (2010). Measurement of thresholds for reference compounds for the sensory profiling of Sake. J. Brew. Soc. Japan. 105(2). 106-115.

YAMADA, H. et al. (1998). Effect of Location and Year of Production on White-core in Rice Kernels for Sake Brewery Evaluated by Image Data. Japanese J. Breeding. 48(4). 355-357.

YOSHIDA, H., (2003). Transfer of Saké Technology to Korea, Taiwan and China. Senri Ethnological Studies. 64. 35-48.

YOSHIOKA, K., HASHIMOTO, N. (1981). Ester formation by alcohol acetyltransferase from brewer's yeast. Agri. And Biological Chem. 45. 2183–2190.

YOSHIZAKI, Y. et al. (2010). Analysis of Volatile Compounds in Shochu Koji, Sake Koji, and Steamed Rice by Gas Chromatography-Mass Spectrometry. J. Inst. Brew. 116(1). 49–55.

Made in United States
Troutdale, OR
12/28/2024

27357954R00146